The Pan Guide to
Babies' Names

Stuart Wilson

PAN BOOKS

First published 1994 Pan Books
an imprint of Macmillan Publishers Ltd
Cavaye Place London SW10 9PG
and Basingstoke

Associated companies throughout the world

ISBN 0-330-33063-2

Copyright © Stuart Wilson 1994

The right of Stuart Wilson to be identified as the
author of this work has been asserted by him in accordance
with the Copyright, Designs and Patents Act 1988.

All rights reserved. No reproduction, copy or transmission
of this publication may be made without written permission.
No paragraph of this publication may be reproduced, copied or
transmitted save with written permission or in accordance with
the provisions of the Copyright Act 1956 (as amended). Any
person who does any unauthorized act in relation to
this publication may be liable to criminal prosecution
and civil claims for damages.

5 7 9 8 6 4

A CIP catalogue record for this book is available from
the British Library

Typeset by CentraCet Limited, Cambridge
Printed and bound in Great Britain by
Cox & Wyman Ltd, Reading, Berkshire

Contents

Introduction 1
Choosing a Name 6
The Creation of New Names 8
Analysis of Sources 11

A–Z of First Names
15

Concept Index 249
Index of Sources 293
Special Category Index 312
Combinations Index 314
Bibliography 325

Introduction

This is not only a new name dictionary, but a new *kind* of name dictionary. For the first time the whole range of modern and established names is available in a completely indexed form. The unique index system enables the parent to choose a specific concept and home in straight away on the names associated with that idea. For example, if you wished to mark the birth of a daughter at sunrise you would discover in the Concept Index fifteen feminine names listed under 'Dawn'. And if you wanted to give your child an Old English or Greek or Celtic name, you would find these names identified in the Index of Sources. Used in either of these ways this unique index system gives the parent an unprecedented freedom and flexibility in the process of name choosing.

This dictionary is also new in another important respect: it includes many new name combinations (or blends) of existing names, and a wide range of 'progressive' or New Age names (often with some link to ecology as in the case of River, Sky and Leaf).

The richness and variety of first names is one of the great glories of the English-speaking peoples. It is both the product and the symbol of a freedom which may be taken for granted, but which is by no means universal. The absence of restrictions in the English-speaking world has resulted in a remarkable flowering

The Pan Guide to Babies' Names

of creativity in naming, not only in variations of spelling, but also in combinations which blend the elements of two or more existing names. Many of these new blends only started to emerge in the 1980s, and consequently a large proportion of them have not appeared in any previous dictionary. (They are listed in the Combinations Index.) Whilst some of these new blends lack style there are many more (such as Loretha and Zaranda) which are appealing names by any standard. It is the attractiveness of a new name which ensures its rapid spread and ultimate survival.

However the core of this book remains the central stock of names which have long been used by English-speaking parents. And an examination of the Index of Sources reveals just how many established names there are in categories such as Hebrew, Latin, and Greek.

The system of first names, surnames and place-names forms an interconnected web, with names flowing from one category to another with increasing rapidity and freedom. Hence many first names may have been derived from surnames, and these in turn may originally have been drawn from place-names. However it is the underlying *meaning* of the name which has been given paramount importance in this dictionary, and hence surname or place-name links are only referred to where the meaning is uncertain.

The entries in this book have been kept brief in order to make it possible to include the maximum number of main entry names (i.e. names that stand in their own right, and are not simply spelling variants of existing names). This dictionary is uniquely rich in these main entry names, and the result is more names, more variety and more choice. However, in addition to

Introduction

these main entry names the principal spelling variants have also been included, especially those that are likely to appeal to the modern parent. Where these variants have diverged markedly from the original form, each is given a separate entry to help the reader identify the source.

In cases where there are several possible origins for a name, the soundest derivation is given, although where two (or more) derivations seem equally viable both (or all) are cited. Even in those cases where the origin is usually considered to be uncertain, an attempt has been made to trace these names back to a viable source, leaving only the most doubtful to be labelled simply 'origin uncertain'.

Hyphenated forms of names (eg Donna-Marie) have generally been avoided here: see the comment in the first paragraph of the Combinations Index. In line with American (and progressive English) usage, accents on names have been omitted.

Throughout the compilation of this book I have borne in mind one main criterion for selection: is the name in question likely to be attractive to the modern English-speaking parent? The application of this principle has ruled out both the more freakish and extreme new names and the archaic names of an unattractive nature. What remains is a larger stock of *usable* names than can be found in any comparable dictionary: a careful selection of names with real potential in the modern world. You will find gathered here over 4600 main entries and a total of over 7300 names – a treasure-house of naming possibilities.

A major feature of this dictionary is the listing of many names that simply do not occur in any other name book. The sources of these names include:

The Pan Guide to Babies' Names

1. New combinations/blends (see Combinations Index).
2. Progressive or New Age names.
3. New spellings of existing names that are now becoming recognized as names in their own right.
4. New names from other languages (especially Celtic languages, Maori, Hawaiian, Japanese and Sanskrit).
5. New names from books, plays, films, etc (see Special Category Index).
6. New names that originated as the professional names of actors and actresses of stage and screen.
7. New names formed with prefixes (notably La- and Sha-). Although many of these names have been listed in other dictionaries (especially in *Everyman's Dictionary of First Names* by Dunkling and Gosling) they appear here for the first time as main entries in alphabetical order.

I must record here my debt to a number of individuals for their help: Shimako Sharpe (Japanese names); Martin Holyoak and Jacqueline Lightband (Sanskrit names); Marjorie Boyt-Morgan of Seattle, Washington; Bob Maddox; and Joanna Woolvett. I am particularly grateful to Tatanya Sophie Prentis for permission to study her unpublished research on unusual names. And my special thanks to Joanna Cobain both for collecting unusual names and for focusing me from the very beginning on the importance of finding the right name. I am also indebted to a number of correspondents in Steiner/Waldorf schools throughout the world who sent me a rich harvest of progressive names.

Introduction

This book offers you more names, more variety, and more choice: a rich storehouse from which you can select the ideal name for your baby.

Choosing a Name

In the final analysis, our name reflects the essential quality that we express – hence the importance of finding the right name. This book has attempted to make the process of choice more fruitful, both by the provision of a unique index system and through the inclusion of many new and attractive names which appear here for the first time in any dictionary. While it would be unwise to put forward a rigid system for choosing names, there are certain guidelines which may prove helpful:

1. If you feel drawn to several first names, try them out with the surname to see if they flow and sound right, especially when spoken aloud.
2. Remember that nicknames and shortened forms will be used whether you (or the child) like them or not. William Gill may sound fine, but perhaps Bill Gill less so. Any names that rhyme should be treated with caution as they can all too easily verge upon the comic.
3. Check the initials of the full name. If you have a surname beginning with M and call your daughter Delia Isobel her initials will be D.I.M. (a fact that her peer group at school will probably not allow her to forget).
4. Consider the effect upon the child if you use too

Choosing a Name

flamboyant (or too dull), too 'way-out' (or too old-fashioned) a name. Extremes in naming may often seem like a good idea at the time, but the child will have to live with the result.

5. Be cautious about naming a child after some charismatic figure of the time – names of this sort date all too easily, and fall quickly out of fashion with the decline of interest in the hero or heroine concerned.

The Creation of
New Names

Many parents throughout the whole of the English-speaking world are beginning to explore new areas of freedom in naming their children, and to feel a new sense of empowerment. A significant element in this new freedom is the creation or invention of new names. Few guidelines exist at present to facilitate this process, but there are some basic principles that may help the parent who wishes to invent a new name:

1. Consider creating a spelling variant of an existing name. This may involve transposing:
    K for C
    Y for I
    Z for S
    G for J
    IE for EY
    OO for U
    etc
    (or vice versa in each case). Alternatively it might involve doubling up (or singling down) consonants:
    LL for L
    TT for T
    SS for S
    RR for R
    etc

The Creation of New Names

2. Consider combining the elements of two or more existing names, perhaps starting with names within your own extended family. (See the Combinations Index as a guide to what has already been done in this area). Feel free to mix elements of masculine and feminine names in this process – others have certainly done so.

3. Consider producing a phonetic version of an existing name: concentrate on the sound and ignore the original spelling.

4. If you are attracted to one culture or language explore the dictionary of that language for possible names, searching out qualities appropriate to the new child.

5. Examine the many other categories of names that can be transferred to first name use, for example plant names, ship names, gemstone names and literary names (see William Freeman's *Dictionary of Fictional Characters* Dent, 1967).

6. If your family is associated with a certain place, explore the names of nearby rivers, hills, villages, etc, through a dictionary of place-names (see Bibliography).

7. Investigate the meaning of your family surname (see the Bibliography) by consulting the Concept Index. Apply the principles of spelling variants or combination of elements to the group of names emerging from this process.

Feel free to experiment and mix different sources and elements creatively until you arrive at the name

The Pan Guide to Babies' Names

which you feel is right for your child. And remember to check out your newly created name along the lines suggested in the section Choosing a Name.

Analysis of Sources

The Index of Sources identifies the linguistic origins of the names in the main dictionary. By totalling up each category it is possible to analyse the origins of the names in this central stock, and this gives us an insight into where our names come from. The English-speaking peoples have always been outgoing, adventurous and pioneering, and this is reflected in the remarkable diversity of the sources from which we draw our names.

In addition to the names in this breakdown, there are names from other sources in this book, notably spelling variants, combinations, inventions and names of uncertain origin.

Bear in mind that this book is very much linked to the English-speaking peoples *as a whole*, and hence contains American Indian, Hawaiian and Japanese names (from the United States) and Maori names (from New Zealand). The larger categories (involving ten names or more) are also given as percentages of the whole.

SOURCE	NUMBER	PERCENTAGE OF TOTAL
Aborigine	1	
African languages	9	
American Indian languages	25	0.8

The Pan Guide to Babies' Names

SOURCE	NUMBER	PERCENTAGE OF TOTAL
Arabic	39	1.2
Aramaic	16	0.5
Assyrian	1	
Bohemian	1	
Breton	2	
Celtic	63	1.9
Chinese	4	
Cornish	45	1.4
Czech	1	
Danish	4	
Dutch	9	
Egyptian	4	
Fijian	2	
French	148	4.5
Gaelic	85	2.6
German	25	0.8
Greek	314	9.5
Hawaiian	24	0.7
Hebrew	304	9.3
Hindi	1	
Hungarian	5	
Irish	112	3.4
Italian	50	1.5
Japanese	36	1.1
Latin	417	12.8
Malay	1	
Maori	34	1.0
Middle English	57	1.7
Mongolian	1	
Norman French	4	
Norwegian	1	
Old English	680	20.7
Old French	68	2.1

Analysis of Sources

SOURCE	NUMBER	PERCENTAGE OF TOTAL
Old German	190	5.8
Old Norse	61	1.9
Persian	17	0.5
Polish	5	
Quechua	1	
Rumanian	1	
Russian	33	1.0
Sanskrit	77	2.3
Scandinavian	18	0.6
Scottish	20	0.6
Slavonic	23	0.7
Spanish	63	1.9
Swedish	5	
Tahitian	1	
Tibetan	1	
Turkish	2	
Welsh	163	5.0
Yiddish	6	
Total	3282	

The Celtic languages can also be grouped together, giving a total of 490 names (15 percent). This clarifies the position of the top five sources in providing the bulk of our main stock of names:

SOURCE	NUMBER	PERCENTAGE OF TOTAL
Celtic languages	490	15.0
Greek	314	9.5
Hebrew	304	9.3
Latin	417	12.8
Old English	680	20.7
Total	2205	67.3

Aaron A Azure

AARON (m) *Hebrew* High mountain.
ABAGAIL *see* ABIGAIL.
ABBEY, ABBIE *see* ABIGAIL.
ABBOT, ABBOTT (m) *Old English* Abbey father.
ABEL (m) *Hebrew* Breath.
ABELARD (m) *Old German* Noble resolution.
ABIGAIL (f) *Hebrew* Father's joy.
ABNER (m) *Hebrew* Father of light.
ABRA (f) *Hebrew* Earth mother.
ABRAHAM (m) *Hebrew* Father of a multitude.
ABRAM (m) *Hebrew* High father.
ABSALOM, ABSOLOM (m) *Hebrew* Father of peace.
ACACIA (f) *Greek* From the name of the tree meaning 'innocent'.
ACANTHA (f) *Greek* From the name of the tree meaning 'thorny'.
ACCALIA (f) A character in Roman mythology.
ACCORD (f) *Old French* Harmony.
ACE (m, rarely f) Possibly a form of Acelin.
ACELIN (m) *Old German* Noble.
ACIMA (f) *Hebrew* The Lord will judge.
ACKERLEY (m) *Old English* Oak tree meadow.
ACQUILLA *see* AQUILLA.
ACTON (m) *Old English* Oak tree village.
ADA (f) *Old English* Happy.
ADAH (f) *Hebrew* Ornament.

Adair   *Aelita*

ADAIR (m) *Gaelic* Oak tree ford.
ADALARD (m) *Old German* Noble resolution.
ADALEE (f) A blend of Ada and Lee.
ADALINE *see* ADELINE.
ADAM (m) *Hebrew* Red earth.
ADAMINA (f) A feminine form of Adam. *Hebrew* Red earth.
ADARA (f) *Sanskrit* Consideration.
ADDIS *see* ADAM.
ADDISON (m) *Old English* Son of Adam.
ADEANA *see* ADINA.
ADELA (f) *Old German* Noble.
ADELAIDE (f) *Old German* Nobility.
ADELE, ADELIA *see* ADELA.
ADELINE, ADELENE, ADELETTE *see* ADELE.
ADELIZA (f) A blend of Adele and Liza.
ADEN *see* AIDAN.
ADENA (f) *Hebrew* Noble.
ADEOLA (f) *Yoruba* Crown has honour.
ADERYN (f) *Welsh* Bird.
ADIE (f) Possibly a form of Adelaide.
ADINA, ADINE (f) *Hebrew* Desire.
ADITA (f) Origin uncertain. Possibly a form of Adina.
ADLAI (m) *Hebrew* My ornament.
ADLEY (m) *Hebrew* Fair minded.
ADOLPH, ADOLPHUS, ADOLF (m) *Old German* Noble wolf.
ADONCIA (f) *Latin* Sweet.
ADRA (f) Origin uncertain. Possibly a form of Adria.
ADRIA (f) Feminine form of Adrian.
ADRIAN (m) From the Italian place-name.
ADRIANNE, ADRIENNE (f) Feminine forms of Adrian.
AELITA (f) *Welsh* Berry.

AERES (f) *Welsh* Heir.
AERIN (f) Probably a feminine form of Aerion.
AERION (m) *Welsh* Heir.
AERLYN (f) Probably a form of Aeres.
AERON (m) *Welsh* Fruit.
AETHNEN (f) *Welsh* Aspen.
AFINA (f) *Rumanian* Blueberry.
AFON (m) *Welsh* River.
AGATHA (f) *Greek* Good.
AGNES (f) *Greek* Pure.
AGNETA, AGNETTA, AGNITA, AGNEATHA *see* AGNES.
AHREN (m) *Old German* Eagle.
AHULANI (f) *Hawaiian* Heavenly shrine.
AIA (f) *Hebrew* Wife.
AIDAN, AIDEN (m) *Gaelic* Fire.
AIDEEN (f) Feminine form of Aidan.
AIKEN (m) *Old English* Made of oak.
AILAN (m) Origin uncertain. Possibly a form of Aidan.
AILEEN, AILENE *see* EILEEN.
AILITH (f) Origin uncertain. Possibly a form of Alitha.
AILSA (f) *Gaelic* From the Scottish island name.
AIMEE (f) The French form of Amy.
AINA (f) *Scandinavian* Always (implying constancy).
AINE (f) A feminine form of Aidan.
AINGEAL (f) *Irish* Angel.
AINSLIE, AINSLEY (m) *Gaelic* One's own meadow.
AINSWORTH (m) *Old English* From Ann's estate.
AISHA, AISSA (f) *Arabic* Woman.
AISLING (f) *Irish* Dream, vision.
AITHNE (f) *Irish* Little fire.
AKAN (m) *Egyptian* Migrant people.

AKI (f, rarely m) *Japanese* Autumn.
AKI (m) *Maori* Boy.
AKILINA (f) *Latin* Eagle.
AKIMA (f) Origin uncertain. Possibly a form of Kim.
AKIRA (f) *Japanese* Intelligence.
ALAN (m) Meaning uncertain. Possibly *Celtic* harmony, or *Gaelic* bright, handsome.
ALANA, ALANNA, ALAYNA, ALANNAH (f) Feminine forms of Alan.
ALANDALE (m) Origin uncertain. Possibly a form of Alan.
ALARIEL, ALARIELLE (f) Blends of Lara and Ariel.
ALANI (f) *Hawaiian* Orange.
ALARIC (m) *Old German* Noble ruler.
ALATHEA, ALATHIA see ALETHEA.
ALASTAIR, ALASDAIR (m) Gaelic forms of Alexander.
ALAULA (f) *Hawaiian* Dawn (or sunset).
ALBAN (m) *Latin* White.
ALBERN (m) *Old English* Noble warrior.
ALBERT (m) *Old German* Noble-bright, Illustrious.
ALCINA, ALCINE (f) *Greek* Sea maiden.
ALDA (f) *Old German* Old.
ALDEN, ALDON (m) *Old English* Two possible origins: 1. River source on the hill; 2. Elf hill down.
ALDER (m) *Middle English* The alder tree.
ALDORA (f) *Old English* Noble gift.
ALDOUS, ALDUS (m) German forms of Alder.
ALDRICH (m) *Old English* Old/elf/noble rule.
ALDRIDGE (m) *Old English* Ridge of the alders.
ALDWIN (m) *Old English* Old friend.
ALECIA (f) A variant of Alice.

Aled　　　　　　　　　　　　　　　Alistair

ALED (m) Meaning uncertain. Probably derived from *Welsh* word *alledu* meaning 'to effuse, pour forth'.

ALEKA (f) *Greek* Defender of mankind.

ALENA, ALENE see ALANA.

ALETHEA, ALITHEA, ALETHIA (f) *Greek* Truth.

ALETTE (f) *Latin* A diminutive of 'wing'.

ALEX see ALEXANDER or ALEXANDRA.

ALEXA (f) Variant of Alexandra.

ALEXANDER (m) *Greek* Protector of men.

ALEXANDRA (f) A feminine form of Alexander.

ALEXANDRIA, ALEXANDRINA see ALEXANDRA.

ALEXIA, ALEXIE, ALEXINA see ALEXANDRA.

ALEXIS (f and m) *Greek* Helper, defender.

ALFORD (m) *Old English* Two possible origins: 1. Elf ford; 2. Alder ford.

ALFRED (m) *Old English* Elf counsel, hence wise counsel.

ALGAR (m) *Old English* Noble/elf spear.

ALGERNON (m) *French* Man with moustache.

ALI, ALY (m and f) Short forms of Alistair, Alison, Alice, etc.

ALIANNE (f) A blend of Alice and Anne.

ALIBETH (f) A blend of Alice and Elizabeth.

ALICE (f) *Old German* Nobility.

ALICIA, ALISA see ALICE.

ALIENOR (f) *Greek* Light.

ALIKA (f) *Nigerian* Outstanding beauty.

ALIM (m) *Arabic* Wise.

ALIMA (f) *Arabic* Musical.

ALINE, ALINA see ADELINE.

ALISHA, ALISSA see ALICIA.

ALISON, ALLISON (f) *Old German* Nobility.

ALISTAIR see ALASTAIR.

ALITHA, ALITHEA, ALITHENE see ALETHEA.
ALIX (m and f) see ALEX.
ALIYA (f) *Hebrew* To ascend.
ALIZA (f) A blend of Alix and Elizabeth.
ALLARD, ALARD (m) *Old German* Noble, hard, enduring.
ALLEN see ALAN.
ALLIDA (f) Origin uncertain. Possibly a form of Alda.
ALLIE see ALYSON.
ALMA (f) *Hebrew* Maiden.
ALMEDHA (f) *Welsh* Shapely.
ALMENA (f) A form of Wilhelmina.
ALMIRA (f) *Arabic* Princess.
ALMON (f) *Welsh* Almond.
ALMITA (f) Origin uncertain. Possibly a form of Almira.
ALNOD (m) *Old English* Elf salutation.
ALODIE (f) *Old English* Rich.
ALOMA (f) From the name of the plant.
ALONZO (m) *Old German* Spanish form of Alphonso, meaning 'noble estate'.
ALORA, ALORAH Blends of Ali and Lora.
ALOYSIA, ALOISA (f) *Old German* Glorious battle.
ALPIN (m) *Latin* White.
ALSTONE, ALSTON (m) *Old English* Two possible origins: 1. Elf stone; 2. Alfred's village.
ALTAY (m) Origin uncertain. Possibly a form of Alton.
ALTHEA (f) *Greek* Wholesome.
ALTON (m) *Old English* Old/elf stream source.
ALULA (f) *Latin* Winged one.
ALURA (f) *Old English* Wise counsellor.

ALVA (f) *Latin* White, blonde.

ALVA (m) *Latin* Rare masculine use of this name. White.

ALVADA (f) A blend of Alva and Vada.

ALVAN (m) *Old German* Old friend.

ALVAR (m) *Old German* Elf army.

ALVASTON (m) *Old English* Two possible origins: 1. Elf place; 2. Alfwald's place.

ALVENA (f) A feminine form of Alvin.

ALVEY (m) *Old English* Elf war.

ALVIN, ALVYN see ALVAN.

ALVINA (f) *Old German* Old friend.

ALVIRA (f) *Old German* Elf arrow.

ALVIS (m) *Old Norse* All knowing.

ALVITA (f) *Latin* Vivacious.

ALWYN see OLWEN.

ALYENA (f) A character in the novel *Tribesmen of Gor* by John Norman.

ALYSON, ALLYSON, ALYSSON see ALISON.

ALYSSA (f) *Greek* Wise.

ALZENA (f) *Arabic* Woman.

ALZINA see ALCINA.

AMABEL (f) *Latin* Lovable.

AMABETH (f) A blend of Amanda and Elizabeth.

AMADELLE (f) A blend of Amanda and Delia.

AMALANDRA (f) A blend of Amalia and Sandra.

AMALETTE (f) A diminutive of Amalia.

AMALIA see EMILY.

AMALINA, AMALINE (f) Blends of Amanda and Caroline.

AMALINDA (f) A blend of Amanda and Linda.

AMALISSA (f) A blend of Amanda and Alice.

AMALY see EMILY.

Amanda   Ameranda, Amerinda

AMANDA (f) *Latin* Lovable. Appears in several seventeenth century plays, but the original inventor is uncertain.

AMANITA, AMANETTE (f) Blends of Amanda and Anita.

AMANTINE (f) A blend of Amanda and Tina.

AMARA (f) *Sanskrit* Immortal.

AMARANDA (f) A blend of Amanda and Miranda.

AMARANTHA (f) *Greek* Unfading.

AMAREL, AMARELLE, AMARELLA (f) Blends of Amara and Ella.

AMARENA, AMARINA (f) Blends of Amara and Rena.

AMARETTE, AMARETTA (f) Diminutives of Amara.

AMARINDA (f) *Greek* Long-lived.

AMARINTHA (f) A blend of Amara and Cynthia.

AMARIS (f) *Hebrew* Whom God has promised.

AMARYLLIS (f) *Greek* Fresh stream.

AMATHEA, AMATHETTE (f) Blends of Amanda and Anthea.

AMBA (f) *Sanskrit* Universal Mother.

AMBER (f) *Arabic* From the name of the precious stone.

AMBIKA (f) *Sanskrit* Benevolent mother.

AMBROSE (m) *Greek* Immortal.

AMBROSINE (f) A feminine form of Ambrose.

AMECIA *see* AMY.

AMEENA (f) Possibly a form of Amelia.

AMELINDA (f) *Latin* Beloved and pretty.

AMELIA (f) *Old German* Industrious.

AMERA (f) A blend of Amy and Vera.

AMERAL (f) Origin uncertain. Possibly a form of Amera.

AMERANDA, AMERINDA *see* AMARANDA.

AMERY (m) *Old German* A form of Almeric. Hardworking, conscientious ruler.
AMETHA (f) Origin uncertain. Possibly a form of Amethyst.
AMETHYST (f) *Greek* From the name of the gem meaning 'not drunken'. (The stone was supposed to prevent intoxication).
AMIA (f) *Latin* Love.
AMICA (f) *Latin* Friend.
AMINA (f) *Arabic* Faithful.
AMINTA (f) *Latin* Loving.
AMIRA (f) *Hebrew* Speech.
AMMA (f) Two possible origins: 1. *Hebrew* Servant; 2. *Old Norse* Grandmother.
AMORETTA (f) *Latin* Little loved one.
AMORY (m) A form of Amery.
AMY (f) *Latin* Love.
ANABETH, ANNABETH (f) Blends of Ann and Elizabeth.
ANAHERA (f) *Maori* Angel.
ANAN (m) *Hebrew* Cloud.
ANANDA (m) *Sanskrit* Bliss.
ANASTASIA (f) *Greek* Resurrection.
ANCEL (m) *Old German* Of God.
ANCILLA (f) *Latin* Handmaiden.
ANDEANA (f) *Spanish* Walker.
ANDERS (m) *Greek* Manly.
ANDOR *see* ANDREW.
ANDORA (f) A blend of Ann and Dora.
ANDRA (f) A feminine form of Andrew.
ANDREA (f) *Greek* Brave.
ANDREW (m) *Greek* Brave.
ANDREY (m) Origin uncertain. Possibly a form of Andrew.

ANDRIANA (f) A feminine form of Andrew.
ANDRIS (f) *Welsh* Very fair.
ANDY *see* ANDREW.
ANELLA (f) A blend of Ann and Ella.
ANETTA *see* ANNETTA.
ANGELA (f) *Greek* Angel.
ANGELICA, ANGELIKA (f) Variants of Angela.
ANGELINA, ANGELINE, ANGELITA (f) Diminutives of Angela.
ANGHARAD (f) *Welsh* Much loved.
ANGUS (m) *Gaelic* Unique choice.
ANGWEN (f) *Welsh* Beautiful.
ANIKA, ANICA (f) *Hausa* Sweetness of face.
ANIRA (f) A blend of Ann and Vera.
ANISA (f) A blend of Ann and Lisa.
ANITA (f) *Hebrew* Graceful.
ANJELICA, ANJELIKA *see* ANGELICA.
ANJENETTE, ANJANETTE (f) Blends of Anjelica and Jeanette.
ANN, ANNA, ANNE (f) *Hebrew* Graceful.
ANNABEL (f) *Latin* Lovable.
ANNABETH (f) A blend of Ann and Elizabeth.
ANNADA (f) A blend of Ann and Ada.
ANNALEE, ANNALIA, ANNALIE (f) Blends of Ann and Lee.
ANNALEEN, ANNALETTE (f) Diminutives of Ann.
ANNALISA (f) A blend of Ann and Lisa.
ANNALYN (f) A blend of Ann and Lyn.
ANNATHEA (f) A blend of Ann and Thea.
ANNATHELLA (f) A blend of Ann and Ella.
ANNATHETTE (f) Diminutive of Ann.
ANNAZETTE (f) A blend of Anna and Suzette.
ANNEKA (f) *Dutch* Diminutive of Ann.
ANNELLA, ANNELLE (f) Blends of Ann and Ella.

ANNELIESE (f) A German form of Ann.
ANNETHA, ANNETHEA see ANNATHEA.
ANNETTE, ANNETTA (f) Diminutives of Ann.
ANNIE, ANNEE see ANN.
ANNIKI (f) A variant of Ann.
ANNINA (f) A blend of Ann and Nina.
ANONA (f) *Latin* Ninth born.
ANNONA (f) A blend of Ann and Nona.
ANNORA (f) *Hebrew* Grace.
ANNWYL (f) *Welsh* Dear.
ANORA see ANNORA.
ANOUSHKA (f) A Russian form of Ann.
ANSELL, ANSEL, ANSELM (m) *Old German* Divine helmet.
ANSLEY see AINSLIE.
ANSON (m) Son of Ann.
ANSTEY (m) *Greek* Resurrection.
ANTHEA (f) *Greek* Flowery.
ANTHELIA (f) A blend of Anthea and Delia.
ANTOINETTE (f) A feminine form of Antony.
ANTON (m) German and Russian form of Antony.
ANTONIA (f) A feminine form of Antony.
ANTONY, ANTHONY (m) From the Roman family name Antonius.
ANTRA (f) Origin uncertain. Possibly a form of Ann.
ANWEN (f) *Welsh* Very fair.
ANYA (f) A Russian form of Ann.
ANYON (m) *Celtic* Anvil.
ANZIL (m) Origin uncertain. Possibly a form of Denzil.
ANZU (f) *Japanese* Apricot.
AO (f) *Maori* Planet Earth.
AOLANI (f) *Hawaiian* Heavenly cloud.
AOSTRA (f) *Greek/Egyptian* Sunrise, dawn.

APHRA (f) *Hebrew* Young deer.
APRIL (f) *Latin* To open (hence springtime).
AQUILA, AQUILLA (m) *Latin* Eagle.
ARA (f) Two possible origins: 1. *Old German* Eagle; 2. *Maori* Path, way, awake.
ARABELLA, ARABEL (f) *Old German/Latin* Beautiful eagle.
ARAMINTA (f) *Latin* Loving.
ARANI (f) *Maori* Orange.
ARAZIE (f) From the name of the Armenian river.
ARCHER (m) *Latin* Bowman.
ARCHIBALD, ARCHIE, ARCH (m) *Old German* Noble, bold.
ARDATH (f) *Hebrew* Flowering field.
ARDELIA (f) *Latin* Zealous.
ARDELL (m) *Old English* Of the dell.
ARDELLE (f) Feminine form of Arden.
ARDEN (m) *Latin* Enthusiastic.
ARDLEY (m) *Old English* The home meadow.
ARELLA (f) Origin uncertain.
ARETHA, ARETA (f) *Greek* Virtue.
ARHLENE *see* ARLEEN.
ARIADNE (f) *Greek* Holy one.
ARIAL (f) *Welsh* Vigour.
ARIAN (f) *Welsh* Silver.
ARIANE, ARIANNA, ARIANA (f) *Greek* Holy one.
ARIANWEN (f) *Welsh* Silver white.
ARIELLA (f) *Hebrew* God's lioness.
ARIKE (m) *Maori* Chief, leader.
ARION (m) Origin uncertain.
ARISTA (f) Origin uncertain. Possibly a form of Aritha.
ARITA (f) *Maori* Eager.

ARITHA (f) From the wood nymph in Greek mythology called Arethusa.
ARLA, ARLANA, ARLANE *see* ARLEEN.
ARLAND, ARLAN *see* ORLANDO.
ARLEIGH, ARLEY (m) *Hebrew* Pledge.
ARLEEN, ARLENE (f) Variants of a feminine form of Charles.
ARLEN (m) *Celtic* Pledge.
ARLETTA, ARLETTE (f) *Old German* Girl.
ARLIN (m) *Old German* Eagle wood.
ARLINGTON (m) *Old German* Settlement at eagle wood.
ARLYNN (f) A blend of Arleen and Lynn.
ARMAND (m) *Old German* Warrior.
ARMINA, ARMINE (f) *Old German* Warrior.
ARNEY (m) *Old German* Eagle.
ARNOLD (m) *Old German* Strong as an eagle.
AROHA (f) *Maori* Love.
ARON *see* AARON.
ARRAN (m) From the name of the Scottish island.
ARTHUR (m) Two possible origins: 1. *Welsh* Bear; 2. *Irish* Stone.
ARUNA (f) *Sanskrit* Dawn.
ARUNDALE (m) *Old English* High meadow.
ARUNDELL (m) *Old English* From the place-name meaning Hoarhound valley.
ARVAL (m) *Latin* Cultivated land.
ARWEN, ARWYN (f) *Welsh* Heroine.
ASA (m) *Hebrew* Healer.
ASA (f) *Japanese* Morning.
ASGELL (f) *Welsh* Chaffinch.
ASHBY (m) *Old English* Farm by the ash trees.
ASHCROFT (m) *Old English* Small farm by ash trees.

Ashe, Asha   Aura

ASHE, ASHA (f) Origin uncertain.
ASHER (m) *Hebrew* Happy.
ASHFORD (m) *Old English* Ford near ash trees.
ASHLEY, ASHLEIGH, ASHLEA, ASHLEE (m and f) *Old English* Ash wood.
ASHLING see AISLING.
ASHTON (m) *Old English* Ash tree village.
ASLAN (m) The lion/sage character in the *Narnia* series of books by C. S. Lewis.
ASMITA (f) *Sanskrit* Self-respect.
ASPEN (m) *Old German* The tree name used as a first name.
ASTA (f) *Greek* Star.
ASTLEY (m) *Old English* Ash tree glade.
ASTON (m) *Old English* Ash tree village.
ASTRA (f) *Latin* Star.
ASTRID (f) *Old Norse* Divine beauty.
ATALIE, ATALIA, TALIE (f) *Scandinavian* Pure.
ATANDRA (f) Origin uncertain.
ATARA (f) *Hebrew* Crown.
ATHALIA (f) *Hebrew* God is exalted.
ATHENE, ATHENA (f) *Greek* Wisdom.
ATHERTON (m) *Old English* The spring village.
ATHOL (m) *Gaelic* New Ireland.
AUBERON (m) *Old German* Little elf ruler.
AUBIN (m) *Latin* Fair, white.
AUBREY (m) *Old German* Elf ruler.
AUDLEY (m) *Old English* Old battle.
AUDREY (f) *Old English* Noble strength.
AUDRENE see AUDREY.
AUGUST (m) *Latin* Majestic.
AUGUSTA (f) *Latin* Majestic.
AULAY (m) Gaelic form of Olaf.
AURA (f) *Greek* Breath.

Aurea   Azura, Azure

AUREA (f) *Latin* Golden.
AURELIA (f) *Latin* Golden.
AURORA (f) *Latin* Dawn.
AUSTIN, AUSTEN *see* AUGUST.
AVA (f) *Latin* Bird.
AVELINA, AVELINE (f) *Old French* Hazel tree.
AVELLANE (f) From the French name for a heraldic cross.
AVALON (f) *Latin* Island.
AVERIL, AVRIL (f) *Old English* Boar battle.
AVERY (m) A variant of Alfred.
AVON (m) *Welsh* River.
AXEL (m) Scandinavian form of Absalom.
AYLA (f) A character in the novels of Jean M. Auel.
AYLMER (m) *Old English* Noble-famous, renowned.
AYLWIN *see* ALVIN.
AYNE (f) Origin uncertain.
AYUMI (f and m) *Japanese* Progress.
AZALEA, AZALIA, AZAELA (f) *Greek* From the name of the flowering plant meaning 'dry'.
AZARA (f) From the plant name.
AZAMI (f) *Japanese* Thistle flower.
AZEA (f) The name of a civilization in the novel *In Conquest Born* by C. S. Friedman.
AZENA (f) Origin uncertain. Possibly a form of Zena.
AZILE (f) Eliza spelt backwards.
AZURA, AZURE (f) *Persian* Sky blue.

Babette B Byron

BABETTE (f) *Hebrew* God is my satisfaction.
BADEN (m) *Old English* Battle.
BAILEY (m) *Middle English* Outer castle wall.
BAIN (m) *Gaelic* White.
BAIRD (m) *Gaelic* Minstrel.
BAKER (m) An occupational surname – maker of bread.
BALDWIN (m) *Old German* Bold friend.
BALLARD (m) *Middle English* Dancing song.
BAMBER (m) *Old English* From the place-name Bimme's bridge.
BANCROFT (m) *Old English* Bean field.
BARANTHA (f) A blend of Barbara and Samantha.
BARBARA (f) *Greek* Stranger.
BARBARELLA, BARBARINA, BARBARETTA (f) Forms of Barbara.
BARCIE (f) Origin uncertain.
BARCLAY (m) *Old English* Birch meadow.
BARDEN (m) *Old English* Valley where barley grows.
BARDOLPH (m) *Old English* Bright wolf.
BARINA (f) A blend of Barbara and Irene.
BARKER (m) *Old English* Logger of birch trees.
BARLOW (m) *Old English* Dweller on barren hills.
BARNABUS, BARNABY, BARNEY (m) *Hebrew* Son of consolation.

BARNARD see BERNARD.
BARNES (m) *Old English* A bear.
BARON, BARRON (m) *Old English* Noble warrior.
BARRETT, BARRET (m) *Old German* Strong as a bear.
BARRIE see BARRY.
BARRINGTON (m) *Old English* The village of Beorn's (or Bara's) people.
BARRY (m) *Gaelic* Spear-like.
BARTHOLOMEW, BART (m) *Aramaic* Son of Tolmai.
BARTON (m) *Old English* Village near the barley field.
BASIL (m) *Greek* Kingly.
BATHSHEBA (f) *Hebrew* Daughter of an oath.
BAXTER (m) *Old German* Baker of bread.
BAYARD (m) *French* Bay colour.
BAZIL, BAZ see BASIL.
BEA see BEATRICE.
BEATRICE (f) *Latin* Bringer of happiness.
BEAU (m) *French* Handsome.
BEAUMONT (m) *French* Beautiful mountain.
BEAVIS (m) *Old English* Strong as an ox.
BEBE see BARBARA.
BECKY see REBECCA.
BEDELIA see BRIDGET.
BEKI see REBECCA.
BELANTHA (f) A blend of Bella and Samantha.
BELDEN (m) *Old English* Beautiful glen.
BELETTA (f) A blend of Belle and Betty.
BELINA (f) A blend of Belle and Carolina.
BELINDA (f) *Latin* Wise beauty.
BELLA see ISABELLA.
BELLAMY (m) *Greek* Fair friend.

BELMONT (m) *Italian* Beautiful mountain.
BEN, BENNY, BENJY see BENJAMIN.
BENA, BINA (f) *Hebrew* Wise.
BENEDETTA (f) Italian form of Benedict.
BENEDICT (m) *Latin* To bless.
BENEDICTA (f) Feminine form of Benedict.
BENITA (f) Spanish form of Benedicta.
BENJAMIN (m) *Hebrew* Son of my right hand.
BENNET, BENNETT, BENET see BENEDICT.
BENSON (m) Son of Ben.
BENTLEY (m) *Old English* Bent grass clearing.
BENTON (m) *Old English* Ben's village.
BERENGER (m) *Old German* Bear spear.
BERENICE (f) *Greek* Bringer of victory.
BERESFORD (m) *Old English* Beaver ford.
BERINTHIA (f) Probably invented by Vanbrugh for his play *The Relapse*.
BERKELEY (m) *Old English* Birch wood.
BERNADETTE (f) Feminine form of Bernard.
BERNARD (m) *Old German* Bold as a bear.
BERNARDINE, BERNARDINA see BERNADETTE.
BERNETTA, BERNETTE see BERNADETTE.
BERNICE see BERENICE.
BERRY (m and f) *Old German* Small fruit.
BERT (m) Diminutive of Albert, Robert, Herbert, etc.
BERTHA (f) *Old German* Bright one.
BERTRAM (m) *Old German* Bright raven.
BERTRAND (m) Possibly a form of Bertram.
BERWICK (m) *Old English* Barley farm.
BERYL (f) *Greek* Precious stone.
BETHANNA (f) A blend of Elizabeth and Anne.
BETHANY (f) *Hebrew* From the place-name meaning house of figs.
BETHIA (f) *Hebrew* Daughter of God.

BETHINA (f) A blend of Elizabeth and Bina.
BETORA (f) A blend of Betty and Lora.
BETSY, BETZY, BETTE *see* BETTY.
BETTINA, BETINA (f) An Italian/Spanish form of Betty.
BETTY *see* ELIZABETH.
BEULAH (f) *Hebrew* Married (woman).
BEVAN (m) *Welsh* Son of Evan.
BEVERLEY, BEVERLY (m and f) *Old English* Beaver stream.
BEVIS (m) *Old French* Possibly 'dear son'.
BIANCA (f) *Italian* White.
BIBI (f) *French* Bauble.
BIDDY, BIDDIE (f) Forms of Bridget.
BILL, BILLY *see* WILLIAM.
BILLIE (f, rarely m) Derived from William.
BINA (f) *Hebrew* Wisdom. Also pet form of Robina, Sabina, etc.
BINNIE, BINKIE (f) *Old English* A bin, receptacle or basket, hence a crib.
BIRCH (m) *Old English* From the tree name meaning 'white'.
BIRON *see* BYRON.
BLAIN, BLAINE (m) *Old English* Source of a river.
BLAIR (m and f) *Gaelic* A field.
BLAISE, BLAIZE (m, rarely f) *Latin* Crippled, stuttering.
BLAKE (m, rarely f) *Old English* Pale.
BLANCHE, BLANCH (f) *French* White.
BLANDON (m) *Latin* Smooth-tongued, flattering.
BLANFORD (m) *Old English* Easy river crossing.
BLASE, BLAZE *see* BLAISE.
BLENDA *see* BELINDA.
BLESSING (m and f) *Old English* Bestowal of grace.

BLISS (f) *Old English* Perfect joy.
BLODWEN (f) *Welsh* White flower.
BLOSSOM (f) *Old English* To open into flower.
BLUE (m) The colour – used as a first name.
BLUEBELL (f) *Middle English/Old English* A flower name – A wild hyacinth.
BLUETTE (f) From the plant name.
BLYSS *see* BLISS.
BLYTHE (f) The word 'blithe' used as a name.
BO (f) *French* Phonetic form of *beau* meaning 'beautiful'.
BOB, BOBBY *see* ROBERT.
BOBBI *see* ROBERTA.
BOLTON (m) *Old English* Dwelling or village.
BONAR (m) *Old French* Gentle, courteous.
BONITA (f) *Spanish* Pretty.
BONNIE, BONNY, BONNI (f) *Scottish* Good.
BOONE (m) *Old French* Good.
BOOTH (m) *Old English* Herdsman.
BORDEN (m) *Old French* Cottage.
BORIS (m) *Russian* To fight.
BOSWORTH (m) *Old English* Estate surrounded by trees.
BOURNE (m) *Old English* A brook.
BOWDEN (m) *Old English* Bow-shaped hill.
BOWEN (m) *Celtic* Son of Owen.
BOYCE (m) *French* Wood.
BOYD (m) *Gaelic* Yellow (hair).
BRACKEN (m) *Old Norse* From the plant name meaning 'a fern'.
BRAD *see* BRADLEY.
BRADEN (m) *Old English* Broad.
BRADFORD (m) *Old English* Broad ford.
BRADLEY (m) *Old English* Broad meadow.

BRADY (m) *Old English* Broad island.

BRAM *see* ABRAHAM.

BRAMBLE (m) *Old English* Blackberry.

BRAMLEY (m) *Old English* Broom clearing.

BRAMWELL (m) *Old English* Bramble well.

BRAN (m) *Welsh* Raven.

BRAND (m) *Middle English* Flaming sword.

BRANDON, BRANDEN (m) *Old English* Hill covered with broom.

BRANNAN, BRANNON (m) *Irish* Sad raven.

BRANSBY (m) *Old Norse* Bran's settlement.

BRANSON (m) Son of Brand.

BRANT *see* BRAND.

BRANTON (m) *Old English* Bran's village.

BRANWELL *see* BRAMWELL.

BRANWEN (f) *Welsh* Beautiful raven.

BREE (f) *Middle English* Broth or soup.

BREELYN (f) A blend of Bree and Lynda.

BREN *see* BRAN.

BRENDA (f) Origin uncertain. Possibly *Old Norse* meaning Sword.

BRENDAN (m) Origin uncertain. Possibly *Irish* meaning Raven.

BRENDELIA (f) A blend of Brenda and Delia.

BRENDELLA (f) A blend of Brenda and Ella.

BRENDINA, BRENDENE (f) Blends of Brenda and Dinah.

BRENDORA (f) A blend of Brenda and Dora.

BRENNA *see* BRENDA.

BRENT (m) *Old English* High place.

BRENTON *see* BRENT.

BRETT (m) *Latin* Briton.

BREWSTER (m) An occupational surname meaning a female brewer.

BRIAHNA, BRIANNA, BRIANNE (f) Feminine forms of Brian.

BRIAN, BRYAN (m) Origin uncertain. Possibly *Irish* meaning Strong or hill.

BRIANTHA (f) A blend of Brianna and Samantha.

BRIAR (m) *Greek* Strong.

BRID, BRIDIE see BRIDGET.

BRIDGET, BRIDGETTE (f) *Irish* The high one.

BRIGHAM (m) *Old English* Hamlet near a bridge.

BRINA (f) *Slavonic* Protector.

BRINDLEY (m) *Old Norse* Burnt wood (or clearing).

BRINK (m) *Old Norse* Steep edge.

BRINLEY see BRINDLEY.

BRINSLEY (m) *Old English* Brin's meadow.

BRIOC see BROCK.

BRION (m) A character in the novel *Deryni Rising* by Katherine Kurtz.

BRIONY see BRYONY.

BRITA, BRITTA, BRITT see BRIDGET.

BRITTINA, BRITTINE (f) Diminutives of Britt.

BROCK (m) *Old English* Badger.

BRODERICK, BRODY (m) *Old Norse* Brother.

BROMLEY (m) *Old English* Dweller in the meadow.

BRON (m) *Old English* Brown.

BRONANDA (f) A blend of Bronwen and Wanda.

BRONESSA (f) *Welsh* White.

BRONIA (f) A feminine form of Bron.

BRONNEN (f) *Cornish* A rush.

BRONSON (m) Son of Brown.

BRONWEN (f) *Welsh* White breast.

BROOK (m and f) *Old English* Dweller by the stream.

BROOKE see BROOK.

BRUCE (m) *French* Woods.

BRUCENA (f) Feminine form of Bruce.
BRUNA (f) Feminine form of Bruno.
BRUNELLA, BRUNETTA see BRUNA.
BRUNO (m) *Old German* Dark or brown complexion.
BRYAN see BRIAN.
BRYANT see BRYAN.
BRYCE (m) Celtic name of unknown origin.
BRYDEN (m) *Old English* Bird valley.
BRYN (m, rarely f) *Welsh* Hill.
BRYNA (f) *Irish* Strength with virtue.
BRYNLEY see BRINLEY.
BRYNN, BRYN, BRYNA (f) Feminine forms of Bryan.
BRYOLA (f) A blend of Brynn and Lola.
BRYON see BRIAN.
BRYONY, BRIONY (f) *Greek* The plant name used as a first name.
BRYSON (m) Son of Brice.
BRYTHER (m) Origin uncertain.
BUCK (m) *Old English* A male deer (hence a dashing man).
BUCKLEY (m) *Old English* Beech meadow.
BUDDY, BUD (m) Friend (a variation of 'brother').
BUNNY (f) A pet form of Berenice, Roberta, etc.
BUNTY (f) Probably derived from the nursery rhyme *Bye Bye Baby Bunting*.
BURCHARD (m) *Old English* Fortified enclosure.
BURGESS (m) *Latin* Fortified place.
BURKE (m) *Old German* Castle.
BURL (m) *Latin* Coarse hair.
BURNETT, BURNET (m) *Old French* Brownish.
BURNFORD, BUFORD (m) *Old English* Stream ford.

BURRELL, BURRILL, BURR (m) *Middle English* A prickly plant.
BURT, BURTT *see* BURTON.
BURTON (m) *Old English* Village on a hill.
BUSTER (m) Nickname for an active boy.
BURWOOD, BURWARD (m) *Old English* Hillside wood.
BUX (m) Possibly a form of Bud.
BYRAM (m) *Old English* Ancient byre.
BYRNE (m) *Old English* Coat of armour.
BYRON (m) *Old English* Byre or barn.

Cachel **C** *Cyrus*

CACHEL, CACHELLA, CACHELLE (f) From the French *cacher* meaning 'to hide', hence 'hidden talents,' 'hidden wisdom'.
CACIE *see* ACACIA.
CADE (m) *Welsh* Battle.
CADELL (m) *Welsh* Warrior.
CADENCE (f) *Latin* Movement of sound.
CADOR (m) *Cornish* Warrior.
CAEL, CALE (m) Variants of Caleb.
CAI (m) *Latin* Welsh form of Caius, meaning 'to rejoice'.
CAIETTA (f) Feminine form of Cai.
CAILIN (f) *Gaelic* Girl.
CAIN (m) *Hebrew* A spear.
CAIRD (m) *Gaelic* A blacksmith.
CAITANYA (f) A blend of Caitlin and Tanya.
CAITLIN (f) An Irish form of Kathleen.
CAITRIONA *see* CATRIONA.
CAITRIN *see* KATHARINE.
CAIUS (m) *Latin* Rejoice.
CAJA (f) *Cornish* Daisy.
CAL (m) A character in the *Wraeththu* trilogy of novels by Storm Constantine.
CALANDRA (f) *Greek* A lark.
CALANTHA, CALANTHE (f) *Greek* Beautiful blossom.

CALDER (m) *Celtic* Stony river.
CALDORA (f) *Greek* Beautiful gift.
CALDWELL (m) *Greek* Warrior.
CALEB (m) *Hebrew* A dog (hence 'bold' and 'faithful').
CALELLA (f) *Celtic* Handmaid.
CALENDULA (f) *Latin* Marigold.
CALIDA (f) *Spanish* Ardently loving.
CALINDA, KALINDA (f) A traditional Spanish dance.
CALISTA, CALLISTA, CALISE (f) *Greek* Most lovely.
CALLA (f) *Greek* Beautiful.
CALLENA (f) *Old German* Talkative.
CALLUM, CALUM (m) Gaelic forms of Columba.
CALLY (f) Pet form of Calandra, Calanthe, etc.
CALOSA (f) Possibly a form of Celosia.
CALTHA (f) *Latin* Marigold.
CALVERT (m) *Old English* Calf-herder.
CALVIN (m) *Latin* Bald.
CAMARA (f) A blend of Camilla and Mary.
CAMELIA (f) From the flowering plant *Camellia*, named after the botanist George Joseph Kamel.
CAMEO (f) *Italian* A carving (the term for a sculptured jewel).
CAMERON (m) *Celtic* Bent nose.
CAMIE (f) Pet form of Camilla, Camina, etc.
CAMILLA, CAMILLE (f) *Latin* Feminine form of the Roman name Camillus, meaning 'attendant' or 'messenger'.
CAMINA (f) A blend of Camilla and Nina.
CAMINDA (f) A blend of Camilla and Linda.
CAMIRA (f) A blend of Camilla and Mira.
CAMITA (f) A blend of Camilla and Rita.
CAMORA (f) A blend of Camilla and Dora.

CAMPBELL (m) *Gaelic* Crooked mouth.
CAMPION (m) *Greek* From the plant name.
CANACE (f) *Greek* Daughter of the wind.
CANDACE (f) *Greek* Fire white.
CANDI, CANDIE, CANDY *see* CANDACE.
CANDIA (f) *Greek* Woman from Candia (now called Heraklion) the capital of Crete.
CANDICE, CANDIS, CANDYCE *see* CANDACE.
CANDIDA (f) *Latin* White.
CANDORA (f) A blend of Candace and Dora.
CANDRA (f) *Sanskrit* Moon.
CANLI (f) A blend of zodiac signs Cancer and Libra.
CAPRICE (f) *Latin* A head with bristling hair.
CARA (f) A form of Caroline, Charlotte, etc.
CARADOC (m) *Welsh* Love.
CARALYN, CARALINE *see* CAROLYN.
CARANA (f) A blend of Cara and Nana.
CARANDA (f) A blend of Cara and Amanda.
CARANTHA (f) A blend of Cara and Samantha.
CARAWAY (f) *Greek* From the plant name.
CARDEN (m) *Old French* To card, comb out.
CAREL, CARELLA, CARELLE (f) *Old English* Care, hence 'carer,' 'caregiver'.
CAREMA (f) A blend of Cara and Emma.
CAREN *see* KAREN.
CARESS (f) *Latin* Fondly touch. Made popular as the name of a character in the television soap opera *Dynasty*.
CARETTA (f) A blend of Cara and Etta.
CAREY, CARI (f, rarely m) *Old English* Pleasant stream.
CARIAD (f) *Welsh* Sweetheart.
CARIN, CARYN *see* KAREN.
CARINA (f) *Latin* A keel.

CARIS (f) *Greek* Favour, grace.

CARISMA (f) *Greek* From 'charisma' meaning favour, grace.

CARISSA (f) A blend of Cara and Larissa.

CARITA (f) *Latin* Charity.

CARL, KARL *see* CHARLES.

CARLA (f) A feminine form of Charles.

CARLANA *see* CHARLENE.

CARLENE, CARLEEN *see* CAROLINE.

CARLETON, CARLTON (m) *Old English* Carl's village.

CARLETTA *see* CARLOTTA.

CARLEY, CARLIE, CARLI *see* CARLENE.

CARLILE, CARLISLE, CARLYLE (m) Two possible origins: 1. *Old English* Carl's island, 2. *Celtic* Fortress of Luel (Lugh was the Celtic sun-god).

CARLIN (m) *Gaelic* Little champion.

CARLINE (f) *Latin* From the plant name, meaning 'thistle'.

CARLINA, CARLINE, CARLYNE *see* CAROLINE.

CARLOTTA (f) Italian feminine form of Charles.

CARLY *see* CARLENE.

CARLTON *see* CARLETON.

CARY *see* CAREY.

CARMEL, CARMELLA, CARMELLE (f) *Hebrew* A vineyard.

CARMELINA, CARMELITA *see* CARMEL.

CARMEN (f) Spanish form of Carmel.

CARMILLA, CARMILA (f) Italian form of Carmel.

CARNEY (m) *Celtic* A fighter.

CARO *see* CAROLINE.

CAROL, CARROL, CARROLL (f and m) Forms of Caroline or Charles.

CAROLA, CAROLE see CAROL.

CAROLEEN (f) A blend of Carol and Kathleen.

CAROLINDA (f) A blend of Carol and Linda.

CAROLINE, CAROLYNE (f) Italian feminine form of Charles.

CAROLYN, CAROLIN (f) Forms of Caroline.

CAROMEL (f) *Latin* Dear honey.

CAROMY (f) *Celtic* Friend.

CARON, CARRON (f) Derived from a Welsh word meaning 'to love', but often seen as a variant of Karen.

CARREN (f) Variant of Caron or Karen.

CARRIE, CARRI see CAROLINE.

CARSON (m) Son of Carr.

CARY see CAREY.

CARYL see CAROL.

CARYN see KAREN.

CARYS (f) *Welsh* Loved one.

CASEY (m and f) *Irish* Watchful.

CASPAR see JASPER.

CASS, CASSY see CASSANDRA.

CASSADY (f) Feminine form of Cassidy.

CASSANDRA (f) *Greek* One whose warnings are ignored.

CASSANTHA (f) A blend of Cassandra and Samantha.

CASSARA (f) A blend of Cassandra and Sara.

CASSENA (f) A variant of Cassia.

CASSIA (f) A broadleaved group of trees which includes the Indian Laburnum.

CASSIDY (m) *Celtic* Ingenious.

CASSIE see CATHERINE.

CATARINA, CATORINA see CATHERINE.

CATHERINE (f) *Greek* Pure.

CATHLEEN (f) Irish form of Catherine.
CATHRINE, CATHRYN *see* CATHERINE.
CATHY *see* CATHERINE.
CATRIN, CATRINA *see* CATRIONA.
CATRIONA (f) Gaelic form of Catherine.
CAVAN (m) *Irish* Comely birth.
CAVENDISH (m) *Old English* Bold pasture.
CAZ (f) Origin uncertain. Possibly a form of Cass.
CECELIA *see* CECILIA.
CECIL (m) *Latin* Blind.
CECILE (f) Feminine form of Cecil.
CECILIA, CECILIE, CECILY (f) Variants of Cecile.
CEDAR (m) The name of a group of coniferous trees.
CEDRIC, CEDRICK (m) *Welsh* Bounty, pattern.
CELARA (f) A blend of Celia and Lara.
CELANDINE (f) A flower name. *Greek* The swallow.
CELANTHA (f) A blend of Celia and Samantha.
CELENA *see* SELENA.
CELESTE (f) *Latin* Heavenly.
CELESTINE, CELESTINA *see* CELESTE.
CELIA (f) The feminine form of a Roman clan name.
CELINA, CELINE *see* SELINA.
CELOSIA (f) *Greek* A flame.
CENTA (f) Possibly a phonetic form of 'centre'.
CERELIA, CERELLIA (f) *Latin* Fruitful woman.
CERI, CERIAL, CERYS (f) *Welsh* To love.
CERIA *see* CERIAL.
CERIDWEN (f) *Welsh* Fair poetry (one of the names of The Goddess or Gaia).
CERISE (f) *French* Cherry.
CHAD (m) *Celtic* Battle or warrior.
CHADWICK (m) *Old English* Warrior town.
CHALCONEL (f) A modern invention meaning 'chalice of the elves'.

CHALFONT (m) *Old English* Ceadel's spring.
CHALLAH (f) *Hebrew* Bread.
CHALLIS, CHALIS (f) Phonetic forms of 'chalice'.
CHAMARA (f) A blend of Chana and Mary.
CHAMEL, CHAMELLA (f) Blends of Chana and Ella.
CHANA see HANNAH.
CHANDELLE (f) *French* Candle.
CHANDLER (m) *French* Seller of candles.
CHANDRA (f) *Sanskrit* Moon.
CHANEL (f) The name of the French perfume used as a first name.
CHANEY (m) *French* Chain of rocks.
CHANNING (m) *Old English* Knowing.
CHANTAL (f) *Latin* A song.
CHANTELLE (f) A blend of Chantal and Ella.
CHAREEN, CHARENE see SHARON.
CHAREL, CHARELLE (f) Blends of Charles and Eleanor.
CHARELLA, CHARETTE, CHARINE, CHARINE (f) Diminutives of Charel.
CHARIS, CHARISSE (f) *Greek* Grace, beauty.
CHARITY (f) *Latin* Affection.
CHARLA (f) Feminine form of Charles.
CHARLAINE, CHARLAYNE see CHARLENE.
CHARLENE, CHARLEEN, CHARLAYNE (f) Forms of Charlotte.
CHARLES (m) *Old English* Man, husbandman (hence manly).
CHARLESENA (f) Diminutive of Charla.
CHARLINDA, CHARLYNDA (f) A blend of Charles and Linda.
CHARLOTTA, CHARLOTTI (f) Variants of Charlotte.

CHARLOTTE (f) French feminine form of Charles.
CHARLTON (m) *Old English* Charles's village.
CHARMAINE, CHARMANE (f) A feminine form of the Roman family name Carmineus.
CHARMIAN (f) *Greek* A little joy.
CHARON see SHARON.
CHAS see CHARLES.
CHATTY see CHARLOTTE.
CHAUNCEY (m) *Old French* Chance, luck.
CHAVONNE, CHAVON (f) Forms of Siobhan.
CHAY see CHARLES.
CHAYA (f) *Hebrew* Life.
CHAYLE, CHAYLEE (f) Origin uncertain.
CHAZ see CHARLES.
CHEL (m) Perhaps a variant of 'chiel', a Scottish form of 'child'.
CHELSEA (f) *Old English* Landing place for chalk.
CHELSTON (m) *Old English* Ceolwulf's village.
CHEM (m) Origin uncertain.
CHENCA (f) Origin uncertain.
CHNNEY, CHEYNI see CHANEY.
CHER, CHERE (f) *French* Dear one.
CHERALYN see CHERILYN.
CHEREDITH (f) A blend of Chere and Edith.
CHEREEN, CHERENE, CHERINA (f) Blends of Chere and Doreen.
CHERELLA, CHERELLE (f) Blends of Chere and Ella.
CHERETTE, CHERETTA (f) Blends of Chere and Betty.
CHERIE, CHERRIE, CHERI (f) *French* Dear one.
CHERILYN, CHERILENE (f) Blends of Cheryl and Linda.

CHERINE, CHERISE, CHERISSA, CHERITA (f) Variants of Cherie.

CHERITH (f) *Latin* Hold dear, cherish.

CHERRIL *see* CHERYL.

CHERRILYN (f) A blend of Cheryl and Linda.

CHERRY (f) Two possible origins: 1. The fruit name used as a first name; 2. A variant of Charity.

CHERYL, CHERIL, SHERYL (f) Variants of Cherry.

CHERYLYN (f) A blend of Cherry and Linda.

CHESLEY (m) *Old English* A camp on the meadow.

CHESNEY (m) *French* Oak grove.

CHESTER (m) *Latin* Fort.

CHET *see* CHESTER.

CHEVY (m) *Welsh* A ridge.

CHEYNE (f) Origin uncertain. Possibly a form of Cheney.

CHIARA (f) *Italian* Clear.

CHILTON (m) *Old English* Village spring.

CHIRITA (f) From the name of the flowering plant.

CHONDA (f) Origin uncertain.

CHLOE, CLOE (f) *Greek* Young green shoot (hence blooming).

CHLOREL, CHLORELLA, CHLORELLE (f) Blends of Chloris and Ella.

CHLORIS (f) *Greek* Blooming.

CHRIS, CRIS, KRIS *see* CHRISTOPHER and CHRISTINE.

CHRISANDA (f) A blend of Christine and Amanda.

CHRISANTHA (f) A blend of Christine and Samantha.

CHRISSIE, CRISSY *see* CHRIS.

CHRISTA (f) German form of Christine.

Christabel, Christobel — Ciprian

CHRISTABEL, CHRISTOBEL (f) *Latin* Fair follower of Christ.
CHRISTAL, CHRISTEL see CRYSTAL.
CHRISTELLE, CHRISTELLA see CHRISTABEL.
CHRISTIAN, KRISTIAN (m and f) *Latin* A Christian.
CHRISTIE (m) A Scottish form of Christopher or Christian.
CHRISTINE, CHRISTINA, KRYSTYNA (f) *Latin* A Christian.
CHRISTOBEL see CHRISTABEL.
CHRISTOPHER (m) *Greek* One who carries Christ (in his heart).
CHRISTMAS (m) *Old English* Christ's Festival (or Mass).
CHRISTY see CHRISTIE.
CHRYSTAL see CRYSTAL.
CHUCK (m) A form of Charles.
CHUNKY (m) Small and sturdy. Source uncertain.
CHURSTON, CHURSTAN (m) *Old English* Church stone.
CHYLAN (f) Origin uncertain.
CIARA (f) *Irish* Dark haired.
CIARAN see KIERAN.
CICELY see CECILIA.
CIJI (f) Origin uncertain. Possibly a form of Cissy.
CILLA see PRISCILLA.
CINDERELLA (f) *French* Little cinder girl.
CINDERINA, CINDERETTA (f) Variants of Cinderella.
CINDORA (f) A blend of Cinderella and Dora.
CINDY, CINDI, SINDY, CINDEE see CYNTHIA, LUCINDA, etc.
CINNAMON (f) *Hebrew* From the name of the spice.
CIPRIAN (m) Man from Cyprus.

CIRRA (f) Possibly from 'cyrrus', a type of cloud.
CIS, CISSY, CISSIE see CICELY.
CIVIA (f) *Hebrew* A deer.
CLAIRE, CLARE see CLARA.
CLAIRINE, CLAIRENE see CLARA.
CLAIRMOND (m) *Old German* Famous protection.
CLAIRONA (f) A blend of Claire and Rona.
CLANCY (m) *Irish* Tribe.
CLARA, CLARE, CLARRIE, CLARRY (f) *Latin* Clear, bright.
CLARAN (f) Origin uncertain. Possibly a form of Clare.
CLARANDA (f) A blend of Clara and Amanda.
CLARANTHA (f) A blend of Clara and Samantha.
CLARE see CLARA.
CLARENCE (m) *Latin* Clear, illustrious.
CLARENDON (m) *Old English* Clover hill.
CLARIBEL (f) A blend of Clare and Bella.
CLARICE (f) A French form of Clare.
CLARINA (f) A blend of Clare and Marina.
CLARINDA (f) Variant of Clare.
CLARISSA, CLARISSE see CLARICE.
CLARITA (f) Spanish form of Clare.
CLARITY (f) *Latin* Clearness.
CLARK, CLARKE (m) From the occupational surname: a clerk.
CLARRIE, CLAREE see CLARA, CLARICE.
CLAUD, CLAUDE (m) *Latin* From the Roman name Claudius, meaning 'lame'.
CLAUDETTE, CLAUDINE, CLAUDELLE (f) Diminutive feminine forms of Claud.
CLAUDIA (f) Feminine form of Claudius (see CLAUD).
CLAUDINE, CLAUDINA see CLAUDIA.

CLAVIL (m) Origin uncertain. Possibly a form of Clay.

CLAY (m) *Old German* To stick together.

CLAYBORN, CLAIBOURNE (m) *Old German* Clover boundary.

CLAYTON (m) *Old English* Village built on clay land.

CLEA *see* CHLOE.

CLEANDRA (f) A blend of Clea and Sandra.

CLEANTHA (f) A blend of Clea and Samantha.

CLEDRA (f) A Cornish name of uncertain meaning.

CLEARY (m) *Gaelic* Scholar.

CLEM, CLEMMIE *see* CLEMENT, CLEMENTINE.

CLEMENCE (f) Feminine form of Clement.

CLEMENT (m) *Latin* Gentle, merciful.

CLEMENTINE (f) French feminine form of Clement.

CLEO *see* CLIO.

CLEODEL (f) *Greek* Famous place.

CLEOME (f) *Greek* From the name of the flowering plant.

CLEONE (f) *Greek* Light, clear.

CLEOPATRA (f) *Greek* Fame of her father.

CLEORA *see* CLIO.

CLETA (f) French form of Cleopatra.

CLETE (m) Masculine form of Cleta.

CLEVELAND (m) *Old English* Land near the steep bank.

CLIANDRA (f) A blend of Clio and Sandra.

CLIANTHA (f) *Greek* Flower of glory.

CLIFFORD, CLIFF (m) *Old English* A crossing near the cliff.

CLIFTON (m) *Old English* Village near the cliff.

CLINTON, CLINT (m) *Old English* Village on a hill.

CLIO (f, rarely m) *Greek* To praise.
CLIVE (m) *Old English* Steep bank.
CLODAGH (f) The name of a river in Ireland.
CLOE *see* CHLOE.
CLORINDA *see* CLARA.
CLORIS *see* CHLORIS.
CLOTILDA, CLOTILDE, CLO (f) *Old German* Famous in battle.
CLOVER (f) *Old English* From the plant name meaning 'to adhere'.
CLOYCE (f) A blend of Clare and Joyce.
CLYDE (m) *Welsh* Heard from afar.
COBURN (m) *Middle English* Small stream.
CODY (m) *Old English* A cushion.
COLBY (m) *Old English* Coal town.
COLE *see* COLEMAN.
COLEEN *see* COLLEEN.
COLETTE *see* COLLETTE.
COLEMAN (m) *Middle English* Coal miner.
COLENA *see* COLLEEN.
COLIN (m) A form of Nicholas.
COLINA (f) Feminine form of Colin.
COLISTA (f) Origin uncertain. Possibly a form of Calista.
COLLEEN (f) *Irish* Girl.
COLLETTE (f) *Latin* Victorious.
COLLINGWOOD (m) *Old English* The wood of Cola's people.
COLMAN (m) *Irish* Dove.
COLSTON (m) *Old English* The village of Cola's people.
COLUM (m) *Gaelic* Dove.
COLUMBA (m) *Latin* Dove.

COLVILLE (m) *Old English* Coal town.
COLVIN (m) *Middle English* and *Old German* Coal friend.
COMFORT (f) *Latin* Consolation.
COMAN (m) *Irish* Bent.
COMPTON (m) *Old English* Village in a narrow valley.
CONAL, CONNAL (m) *Irish* Mighty or high.
CONAN *see* CONAL.
CONCORD (f) *Latin* Harmony.
CONELLA, CONETTA *see* CONNIE.
CONLAN (m) Origin uncertain. Possibly a form of Conal.
CONN (m) *Irish* Sense, intelligence.
CONNIE *see* CONSTANCE.
CONNOR *(m) Irish* High desire.
CONRAD (m) *Old German* Brave counsel.
CONROY (m) *Irish* Hound of the plain.
CONSTANCE (f) *Latin* Steadfast.
CONSTANT, CONSTANTINE (m) *Latin* Steadfast.
CONWAY (m) *Welsh* Head river.
COOPER (m) *Middle English* Cask-maker.
CORA, KORA (f) *Greek* Maiden.
CORABETH (f) A blend of Cora and Elizabeth.
CORAL (f) *Greek* A jewel name.
CORALIE, CORALEE (f) Forms of Coral.
CORALINE, CORALINE, CORALYN (f) Blends of Coral and Linda.
CORAN (m) Origin uncertain. Possibly a form of Conan.
CORANDA (f) A blend of Cora and Amanda.
CORANTHA (f) A blend of Cora and Samantha.
CORBET, CORBIN, CORBYN (m) *Old French* Raven.

CORBY (m) A form of Corbet.
CORDELIA (f) *Celtic* Daughter of the sea.
CORDELLE (f) *French* A rope.
CORETTA, CORETTE *see* CORA.
COREY (f) *Gaelic* A ravine.
CORIANDER, KORIANDER (m) *Greek* From the herb name.
CORIANTHA, KORIANTHA (f) A feminine form of Coriander.
CORIN *see* CORINNE.
CORINA, CORINNE, CORINNA, CORRINNE *see* CORA.
CORINTHE (f) A blend of Cora and Ianthe.
CORIS, KORIS (f) *Greek* From the name of the flowering plant.
CORISANDE, CORISANDA (f) *Greek* Singer in a chorus.
CORISSA, CORITA (f) Variants of Cora.
CORMAC, CORMICK (m) *Greek* The trunk of a tree.
COROMEL (f) *Latin* A combination of 'crown' and 'honey' meaning 'sweet ruler'.
CORONA, KORONA (f) *Latin* Crown.
CORRAN (m) Origin uncertain. Possibly a form of Conan.
CORREEN, CORRENE *see* CORINNE.
CORREY, CORRIE *see* COREY.
CORY *see* COREY.
COSINA, COSIMA (f) *Greek* World harmony.
COSMO (m) *Greek* The universe.
COSTIN (m) A form of Constantine.
COURTENAY, COURTNAY, COURTNEY (m, rarely f) *Latin* An enclosed place.
COZETTA (f) Origin uncertain. Possibly a form of Cosina.

CRADDOCK (m) *Welsh* Amiable.
CRAIG (m) *Celtic* Rocky crag.
CRAMER (m) *Middle English* To cram in.
CRANFORD (m) *Old English* Crane ford.
CRANLEIGH, CRANLEY (m) *Old English* Crane wood.
CRANSTON (m) *Old English* Village where cranes gather.
CRAWFORD (m) *Old English* Crow ford.
CRESSIDA, CRESSYDA (f) *Greek* Gold.
CRESTA (f) *Old French* Mountain top.
CRICHTON, CREIGHTON (m) *Welsh* Village on the hill.
CRIS see CHRIS.
CRISANN (f) A blend of Christine and Ann.
CRISPIN, CRISPIAN (m) *Latin* Curly hair.
CRISTA see CHRISTA.
CRISTAL, CRISTALLA see CRYSTAL.
CRISTELLA, CRISTELLE (f) Blends of Christine and Ella.
CRISTINE see CHRISTINA.
CROFTON (m) *Old English* Village in the field.
CRONAN (m) *Greek* Companion.
CRYSTAL, KRYSTAL (f) *Greek* Clear glass.
CRYSTONEL (f) A modern invention meaning 'crystal of the elves'.
CULLUM see COLUM.
CULVER (m) *Old English* Dove.
CURTIS, CURT (m) *Latin* Courtyard.
CURZON (m) *Old German* Tree stump.
CY (m) A form of Cyrus, Cyril, Simon, etc.
CYAN (f) *Greek* Dark blue.
CYBIL see SIBYL.
CYD see SIDONIE.

CYMA (f) *Greek* To grow, flourish.
CYNARA (f) *Greek* Artichoke.
CYNDEE, CYNDY *see* CINDY.
CYNDORA (f) A blend of Cyndy and Dora.
CYNTHIA (f) *Greek* Moon goddess.
CYPRIAN (m) *see* CIPRIAN.
CYRIL (m) *Greek* Lord, ruler.
CYRUS (m) *Persian* Sun.

D

Dacey — Dyson

DACEY (m) *Gaelic* Southerner.
DACIA (f) *Latin* The far land.
DACIAN (m) Origin uncertain. Possibly a form of Dacia.
DACK (m) Origin uncertain. Possibly a form of Dacian.
DACRE (m) From the town in Palestine called Acre.
DAENA *see* DIANA.
DAEVID *see* DAVID.
DAGAN (m) *Scandinavian* Sunrise, dawn.
DAHLIA (f) From the flower, named after the Swedish botanist A. Dahl.
DAIEN (f) Origin uncertain. Possibly a form of Diane.
DAIMEN *see* DAMON.
DAIN (m) *Old English* A form of Dainard, meaning 'hardy Dane'.
DAINTRY (f) Origin uncertain. Possibly a form of Dain.
DAISHA (f) Origin uncertain. Possibly a form of Daisy.
DAISY, DASEY, DASIE (f) *Old English* From the name of the flower, meaning 'day's eye'.
DALBY (m) *Old Norse* Valley farm.
DALE, DAL (m) *Old English* Inhabitant of the valley.

Daley · Danita

DALEY, DALY (m) *Irish* Assembly.
DALILA *see* DELILAH.
DALINDA (f) A blend of Dalila and Linda.
DALMOR (m) Origin uncertain. Possibly a form of Delmar.
DALLAS, DALLACE (m and rarely f) *Old English* House in the valley.
DALTA (f) *Gaelic* Favourite child.
DALTON (m) *Old English* Village near the valley.
DAMAE (f) A blend of Daisy and Mae.
DAMALA (f) A blend of Daisy and Mala.
DAMARA (f) *Greek* Taming.
DAMAREL (f) A modern invention meaning 'lady elf'.
DAMARIS (f) From the name of the evergreen tree.
DAMEN *see* DAMON.
DAMIAN, DAMIEN (m) *Greek* To tame.
DAMITA (f) *Latin* A form of Dama, meaning 'lady'.
DAMON (m) A form of Damian.
DAMSON (f) *Latin* Plum from Damascus.
DANA (f, rarely m) Two possible origins: 1. *Hebrew* Judge; 2. *Gaelic* Brave.
DANBY (m) *Old Norse* Settlement of the Danes.
DANDO *see* DANDY.
DANDY (m) A form of Andrew.
DANE (m) *Old English* A Danish settler.
DANELLA, DANETTE, DANETTA (f) Variants of Dana.
DANICA (f) *Slavonic* Morning star.
DANICE (f) Feminine form of Daniel.
DANIEL (m) *Hebrew* God is my judge.
DANIELLE, DANIELLA (f) Feminine forms of Daniel.
DANITA, DANIKA, DANITRA *see* DANICA.

DANNY, DANNIE, DANY *see* DANIEL, DANIELLE.

DANYA (f) A blend of Danielle and Anya.

DAOMA (f) Origin uncertain.

DAPHNE (f) *Greek* The laurel or bay tree.

DARA, DARAH (f) *Middle English* To dare.

DARAN *see* DARREN.

DARANDA (f) A blend of Dara and Amanda.

DARANTHA (f) A blend of Dara and Samantha.

DARBY (m) *Middle English* Home near the water.

DARCY (m) *French* Of the Oise river.

DAREL (m) *French* Beloved one.

DAREN *see* DARREN.

DARIA, DARICE (f) *Persian* Queenly.

DARIAN (m) *Persian* Kingly.

DARIEN *see* DARIAN.

DARILYN (f) A blend of Dara and Lynda.

DARIN *see* DARREN.

DARINA (f) A blend of Dara and Rina.

DARINKA (f) A blend of Dara and Katinka.

DARIO (m) A blend of Darren and Mario.

DARISSA (f) A blend of Dara and Clarissa.

DARIUS (m) *Persian* Kingly.

DARLA (f) *Middle English* Loved one.

DARLENE (f) *Old English* Dearly beloved.

DARLEY (m) *Old English* Wood frequented by deer.

DARLIN, DARLYN (f) *Old English* Loved one.

DARNEL (m) *Middle English* A weed found in grain fields.

DARNELL Variant of Darnel.

DAROL *see* DARREL.

DARON *see* DARREN.

DARREL, DARRELL (m) *Old English* Grove of oak trees.

DARREN, DARRIN (m) *Old English* Small rocky hill.
DARRINGTON (m) *Old English*. The village of Dagheard's people.
DARROW (m) *Old English* Spear.
DARRY see DARRYL.
DARRYL, DARYL, DARRELL (m) *Old English* Loved one.
DARSHA (f) Feminine form of Darshan.
DARSHAN (m) *Sanskrit* Gift of God.
DARTON (m) *Old English* Village near the water.
DARVIN (m) A blend of Darren and Marvin.
DARVINIA (f) Feminine form of Darvin.
DARWIN (m) *Old English* River where oaks grow.
DARY (m) A blend of Darren and Gary.
DARYL (originally m, now mainly f) A form of Darryl.
DARYN see DARREN.
DASHA (f) *Old French* The ash tree.
DASHIEL, DASHIELL (m) Origin uncertain. Possibly *Old French/Old English* 'Ash tree of the elves'.
DASHWOOD (m) *Old French* The ash wood.
DAVE see DAVID.
DAVEEN, DAVENE see DAVINA.
DAVEN (m) *Scandinavian* Two rivers.
DAVIAN (m) A blend of David and Adrian.
DAVID (m) *Hebrew* Beloved by God.
DAVIDENE (f) Feminine form of David.
DAVINA, DEVINA, DAVIDA (f) Scottish feminine forms of David.
DAVIS see DAVID.
DAVITA (f) Spanish feminine form of David.

Davon — Deena

DAVON (m) Origin uncertain. Possibly a form of Daven.

DAVORA (f) A blend of Davina and Dora.

DAVY, DAVIE *see* DAVID.

DAWN (f) *Middle English* Daybreak.

DAWNELLA, DAWNELLE (f) Blends of Dawn and Ella.

DAWSON (m) A surname linked with David.

DAX (m) Possibly from the French place-name.

DAY (m) A British saint's name of uncertain origin.

DAYA (f) *Hebrew* A bird.

DAYALA (f) *Sanskrit* Mercy.

DAYLE *see* DALE.

DAYMER (f) A Cornish name of uncertain meaning.

DAYNA *see* DANA.

DAYTON (m) *Old English* Day (i.e. bright) village.

DAYVA (f) Phonetic form of Deva.

DAYVID *see* DAVID.

DEAN, DENE (m) *Old French* Leader.

DEANA, DEANE, DEANN *see* DIANE.

DEBBIE, DEBI, DEBBY *see* DEBORAH.

DEBORAH, DEBRA (f) *Hebrew* A bee.

DEBRELLE (f) A blend of Deborah and Elle.

DEBROY (m) Origin uncertain.

DECHEN (f) *Tibetan* Great bliss.

DECIA (f) *Latin* Possibly a form of 'Decima' meaning 'tenth'.

DECLAN (m) Irish saint's name of uncertain meaning.

DEDRA (f) Origin uncertain. Possibly a form of Deirdre.

DEE (f, rarely m) *Old English* The Goddess.

DEEANN, DEANA *see* DIANE.

DEENA *see* DINAH.

Deidre   Delola

DEIDRE see DEIRDRE.
DEION see DIONE.
DEIRDRE (f) *Irish* Young girl.
DEKE see DEKEL.
DEKEL (m) *Hebrew* Palm tree.
DEL (f) *Welsh* Pretty.
DELANA (f) A blend of Del and Lana.
DELANDRA (f) A blend of Del and Sandra.
DELANE (f) A blend of Del and Elaine.
DELANEY (m) *Old French* Of the alder grove.
DELANNE (f) A blend of Del and Anne.
DELANIE (f) A blend of Del and Melanie.
DELARA (f) A blend of Del and Lara.
DELAURA (f) A blend of Del and Laura.
DELCINE (f) *Latin* Sweet.
DELENA (f) A blend of Del and Lena.
DELIA (f) *Latin* From the Greek island of Delos.
DELICIA (f) *Latin* Delight.
DELILAH, DALILAH (f) *Hebrew* Alluring, amorous.
DELINA (f) A blend of Del and Lina.
DELINDA (f) *Old German* Gentle.
DELISE, DELISA see DELICIA.
DELITA (f) A blend of Del and Lita.
DELIZA, DELISHA see DELICIA.
DELL (m) *Old English* Inhabitant of a dell.
DELLA see ADELA.
DELLEN (f) *Cornish* Petal.
DELLENE (f) A variant of Della.
DELMA see FIDELMA.
DELMAR (m) *Spanish* By the sea.
DELMELDA (f) *Greek* To announce.
DELOIS (f) A blend of Del and Lois.
DELOLA (f) A blend of Del and Lola.

Delora — Denice

DELORA (f) *Latin* Seashore.

DELORES (f) Spanish form of Dolores.

DELORIS see DOLORES.

DELORNA (f) A blend of Del and Lorna.

DELOSA (f) A blend of Del and Rosa.

DELPHA (f) *Greek* Dolphin.

DELPHINE, DELPHI (f) *Greek* Woman from Delphi.

DELROY see ELROY.

DELSHAY (f) A blend of Del and Shayla.

DELSIE see DULCIE.

DELVIN (m) *Greek* Dolphin.

DELWYN see DELVIN.

DELYNDA, DELYN (f) A blend of Del and Lynda.

DELYS see DELICIA.

DELYTH (f) *Welsh* Pretty.

DEMAREL see DEMEREL.

DEMELZA (f) From the Cornish place-name which may mean 'hill fort of Maeldaf'.

DEMEREL (f) Possibly a form of Denerel.

DEMPSEY (m) *Old French* Deserving blame.

DENA see DINAH.

DENBY (m) *Old Norse* Danish settlement.

DENCY (f) Possibly a form of Denise.

DENE see DEAN.

DENEREL (f) A modern invention meaning 'valley of the elves'.

DENESE see DENISE.

DENETTE (f) A form of Jenette (Jeanette).

DENHOLM (m) *Old Norse* Home of the Dane.

DENIA (f) *Greek* Of Dionysus, god of wine.

DENICA (f) Origin uncertain. Possibly a form of Denia.

DENICE see DENISE.

DENINE (f) A blend of Denise and Caroline.
DENIS, DENNIS (m) The French form of Dionysus, the Greek god of wine.
DENISE (f) Feminine form of Denis.
DENMAN (m) *Old English* Dweller in a valley.
DENNA (f) *Old English* Valley.
DENNING (m) *Old English* Dane gift.
DENNY see DENIS.
DENSIL see DENZIL.
DENTON (m) *Old English* Dean's village.
DENVER (m) *Old English* Green valley.
DENYS see DENIS.
DENZIL, DENZEL (m) Variants of Denis.
DEREK, DERRICK (m) *Old German* Famous ruler.
DERENDA (f) A blend of Deri and Brenda.
DERI (m) *Welsh* Oak.
DERIC, DERIK see DEREK.
DERMAN (m) *Old English* Waterman, boatman.
DERMOT (m) *Old English* Moat surrounding a castle.
DERON (m) *Old English* Water.
DERORA (f) *Hebrew* Flowing stream.
DERREN see DARREN.
DERRICK see DEREK.
DERRY (m) *Old English* Oak tree.
DERWENT (m) *Old English* River where oaks grow.
DERWIN (m) *Old German* Animal lover.
DERYL (f) Variant of Beryl.
DERYN, DERREN, DERRINE (f) *Welsh* Bird.
DES see DESMOND.
DESI (m) A form of the Latin word 'Desiderio' meaning 'desire'.
DESIREE (f) *Old French* Desired one.
DESMA (f) *Greek* Bond.

DESMOND (m) *Latin* The world.

DESSA (f) Perhaps a variant of Tessa.

DEVA (f) *Sanskrit* Angel; being of light.

DEVAN see DEVIN.

DEVERIE see DEVORA.

DEVERNE (f) Verna with the De- prefix.

DEVIN (m) *Celtic* Poet.

DEVINA, DEVINDA (f) Possibly feminine forms of Devin.

DEVITA (f) Vita with the De- prefix.

DEVLYNN (f) A variant of Evelyn.

DEVON (m) **DEVONA** (f) *Old English* Dweller in the deep valley.

DEVORA, DEVORAH see DEBORAH.

DEVRA see DEBORAH.

DEWAR (m) *Gaelic* A pilgrim.

DEWEY, DEWI (m) A Welsh form of David.

DEX see DEXTER.

DEXTER (m) *Latin* Right-handed (hence skillful).

DEXY (f) A feminine form of Dexter.

DEZO (f) A feminine form of Desi.

DI see DIANA.

DIADORA (f) A blend of Diana and Dora.

DIAHANN see DIANA.

DIAMANDA (f) A blend of Diamond and Amanda.

DIAMOND (f) The Greek name of the precious stone used as a first name.

DIAN see DIANA.

DIANA (f) *Latin* Divine.

DIANDRA (f) *Greek* Flower with two stamens.

DIANNA see DIANA.

DIANORA (f) *Latin* Divine.

DIANTHA (f) *Greek* Divine flower.

DICK see RICHARD.

DICKON, DIKKEN (m) Origin uncertain. Possibly a form of Dickson.
DICKSON (m) Son of Dick.
DIGBY (m) *Dutch* Dike.
DIELLA (f) *Latin* Holy girl.
DIERDRE *see* DEIDRE.
DIGGORY (m) *Middle English* Possibly 'dike'.
DILLARD (m) Possibly a form of Dale.
DILLON, DILL *see* DALE.
DILLYS, DILYS (f) *Welsh* Genuine.
DINAH, DINA, DYNAH (f) *Hebrew* Judgement.
DINSDALE (m) *Old English* The enclosure belonging to Deighton.
DIONA, DIONNA, DION *see* DIONE.
DIONE, DIONNE (f) The Greek form of the Latin name Diana.
DIONARA, DIONELLA, DIONETTA (f) Variants of Dione.
DIORELLA (f) A blend of Dione and Morella.
DIRETTA (f) *Italian* To direct, control.
DIRK (m) *Old German* Famous ruler.
DISA (f) *Norwegian* Active spirit.
DIVINA *see* DAVINA.
DIXIE (f) *Old English* Dike.
DIXON (m) Richard's son.
DOANNA (f) A blend of Dorothy and Anna.
DOLAN (m) Two possible origins: 1. *Irish* Black-haired 2. *Old English* Bend in a stream.
DOLINDA (f) A blend of Dora and Linda.
DOLISA (f) A blend of Dora and Lisa.
DOLITA (f) A blend of Dora and Lita.
DOLLY *see* DOROTHY.
DOLORES (f) *Spanish* Lady of sorrows.
DOLVENE (f) A blend of Dolores and Vena.

DOM, DOMI, DOMONIC see DOMINIC.
DOMINIC, DOMINICK (m) *Latin* Belonging to God.
DOMINIQUE, DOMINICA (f) Feminine forms of Dominic.
DOMINO (f) *French* Masquerade cloak and mask.
DON, DONNY, DONNIE (m) Variant of Donald.
DONA, DONAH see DONNA.
DONAL, DONALD (m) *Irish* World rule, hence world ruler.
DONALDA (f) Feminine form of Donald.
DONAVON see DONOVAN.
DONELLA (f) A blend of Dona and Ella.
DONNA (f) *Italian* Lady.
DONNAN (m) *Irish* Brown.
DONNELL (m) *Celtic* Hill.
DONOVAN see DONALD.
DONYA (f) A blend of Dora and Sonya.
DORA see DOROTHEA.
DORAL (f, rarely m) *Greek* Goldfish.
DORAN (m) *Hebrew* Gift.
DORANDA (f) A blend of Dora and Amanda.
DORANN (f) A blend of Dora and Ann.
DORANTHA (f) A blend of Dora and Samantha.
DORATA (f) Variant of Dora.
DORCAS (f) *Greek* Gazelle.
DOREA (f) *Greek* Gift.
DOREEN, DORENE (f) Variants of Dorothy.
DORELLA, DORELLE (f) Blends of Dora and Ella.
DORENA (f) *Greek* Bountiful.
DORENDA see DORINDA.
DORETHA see DOROTHEA.
DORETTA, DORETTE (f) French forms of Dorothea.
DORI, DORIA, DORIE see DORIS.

Dorian　　　　　　　　　　　　　　　Duane

DORIAN (m) *Greek* Gift.
DORINA (f) *Hebrew* Perfection.
DORINDA (f) A blend of Dora and Belinda.
DORINE *see* DOREEN.
DORIS (f) *Greek* Woman from Doris, an area in central Greece.
DORITA (f) Spanish form of Doris.
DORKA (f) Origin uncertain. Possibly a form of Dorcas.
DORNA (f) A blend of Dora and Lorna.
DORO *see* DOROTHEA.
DORONA (f) A blend of Dora and Rona.
DOROTA (f) Origin uncertain. Possibly a form of Dorothea.
DOROTHEA (f) The original form of Dorothy.
DOROTHY (f) *Greek* Gift of God.
DORRIEN *see* DORIAN.
DORTHEA *see* DOROTHEA.
DORY *see* ISIDORE.
DOT, DOTTIE *see* DOROTHY.
DOUGAL (m) *Irish* Black stranger.
DOUGLAS (m) *Gaelic* Dark blue water.
DOYLE (m) *Irish* Assembly.
DRAKE (m) *Latin* Dragon.
DREENA *see* DRINA.
DREW, DRUE, DRU *see* ANDREW.
DRINA *see* ALEXANDRINA.
DRUCE (m) *Celtic* Wise man.
DRUELLA (f) *Old German* Elfin vision.
DRUMMOND (m) From the Scottish surname of uncertain meaning.
DRUSILLA, DRUCELLA (f) From the Roman family name Drusus.
DUANE (m) *Irish* Black.

DUDLEY (m) *Old English* Dod's meadow.

DUKE (m) *Latin* Leader.

DULCIE (f) *Latin* Charming, sweet.

DUMA (f) *Hebrew* Quiet, gentle woman.

DUNCAN (m) *Celtic* Warrior with dark skin.

DUNIA (f) Origin uncertain.

DUNSTAN (m) *Old English* Brown stone quarry.

DURAND, DURAN (m) *Latin* Enduring.

DURETTA (f) *Spanish* Little steadfast one.

DURIAN (m) From the name of the evergreen Asian tree.

DURRANT see DURAND.

DURSTEN (m) A character in the novel *Bearing an Hourglass* by Piers Anthony.

DUSTIN see DUNSTAN.

DWAYNE, DUWAYNE see WAYNE.

DYANA (f) *Sanskrit* Meditation.

DYAN, DYANNE see DIANA.

DWIGHT (m) *Old English* White, fair.

DYLAN (m) *Welsh* The sea.

DYSIS (f) *Greek* Sunset.

DYSON (m) From the surname linked to Dennis.

E
Eamonn — *Ezra*

EAMONN, EAMON (m) Irish form of Edmund.
EARL, EARLE (m) The title of nobility used as a name.
EARLENE (f) Feminine form of Earl.
EARNEST *see* ERNEST.
EARTHA (f) *Old English* Earth.
EARTHAN (m) *Old English* Of the Earth.
EASTER (f) *Old German* Name given to a child born during this Christian festival.
EASTMAN (m) *Old English* Protector of grace.
EASTON (m) *Old English* Inhabitant of an eastern village.
EBEN, EB (m) *Hebrew* Forms of Ebenezer, meaning 'foundation stone'.
EBONY (f) *Greek* Hard, dark wood.
EBREL (f) *Cornish* April.
ED, EDDY, EDDIE *see* EDWARD.
EDGAR (m) *Old English* Spear of prosperity.
EDINA (f) *Old English* Rich friend.
EDITH (f) *Old English* Name meaning 'prosperity' and 'war' or 'strife'.
EDLAN (m) *Old English* Prosperous village.
EDLIN (m) *Old German* Nobility.
EDLYN (f) *Old English* Happy brook.
EDMAR, EDMER (m) *Old English* Rich sea.
EDMOND, EDMUND (m) *Old English* Rich warrior.

EDNA, EDNAH (f) *Hebrew* Delight, desired.
EDRIC (m) *Old English* Rich ruler.
EDSON (m) Son of Ed(ward).
EDWARD (m) *Old English* Happy, fortunate guardian.
EDWIN (m) *Old English* Happy, fortunate friend.
EDWINA (f) Feminine form of Edwin.
EDYTH *see* EDITH.
EFFRO (m) *Welsh* Awake.
EFRONA (f) *Hebrew* Sweet-singing bird.
EGAN (m) *Old English* Formidable, strong.
EIA (f) Celtic saint's name of uncertain meaning.
EILAN (m) *Irish* Light.
EILEEN, AYLEEN (f) Irish form of Helen.
EINAR (m) *Old Norse* Warrior chief.
EIRA (f) *Welsh* Snow.
EIRAN (m) *Irish* Peace.
EIRIAN (f) *Welsh* Silver.
EITHNE *see* ETHNE.
ELA *see* ELLA.
ELAIA (f) Origin uncertain. Possibly a form of Elain.
ELAILA (f) A blend of Elaine and Leila.
ELAIN (f) *Welsh* Fawn.
ELAINE (f) The Old French form of Helen.
ELAMARA (f) A blend of Ella and Mary.
ELAN (f) *French* Grace, style.
ELAN *see* ELLEN.
ELAN (m) *Old English* Two possible origins: 1. The name of four rivers in Wales; 2. Island.
ELANA (f) *Hebrew* A tree.
ELANDRA (f) A blend of Elana and Sandra.
ELANOR *see* Eleanor.
ELANTHA (f) A blend of Elana and Samantha.

Elara   Elga

ELARA (f) The granddaughter of Zeus in Greek mythology.

ELATA (f) Origin uncertain. Possibly a form of Elara.

ELAVRA (f) Origin uncertain.

ELAYN see ELAINE.

ELBER (m) *Old English* Elf grove.

ELBOURNE (m) *Old English* Elf stream.

ELDEN (m) From the name of the Elder tree.

ELDON (m) *Old English* Two possible origins: 1. Ella's down: 2. Elf down.

ELDORA (f) *Spanish* Gilded or golden.

ELDRIDGE (m) *Old English* Wise adviser.

ELEANA, ELEA see ELEANOR.

ELEANOR (f) *Greek* Origin uncertain. Possibly 'pity, mercy'.

ELEANORA, ELINOR see ELEANOR.

ELENA, ELEENA, ELYNA (f) *Greek* Light.

ELENDA (f) A blend of Elen and Brenda.

ELENDIL (m) A character whose name means 'elf-friend' in the Tolkien trilogy of novels *Lord of the Rings*.

ELENI see ELENA.

ELENOR see ELEANOR.

ELENYA (f) According to Tolkien, the first day of the week in the Elven calendar, meaning 'star's day'.

ELESTREN (f) *Cornish* Iris.

ELFED (m) *Welsh* Autumn.

ELFEN (f) *Welsh* Element.

ELFIN (f) *Old English* Elf-like.

ELFORD (m) *Old English* Three possible origins: 1. Elf ford; 2. Elder ford; 3. Ella's ford.

ELFYN (m) *Welsh* Brow of hill.

ELGA (f) Origin uncertain. Possibly a form of Helga.

Elgar   Elma

ELGAR (m) *Old English* Noble spear.

ELI (m) *Hebrew* On high.

ELIAN (m) *Latin* Bright.

ELIANA (f) *Hebrew* God has answered me.

ELIAS (m) Greek form of Elijah.

ELIJAH (m) *Hebrew* The Lord is my God.

ELIN see ELLEN.

ELINGDON (m) *Old English* Two possible origins: 1. Elf down; 2. Elder tree down.

ELINOR see ELEANOR.

ELIORA (f) *Hebrew* God is my light.

ELISABETH, ELISE, ELYSE, ELISSA see ELIZABETH.

ELISENA (f) From the name of the flowering plant.

ELISHA (m) *Hebrew* God is my salvation.

ELIZABETH, BETTY, ELSA, LIZA (f) *Hebrew* God's oath.

ELKA, ELKE, ELKIE (f) German forms of Alice.

ELLA, ELLIE, ELLE (f) *Old German* All, entirely.

ELLAINE see ELAINE.

ELLANA (f) A blend of Ellen and Lana.

ELLEN (f) A form of Eleanor.

ELLENDEA (f) *Greek* God's light.

ELLENOR see ELEANOR.

ELLERY (m) *Old German* Alder tree.

ELLINOR see ELEANOR.

ELLIOTT, ELIOT (m) Forms of Elijah.

ELLIS, ELLICE (m) Forms of Elisha.

ELLISON (m) Son of Elijah.

ELLON see ELLEN.

ELLWOOD (m) *Old English* The woods of Ellis.

ELLY, ELLIE, ELLI see ELEANOR.

ELLYN see ELLEN.

ELMA (f) *Greek* Pleasant, fair.

ELMENA, ELMINA see ALMINA.
ELMER (m) *Old English* Noble fame.
ELMIRA (f) Feminine form of Elmer.
ELMORE (m) *Old English* Elf moor.
ELMSTONE (m) *Old English* Two possible origins:
 1. Place near the elms; 2. Elf place.
ELNA (f) Swedish form of Elina (Ellen).
ELODIE (f) *Greek* Fragile flower.
ELOISE, ALOISA (f) Forms of the French name Heloise.
ELOLA (f) A blend of Ella and Lola.
ELORA, ELLORA (f) *Greek* Happy.
ELOUISA (f) A blend of Eloise and Louisa.
ELOWEN (f) *Cornish* Elm.
ELPHIN (m) *Welsh* Brow of hill.
ELPHINE (f) *Welsh* Brow of hill.
ELRA (f) *Old German* Elfin wisdom.
ELRIC (m) *Old German* Ruler of all.
ELRICA (f) Feminine form of Elric.
ELROY see LEROY.
ELSA, ELSE (f) German forms of Elizabeth.
ELSENA (f) A blend of Elora and Cynthia.
ELSBETH see ELSPETH.
ELSDUN (m) *Old English* Elf valley.
ELSON (m) Son of Elias.
ELSPETH, ELSPET (f) Scottish forms of Elizabeth.
ELSTAN (m) *Old English* Small stone.
ELSTEAD, ELSTON (m) *Old English* Place of the elves.
ELTON (m) *Old English* Old village.
ELUNED (f) *Welsh* Idol.
ELVA (f) Phonetic form of the Irish name Ailbhe.
ELVASTON (m) *Old English* Two possible origins:
 1. Alfwald's village; 2. Elf village.

Elvedon — Emma

ELVEDON (m) *Old English* Two possible origins: 1. Swan valley; 2. Valley of the elves.
ELVERA see ELVIRA.
ELVIN see ALVIN.
ELVINA (f) *Old English* Noble/elf friend.
ELVIRA (f) From the Spanish place-name.
ELVIVA (f) Origin uncertain. Possibly a form of Elvira.
ELVIS, ELVY, ELWIN, ELWYN see ELVIN.
ELWOOD (m) *Old English* Noble woods.
ELYSE (f) A form of Elizabeth.
ELYSSA (f) A form of Alicia.
EMALINE, EMELYNE see EMILY.
EMANUEL (m) *Hebrew* God is with us.
EMBLYN see EMELINE.
EMELIA see AMELIA.
EMELINE, EMELYN see EMILY.
EMER (f) A variant of Emma.
EMER (m) *Old English* Uncle.
EMERALD (f) *Greek* After the name of the precious stone.
EMERE (f) Maori form of Emily.
EMERIC, EMERICK (m) *Old German* Ruler.
EMERSON (m) Son of Emery.
EMERY (m) *Old German* Home-power, hence 'ruler of the home'.
EMI (f) *Japanese* Smile.
EMILE (m) *Latin* Eager.
EMILENE see EMELINE.
EMILIA see AMELIA.
EMILY (f) *Latin* Ambitious, industrious.
EMINA (f) *Latin* Noble maiden.
EMLYN, EMLIN (m) Emil's lake.
EMMA (f) *Greek* Grandmother.

EMMELINE, EMMALINE, EMMILINE (f) Forms of Emily.

EMMERSON *see* EMERSON.

EMMERT (m) Variant of Emmet.

EMMERY *see* EMERY.

EMMET, EMMETT (m and f) Two possible origins: 1. *Hebrew* Truth; 2. *Old English* An ant.

EMRYS (m) Welsh form of Ambrose.

ENA *see* HELENA.

ENFYS (f) *Welsh* Rainbow.

ENID (f) *Welsh* Soul, life.

ENITA *see* ANITA.

ENNIS (m) A form of Angus.

ENOCH (m) *Hebrew* Dedicated.

ENYA (f) Feminine form of Enyou.

ENYON (m) Cornish form of the Latin name Annianus.

EOLA, EOLANDE (f) *Greek* Dawn.

EPHIE *see* EUPHEMIA.

EPHRAIM (m) *Hebrew* Fruitful.

ERANTHA (f) *Greek* From the flower name *Eranthis*.

ERASMUS (m) *Greek* To love.

ERDA (f) *Old German* Child of the earth.

ERIC, ERIK (m) *German* Honourable ruler.

ERICA, ERIKA (f) Feminine form of Eric.

ERIN (f) Poetic name for Ireland.

ERINA (f) *Gaelic* Of Ireland.

ERKAN (m) Origin uncertain. Possibly a form of Eric.

ERLAND, ERLEND (m) *Old German* Honourable country.

ERLE *see* EARL.

ERLINA (f) *Old English* Little elf.

ERLINDA (f) *Hebrew* Lively.

Erma   Eugene

ERMA *see* IRMA.
ERNEST (m) *Old German* Resolute, sincere.
ERNIE, ERN *see* ERNEST.
ERROL (m) *Latin* To wander.
ERSKINE (m) *Gaelic* From the place-name, probably meaning 'projecting height'.
ERVAN (m) From the Cornish saint's name of uncertain meaning.
ERVIN, ERWIN *see* IRVIN.
ERYL (f) Origin uncertain. Possibly a form of Errol.
ESAU (m) *Hebrew* Hairy.
ESMA (f) Feminine form of Esme.
ESME (m and f) *French* To esteem.
ESMERALDA (f) *Spanish* Emerald.
ESMOND (m) *Old English* Name meaning a combination of 'grace' and 'protection'.
ESPRIT (f) *French* Spirit.
ESTA *see* ESTHER.
ESTELAR (f) *Spanish* Star.
ESTELLA (f) *Latin* Star.
ESTELLE, ESTEL *see* ESTELLA.
ESTER *see* ESTHER.
ESTHER (f) *Persian* Star, the planet Venus.
ESWEN (f) *Welsh* Strength.
ETANA (f) *Hebrew* Strong.
ETANDRA (f) A blend of Etana and Sandra.
ETELKA (f) *Slavonic* Noble.
ETHAN (m) *Hebrew* Firm, strong.
ETHEL (f) *Old English* Noble.
ETHENA, ETHINA (f) A blend of Ethel and Lena.
ETHNE (f) *Irish* Little fire.
ETTA (f) A pet form of Henrietta, Marietta, etc.
EVAN *see* EWAN.
EUGENE (m) *Greek* Well-born.

EUNICE (f) *Greek* Victorious.
EUPHEMIA (f) *Greek* Auspicious speech.
EUSTACE (m) *Greek* Fruitful.
EVA (f) *Hebrew* Life.
EVADNE (f) *Greek* Possibly 'good fortune'.
EVALINE, EVALINA see EVELINE.
EVAN, EWEN (m) Welsh form of John.
EVANDER (m) Origin uncertain.
EVANGELINE (f) *Greek* Good news.
EVARA (f) A blend of Eva and Sara.
EVE (f) *Hebrew* Life.
EVELEEN (f) Irish form of Eva.
EVELIA (f) A blend of Eve and Delia.
EVELINE, EVELINA see AVELINA.
EVELYN (f, rarely m) *Celtic* Pleasant.
EVERARD (m) *Old German* Compound of 'boar' and 'hard'.
EVERETT, EVERET see EVERARD.
EVEROL (m) A blend of Everard and Errol.
EVERTON (m) *Old English* Boar farm.
EVETTE (f) A form of Evelyn.
EVINDA (f) A blend of Eve and Linda.
EVITA (f) Spanish form of Eve.
EVON, EVONNE see YVONNE.
EWA (f) Origin uncertain. Possibly a form of Ewan.
EWAN, EWEN (m) Probably a form of Evan.
EWART (m) *Old French* One who serves water.
EZRA (m) *Hebrew* Salvation.

Fabia F Fynn

FABIA (f) Feminine form of Fabian.
FABIAN (m) Possibly derived from the Latin word for 'bean', meaning 'bean farmer'.
FAINE (f) *Old English* Joyful.
FAIRBURN (m) *Old German* Handsome.
FAIRFIELD (m) *Old English* Beautiful field.
FAIRLEY (m) *Old English* Wayside place.
FAITH (f) *Latin* To trust.
FANNY *see* FRANCES.
FANYA (f) A blend of Fanny and Anya.
FARAH (f) *Persian* Joy.
FARAMOND (m) *Old German* Compound of words for 'journey' and 'protection' (i.e. traveller's protector).
FARAND (m) *Old German* Pleasant.
FARICA (f) *Old German* Peace-loving ruler.
FARLAND (m) *Old English* Land by the road.
FARLEY (m) *Old English* Wayside place.
FAROLD (m) *Old English* Mighty traveller.
FARON (m and f) *see* FARREN.
FARQUHAR (m) *Gaelic* Friendly man.
FARRAH (f) *Arabic* Wild ass.
FARRANT (m) *Old French* Journey venture.
FARRAR (m) *Old English* Smith, farrier.
FARREL (m) *Celtic* Valorous one.
FARREN, FARRON (m) English forms of Ferdinand.
FAWN, FAWNE (f) *Latin* Young deer.

Fay — Finbar

FAY (f) *Old French* Fidelity.
FAZ (m) Origin uncertain.
FELANTHA (f) A blend of Felina and Samantha.
FELDA (f) *Old German* The field.
FELICIA, FELICE (f) *Latin* Happiness.
FELICITY *see* FELICIA.
FELINA, FELENE (f) *Latin* Cat-like.
FELISSE *see* FELICIA.
FELIX (m) *Latin* Happy, fortunate.
FELTON (m) *Old English* Village in a garden.
FENELLA (f) *Gaelic* White shoulder.
FENNEL (f) *Latin* From the name of the herb.
FENNER (m) *Old English* Dweller in a marsh or fen.
FENTON (m) *Old English* Settlement in a fen.
FERDINAND (m) *Old German* Peace-boldness, hence 'courageous peacemaker'.
FERGUS, FEARGUS (m) *Gaelic* Supreme choice.
FERN (f, rarely m) *Old German* Plant name used as a first name.
FERNARD (m) A variant of Ferdinand.
FERNLEY (m, rarely f) *Old English* Clearing with ferns.
FERRANT (m) *Old French* Iron grey.
FERRIS (m) *Latin* Iron.
FEYA (f) Phonetic form of 'fair'.
FFODUS (m) *Welsh* Lucky.
FIDEL (m) *Latin* Faithful.
FIDELMA (f) A blend of Fidel and Mary.
FIELDING (m) *Old English* Field-dweller.
FIFE, FYFE (m) From the Scottish shire name.
FIFI (f) Diminutive of French form of Josephine.
FIKA (f) Origin uncertain.
FILIPA *see* PHILLIPA.
FINBAR (m) *Irish* Fair head.

FINDLAY see FINLAY.
FINELLA see FENELLA.
FINESSE (f) *French* Subtle and elegant skill.
FINGAL (m) *Gaelic* A Norwegian.
FINLAY (m) *Gaelic* Fair hero.
FINN (m) *Irish* Fair.
FINNAN (m) *Irish* Fair.
FINOLA see FINELLA.
FINTAN (m) *Irish* Fair.
FIONA (f) *Gaelic* Fair, white.
FIORELLA (f) Variant of Florence.
FIORINA (f) A blend of Fiona and Rina.
FIRTH (m) *Old English* Woodland.
FISHER (m) *Old English* Fisherman.
FITZROY (m) *Latin* Son of the king.
FLAIR (f) *Latin* Instinct for excellence.
FLANN (m) *Old English* An arrow.
FLEET (f) *Old Norse* Swift.
FLETCHER (m) *Old French* Maker of arrows.
FLEUR (f) *French* Flower.
FLINT (m) *Old English* Stone splinter.
FLISS see PHYLLIS.
FLOELLA (f) A blend of Flora and Ella.
FLORA (f) *Latin* A flower.
FLOREEN see FLORENCE.
FLORELLA see FLORA.
FLORENCE (f) *Latin* Blooming.
FLORETTA see FLORA.
FLORIANE (f) A blend of Flora and Diane.
FLORIMEL (f) *Latin* Honey flower.
FLORINA (f) A form of Florentina (Florence).
FLORINDA (f) A blend of Flora and Linda.
FLORIS, FLORICE (f) *Latin* Flower.
FLOS, FLOSSIE see FLORENCE.

Flower   Freya

FLOWER (f) *Latin* Bloom, blossom.
FLOY *see* FLORENCE.
FLOYD *see* LLOYD.
FONDA (m) *French* To melt.
FONDRA (f) A blend of Fonda and Sandra.
FONEDA (f) Variant of Fonda used as a feminine name.
FONTAYNE (f) *Old English* Spring water.
FORBES (m) *Greek* A broadleaved flowering plant.
FORREST (m) *Latin* Woods.
FOSTER *see* FORREST.
FRANCELLE, FRANCELLA (f) Blends of Frances and Ella.
FRANCES (f) *Latin* Free.
FRANCESCA (f) Italian form of Frances.
FRANCETTA, FRANCELLA *see* FRANCESCA.
FRANCEY *see* FRANCES.
FRANCHESCA, FRANCHESKA *see* FRANCESCA.
FRANCINE, FRANCENE *see* FRANCES.
FRANCIS (m) *Latin* Free.
FRANCISCA *see* FRANCESCA.
FRANK *see* FRANCIS.
FRANKLYN (m) *Latin* Freeholder.
FRASER (m) *French* Charcoal maker.
FRED *see* FREDERICK.
FREDA *see* FRIEDA.
FREDERICK (m) *Old German* Peaceful ruler.
FREEMAN (m) *Old English* One born free.
FREEMONT (m) *Old German* Free-protector hence 'protector of freedom'.
FREIDA *see* FRIEDA.
FRENELLE (f) A blend of Federick and Donelle.
FREYA (f) *Old Norse* Norse goddess of love and beauty.

Frieda, Frida — Fynn

FRIEDA, FRIDA (f) *Old German* Peace.
FRITH (m) *Old English* Woodland.
FRITHA (f) Feminine form of Frith.
FRITZ (m) German form of Frederick.
FULKE (m) *Old German* People.
FULLER (m) *Old English* One who works with cloth.
FULTON (m) *Old English* Field near a village.
FYNN (m) *Irish* Fair.

Gabi G Gyles

GABI, GABE, GABIE, GABY see GABRIELLA.
GABRIEL (m), **GABRIELLA, GABRIELLE** (f)
   Hebrew God is my strength.
GADELL See CADELL.
GAEL, GAELLE See GAIL.
GAENOR see GAYNOR.
GAE, GAI see GAY.
GAIA (f) *Greek*: Spirit of planet Earth, The Goddess.
GAIAN (m), **GAIANE** (f) *Greek* Child of Earth.
GAIL, GALE, GAYLE see ABIGAIL.
GAILA, GAYLA (f) Forms of Gail.
GALA (f) *Arabic*. Festive gathering.
GALANTHA (f) *Greek*. Snowdrop.
GALATEA (f) *Greek*. Milky.
GALAXY (f) *Greek*. Star system.
GALE (f) Two possible origins: 1. A form of Abigail;
   2. Storm: Origin uncertain.
GALEN (m) *Greek* Tranquil.
GALENA (f) *Latin* A mineral ore.
GALIENA (f) *Old German*. Tall.
GALINA (f) *Greek* Peace.
GALLEN (m) *Greek* Healer.
GALLIN (m) *Celtic* Little stranger.
GALVIN (m) *Celtic* Sparrow.
GANA see JANA.
GARARD see GERARD.

GARDNER (m) *Dutch* A garden.
GAREN *see* DAREN.
GARETH, GARET *see* GARTH.
GARFIELD (m) *Old English* Triangular field.
GARIN *see* DARIN.
GARION (m) A character in the *Malloreon* novel cycle by David Eddings.
GARLAND (f and m) *Old French* Wreath of flowers.
GARLON *see* GARLAND.
GARNER (m) *Latin* A granary.
GARNET (m) *Latin* Grain, seed.
GARRARD *see* GERARD.
GARRETT (m) *Old French* To watch.
GARREN *see* DARREN.
GARRICK (m) *Old English* Oak Spear.
GARRIE (m) Short form of Gareth, Garner, etc.
GARRISON (m) *Old French* Troops at a fort.
GARRON *see* DARREN.
GARSON *see* GARRISON.
GARVEY (m) *Old English* Spear bearer.
GARVIN (m) *Old German* Warrior friend.
GARWOOD (m) *Old English* From the forest.
GARTH (m) *Old Norse* An enclosure.
GARY, GARRY *see* GARVEY.
GASTON (m) *French* Man from Gascony.
GAVA (m) *Sanskrit* Swift.
GAVIN, GAVAN (m) *Welsh* Little Hawk.
GAVRA (f) *Hebrew* The Lord is my rock.
GAVRICK *see* GARRICK.
GAVRIELLE *see* GABRIELLE.
GAWAIN (m) *Welsh* Courteous.
GAWEN (m) Cornish form of Gawain.
GAY (f) *Middle English* Merry.
GAYLA *see* GAY.

Gayle   Gerard

GAYLE *see* GAIL.
GAYLIN *see* GALEN.
GAYLORD (m) *Old French* Brave.
GAYNOR, GAYNER (m) Son of white-haired man.
GAYORA (f) *Hebrew* Valley of light.
GED *see* JED.
GEENA *see* GINA.
GEETA, GITA (f) *Sanskrit* Song.
GEF *see* GEOFF.
GEM (f and m) *Latin* Jewel.
GEMELLE (f) A blend of Gem and Ella.
GEMMA (f) *Latin* Jewel.
GENA *see* GINA.
GENE *see* EUGENE.
GENETH (f) *Welsh* Girl.
GENEVA, GENEVIA (f) *Latin* Juniper berry.
GENEVIEVE (f) *Celtic* White wave.
GENEVRA *see* GENEVA.
GEOFFREY, JEFFREY, GEOFF, JEFF (m) *Old English* Gift of peace.
GEORDIE (m) Scottish form of George.
GEORGE (m) *Greek* Farmer.
GEORGEANA (f) A blend of George and Anna.
GEORGETTE (f) A form of Georgia.
GEORGIA, GEORGIANA (f) Feminine forms of George.
GEORGIE *see* GEORGE.
GEORGINA, GEORGINE *see* GEORGIA.
GEORGY *see* GEORGIA, GEORGINA.
GERAINT (m) *Welsh* Old.
GERALD, GERRY (m) *Old German* Spear-ruler.
GERALDINE (f) Feminine form of Gerald. Invented by the sixteenth-century poet, the Earl of Surrey.
GERARD (m) *Old German* Spear-brave.

Gerda   Ginny

GERDA (f) *Old Norse* Protection.
GEREMY see JEREMY.
GERMAINE (f) *Latin* Bud or sprout.
GERRITT see GARETH.
GERRY see GERALD.
GERTRUDE, TRUDY, GERTIE (f) *Old German* Adored warrior.
GERVASE, GERVAIS (m) *Old German* Spear.
GERVAISE (f) Feminine form of Gervase.
GETA (f) *Latin* Divine power.
GEVA (m) *Hebrew* Hill.
GEVIRA (f) *Hebrew* Lady, queen.
GIA see REGINA.
GIANETTA (f) Italian form of Janet.
GIBSON (m) Son of Gibb.
GIDEON (m) *Hebrew* Feller of trees.
GIFFORD, GIFFARD (m) *Old French* Chubby-cheeked.
GIG (m) *Middle English* Horse-drawn carriage.
GILBERT (m) *Old German* Will to be bright (or famous).
GILA (f) *Hebrew* Joy.
GILANA (f) *Hebrew* Exultation.
GILDA (f) *Celtic* Servant of God.
GILDAS (m) From the name of the sixth-century Welsh Christian.
GILES (m) *Greek* Young goat (hence a goatskin shield).
GILLIAN see JULIANA.
GILMORE (m) *Celtic* Glen near the sea.
GINA see REGINA.
GINGER (f) Two possible origins: 1. A form of Virginia; 2. A reference to hair colour.
GINNY see VIRGINIA.

Girvan — Glynis, Glinis

GIRVAN (m) *Hebrew* The Lord's grace.
GISA *see* GIZA.
GISELA, GISELLE (f) *Old English* Bright pledge.
GITA (f) Two possible origins: 1. *Sanskrit* Song; 2. *Yiddish* Good.
GITHA (f) *Old Norse* War.
GIZA (f) *Hebrew* Hewn stone.
GLADE (m, rarely f) *Old English* Space between woodland trees, hence to bring light, to be glad.
GLADWIN (m) *Old English* Glad friend.
GLADYS (f) *Latin* Lame.
GLAIN (f) *Welsh* Jewel.
GLAN (m) Masculine form of Glenda.
GLANNA (f) *Latin* Bank of a river.
GLEDA *see* GLADYS.
GLENDA (f) *Welsh* Fair and good.
GLENDALE (m) *Celtic/Old English* Clean, holy valley.
GLENDON (m) *Celtic* Glen fortress.
GLENDORA (f) A blend of Glenys and Dora.
GLENFORD (m) *Celtic/Old English* Clean, holy ford.
GLENN, GLEN (m, rarely f) *Celtic* Secluded wooded valley.
GLENNA (f) Feminine form of Glenn.
GLENTON (m) *Celtic/Old English* Village in a wooded valley.
GLENVILLE (m) *Celtic/French* Town in a wooded valley.
GLENYS (f) *Welsh* Holy, fair.
GLINDA (f) A blend of Glenys and Linda.
GLORIA (f) *Latin* Glory.
GLORIETTE (f) Diminutive of Gloria.
GLYN, GLYNN (m) Welsh forms of Glen.
GLYNIS, GLINIS (f) *Welsh* Little valley.

GODDARD (m) *Old English* Good in counsel.
GODFREY (m) *Old German* God's peace.
GODWIN (m) *Old English* Friend of God.
GOLDA (f) *Old English* Gold.
GOLDIE see GOLDA.
GOLDWIN, GOLDWYN (m) *Old English* Lover of gold.
GOMER (m) *Hebrew* To complete.
GOODWIN (m) *Old English* Good friend.
GOOGIE (f) **GOOGY** (m) Origin uncertain.
GORDON, GORDAN, GORDEN (m) Origin uncertain, but possibly a form of Greek word Gordius meaning 'bold'.
GRACE, GRACIE (f) *Latin* Grace.
GRADY (m) *Gaelic* Illustrious and noble.
GRAHAM, GRAHAME, GRAEME (m) *Old English* Compound name meaning 'gravelly place' plus 'home'.
GRAINGER (m) *Old French* Farm steward.
GRANT (m) *Middle English* Giver.
GRANTLEY, GRANTLEIGH (m) *Old English* A form of Grantland, meaning 'deeded land'.
GRANVILLE (m) *Old French* From the big town.
GRAY (m) *Old English* To shine.
GRAYLING (f) *Old English* From the name of the fish, meaning 'small gray'.
GREENDALE (m) *Old English* Green valley.
GREENWOOD (m) *Old English* Green woodland.
GREER (f) *Greek* Guardian, watchful.
GREGOR (m) German form of Gregory.
GREGORY (m) *Greek* Vigilant.
GRETA, GREETA (f) Variants of Margaret.
GRETCHEN (f) German form of Margaret.
GRETEL (f) Variant of Gretchen.

GREVILLE (m) *Old English/French* Town at the grove or copse.
GREY *see* GRAY.
GRIFFITH, GRIFF (m) *Greek* From the griffin, a mythical creature.
GRISELDA (f) Italian name of uncertain meaning.
GROVER (m) *Old English* One who grows trees.
GUINEVERE (f) *Celtic* White wave.
GUS, GUSSIE *see* AUGUSTA.
GUY (m) *Old French* A guide.
GWEN (f) *Celtic* White.
GWENDA *see* GWEN.
GWENDOLYN (f) Variant of Gwen.
GWENETH, GWENYTH, GWENITH (f) *Welsh* forms of Gwen.
GWENIVER (f) Cornish form of Jennifer.
GWYLAN (m) *Welsh* Seagull.
GWYN (m and f) *Welsh* Fair, white.
GWYNETH, GWYNNETH (f) *Welsh* Happiness.
GWYNFA (f) Feminine form of Gwynfor.
GWYNFOR (m) *Welsh* Good lord.
GYLES *see* GILES.

Haddon H Hywell

HADDON (m) *Old English* A heath.
HADLEY (m) *Old English* Meadow near the heath.
HADRIAN (m) *Greek* Rich.
HAGAN, HAGEN *see* HAVEN.
HAINES (m) From the German form of John.
HAINEY (f) Origin uncertain. Possibly a form of Haines.
HAL *see* HENRY and HAROLD.
HALDEN, HALDON (m) *Old English* Hal's valley.
HALEEN, HALENE (f) A blend of Haley and Eileen.
HALEY (f) *Old Norse* Hero.
HALFORD (m) *Old English* Hal's river crossing.
HALLAM (m) *Old Norse* At the rocks.
HALLEY (m) *Old Norse* Hero.
HALLY (f) *Old Norse* Hero.
HAMILTON (m) *Old English* Crooked hill.
HAMISH (m) Phonetic form of the Gaelic variant of James.
HAMLIN (m) *Old English* Brook near the home.
HAMPTON (m) *Old English* High village.
HANA *see* HANNAH.
HANDLEY, HANLEY (m) *Old English* Hane's meadow.
HANFORD (m) *Old German* Hill ford.
HANIA *see* HANNAH.
HANITA (f) Diminutive of Hannah.

HANK see HENRY.
HANNAH (f) *Hebrew* Gracious, merciful.
HANSON (m) Son of Hans (John).
HAPPY (m and f) Nickname for a contented person.
HARALD see HAROLD.
HARCOURT (m) *Middle English* Army courtyard.
HARDING see HARDY.
HARDY (m) *Middle English* Bold, robust.
HAREL, HARRELL (m) *Hebrew* Mountain of God.
HARFORD (m) *Old English* Hare ford.
HARKER (m) *Old English* Listener.
HARLAND, HARLAN (m) *Middle English* Strand of hemp.
HARLENE (f) Origin uncertain. Possibly a form of Arlene.
HARLEY, HARLEIGH (m) *Old English* Hemp field.
HARMAN, HARMOND (m) *Greek* Peace, harmony.
HARMONEL (f) A modern invention meaning 'harmony of the elves'.
HARMONIA (f) *Greek* Unifying.
HARMONY (f) *Greek* Concord.
HAROLD, HARALD (m) *Old English* Leader of the army.
HAROLYN (f) Origin uncertain. Possibly a form of Carolyn.
HARPER (m) *Old Norse* To grip a harpoon.
HARRIE see HARRY.
HARRIET (f) Feminine form of Harry.
HARRINGTON (m) *Old English* Place of the he-goat.
HARRIS, HARRISON (m) Son of Harry.
HARROLD see HAROLD.
HARRY see HENRY.
HART (m) *Old English* Stag, hart.
HARTLEY (m) *Old English* Stag wood (or clearing).

Harva Hazelwood

HARVA (f) Feminine form of Harvey.
HARVEY (m) *Old German* Worthy of battle.
HARVIE, HARVE see HARVEY.
HARWOOD (m) *Old English* Hare wood.
HASLAM (m) *Old English* Place of hazel trees.
HATTIE, HATTY see HARRIET.
HATTIERENE (f) A blend of Hattie and Irene.
HAUORA (f) *Maori* Lively.
HAVELOCK (m) *Old Norse* Sea sport.
HAVEN (m) *Middle English* Harbour.
HAVILAND (m) *Old English* Land of Hafer's people.
HAVLIN (m) Origin uncertain. Possibly a form of Haviland.
HAVIVA (f) *Hebrew* Beloved.
HAWA (f) *Hebrew* Breath of life.
HAWK (m) *Old Norse* Bird of prey, hawk.
HAWLEY (m) *Old English* Hedged meadow.
HAWTHORNE (m) *Old English* From the tree name.
HAY (m) *Old English* Fence, hedge.
HAYDEN, HAYDON (m) *Old English* Hay pasture.
HAYFORD (m) *Old English* Ford near the hay meadow.
HAYLEY see HALEY.
HAYMON, HAYMAN (m) *Old English* Hill (mountain) fence.
HAYNES (m) A form of Hans (John).
HAYWARD (m) *Middle English* Protective hedge.
HAYWOOD (m) *Old English* Hedged copse.
HAZE, HAIZE, HAYZE (f) Origin uncertain. Mist, haze.
HAZEL, HAZELLE (f) *Old English* From the name of the tree.
HAZELBELLE (f) A blend of Hazel and Bella.
HAZELWOOD (m) *Old English* Wood of hazel trees.

HAZEN see HAVEN.
HAZENA, HAZINE (f) Feminine form of Hazen.
HAZIRA (f) A blend of Hazel and Mira.
HEADLEY see HEDLEY.
HEATH (m) *Middle English* Wasteland, heath.
HEATHER (f) From the plant-name of uncertain origin.
HEATON (m) *Old English* High place.
HEBE (f) *Greek* Youth.
HECTOR (m) *Greek* Holding fast.
HEDDA (f) *Greek* Warfare.
HEDDLE (m) Origin uncertain. Possibly a form of Hedley.
HEDERA (f) *Latin* Ivy.
HEDLI (f) *Old English* Hiding place in a meadow.
HEDLEY (m and f) *Old English* Clearing with heather.
HEDY see HEDDA and HESTER.
HEIDI (f) German form of Adelaide.
HELAINE, HELAYNE (f) Blends of Helen and Elaine.
HELANDRA (f) A blend of Helen and Sandra.
HELANTHA (f) A blend of Helen and Samantha.
HELEN, HELLEN (f) *Greek* Torch, light (hence the shining one).
HELENOR (f) A blend of Helen and Eleanor.
HELGA (f) *Old English* Holly.
HELIANTHA (f) *Greek* Sun flower.
HELINA (f) Hawaiian form of Helen.
HELINDA, HELYNDA (f) A blend of Helen and Linda.
HELISSA (f) A blend of Helen and Lisa.
HELITA (f) A blend of Helen and Lita.
HELIUS (m) *Greek* The sun.

HELMA (f) *Old English* Helm or rudder.
HELOISE, HELOISA (f) French form of Eloise.
HELORA (f) A blend of Helen and Lora.
HENA *see* HANNAH.
HENLY, HENLEY (m) *Old English* High clearing.
HENRI (m) French form of Henry.
HENRIETTA (f) Derived from the French form of Henry.
HENRY (m) *Old German* Home ruler.
HERALD *see* HAROLD.
HERBERT (m) *Old German* Bright, shining army.
HERCULES (m) From the Greek name Heracles, probably meaning 'glory of the goddess Hera'.
HEREWARD (m) *Old English* Army defence.
HERMA (f) *Latin* Square pillar of stone, signpost.
HERMAN (m) *Old German* Soldier.
HERMES (m) From the name of the Greek messenger of the gods.
HERMIA *see* HERMIONE.
HERMIONE (f) Feminine form of Hermes.
HERMON *see* HERMAN.
HERON (m) *Old English* Holy name.
HERRICK (m) Possibly a variant of Eric.
HERTHA (f) *Old German* Earth mother.
HESKELL (m) Origin uncertain. Possibly a form of Hesketh.
HESKETH (m) *Old Norse* Horse track.
HESPER (f) Origin uncertain.
HESTER *see* ESTHER.
HESTIA (f) Greek goddess of the hearth.
HETTA *see* HARRIET.
HETTY, HETTIE *see* HARRIET.
HEW *see* HUGH and HEWLETT.

HEWITT (m) *Old English* Two possible origins: 1. A form of Hugh; 2. Cleared place.
HEWLETT (m) *Old English* Fountainhead of steam.
HEYWOOD (m) *Old English* High wood.
HIAM, HIGHAM (m) *Old English* High homestead.
HICKORY (m) *American Indian* From the name of the broadleaved tree.
HIEDI *see* HEIDI.
HILA (f) *Hebrew* Praise.
HILANA (f) A blend of Hila and Amanda.
HILANTHA (f) A blend of Hila and Samantha.
HILARY (f and rarely m) *Latin* Cheerful.
HILDA *see* HILDEGARDE.
HILDEGARDE (f) *Old German* Warrior.
HILDELITH (f) A blend of Hilda and Delyth.
HILDRETH (m) *Old English* Battle counsellor.
HILLA *see* HILA.
HILLARY, HILLERY *see* HILARY.
HILLELA (f) *Hebrew* Feminine form of Hillel, meaning 'praised'.
HILLMAN (m) *Middle English* Hill farmer.
HILMA *see* WILHELMINA.
HILMER (m) *Old English* Lake on the hill.
HILORA (f) *Hebrew/Maori* Praise to life.
HILTON, HYLTON (m) *Old English* Village on the hill.
HINA (f) From the name of the Tahitian moon goddess.
HIRAM (m) *Hebrew* Noble born.
HIRONDELLE, HIRONDEL (f) *French* A swallow.
HOB, HOBIE (m) Variant of Robin or Robert.
HOBART (m) *Danish* Bart's hill.
HODGSON (m) *Old German* Son of Hodge, meaning 'famous spear'.

HOEL see HOWELL.
HOGAN (m) Irish variant of Hagan.
HOLBROOK (m) *Old English* Stream in the hollow.
HOLDEN (m) *Old English* Deep valley.
HOLLACE (f) Variant of Haley.
HOLLAND (m) *Old English* Land on rising ground.
HOLLIE see HOLLY.
HOLLIS (m) Variant of Halley.
HOLLY (f, rarely m) *Old English* Holly tree.
HOLM (m) *Old Norse* Island.
HOLMAN (m) *Old English* Dweller in a hollow.
HOLMES (m) *Old Norse* Island in a fen.
HOMER (m) *Greek* One who is being led (hence blind).
HONEY (f) *Old Norse* Sweetness (can also be taken to mean 'excellence').
HONOR (f) *Latin* Honour, beauty.
HOPE (f) *Old English* Hope.
HORACE (m) Two possible origins: 1. *Greek*. To see, behold: 2. *Latin*. Hour, hence 'time'.
HORATIA (f) Feminine form of Horatio.
HORATIO (m) From the Roman clan name Horatius, which derives from the Greek name Horace.
HORTENSE (f) *Latin* A garden.
HORTON (m) *Latin* A garden.
HOSHI (f) *Japanese* Star.
HOWARD (m) *Old English* Guardian of the home.
HOWELL (m) *Old English* Well on the hill.
HOWLAND (m) *Old English* Land on the spur of the hill.
HOYT (m) *Middle English* A ship.
HUB see HUBBARD.
HUBBARD (m) A form of Hubert.
HUBERT (m) *Old German* Bright in mind.

HUCKLEBERRY (m) A character in *Huckleberry Finn* by Mark Twain.
HUDSON (m) Son of Hudd.
HUELA (f) Feminine form of Hugh.
HUGH, HUGHIE (m) Variant of Hubert.
HUGO *see* HUGH.
HULANDAH (f) Origin uncertain. Possibly a form of Huldah.
HULDAH (f) *Hebrew* A weasel or mole.
HUMBERT (m) *Old German* Bright home.
HUMPHREY (m) *Old German* A name meaning both 'strength' and 'peace'.
HUNT (m) *Old English* To search, hunt.
HUNTER (m) *Old English* Huntsman.
HUNTLEY, HUNTLY (m) *Old English* Hunting meadow.
HURST (m) *Old English* Wooden hill.
HUW (m) Welsh form of Hugh.
HYACINTH (f) *Greek* A flower-name meaning 'blue gem or sapphire'.
HYLDA *see* HILDA.
HYLTON *see* HILTON.
HYMAN (m) *Old English* Dweller in a high place.
HYONE (f) *Greek* Sea dream.
HYSSOP (m) *Old English* Origin uncertain. Perhaps 'hazel valley'.
HYWEL (m) *Welsh* Eminent.

Iago — Izzy

IAGO (m) Welsh for James.
IAIN (m) Gaelic form of John.
IAN (m) Scottish form of John.
IANTHE (f) *Greek* Violet flower.
IANTO (m) Welsh form of John.
IDA (f) *Old German* Possibly 'youthful'.
IDANA (f) A blend of Ida and Anna.
IDELIA (f) *Old German* Noble.
IDENA (f) A blend of Ida and Dena (Dinah).
IDONA, IDONEA (f) *Old Norse* Literally 'labour'; Idhuna was the Norse goddess of Spring.
IDINA *see* IDONA.
IDRIS (m) *Welsh* Ardent lord.
IDYLLA (f) *Greek* Perfection.
IESTIN, IESTYN (f) Welsh feminine form of Justin.
IEUAN (m) Welsh form of John.
IFOR (m) Two possible origins: 1. *Welsh* Lord; 2. A form of Ivor.
IKE *see* ISAAC.
ILA (f) *Aramaic* The best.
ILARIA (f) *Latin* Cheerful.
ILEANA (f) *Greek* From Troy.
ILEEN, ILENE *see* EILEEN.
ILISE *see* ALISE.
ILKA (f) *Gaelic* Of the same kind or type.
ILMA (f) Origin uncertain.

ILONA (f) Hungarian form of Helen.
ILORA (f) A blend of Ilona and Lora.
ILSE (f) German form of Elizabeth.
ILVA (f) *Old English* Origin uncertain. Possibly 'elven, elfin'.
ILYA, ILIJA (m) Slavonic forms of Elijah.
IMA *see* EMMA.
IMELDA (f) Italian form of German name Irmhild meaning 'all-embracing battle'.
IMMANUEL *see* EMANUEL.
IMOGEN (f) *Latin* Innocent.
INA (f) *Latin* Mother. Also a shortened version of any of the feminine names ending in this syllable.
INARET (f) *Welsh* Much loved.
INCA (f) *Quechua* Lord.
INDIA (f) *Sanskrit* The country name used as a first name. River Indus.
INDIRA (f) *Sanskrit* Moon.
INES, INEZ (f) Italian form of Agnes.
INGA, INGE (f) *Old Norse* Diminutive of Ingeborg meaning 'the protection of Ing' (god of peace in Norse mythology).
INGARET *see* INARET.
INGHAM (m) *Old English* Ing's homestead.
INGRAM (m) *Old German* Angel-raven.
INGRID (f) Scandinavian form of Inga.
INNES (m) *Celtic* Island.
INNIS (m) *Gaelic* Island.
INZA (f) A character in a novel by Frank Merriweather.
IOLA (f) *Greek* Dawn cloud.
IOLANA, IOLANI (f) Hawaiian form of Yolanda.
IOLANTA, IOLANTHE *see* YOLANDE.
IOLE, IOLO (m) *Welsh* Worthy lord.

ION (m) *Greek* Purple-coloured jewel.
IONA (f) Feminine form of Ion.
IONE *see* IONA.
IORA (f) *Latin* Gold.
IORWEN (f) *Welsh* Beautiful.
IRA (m) *Hebrew* Descend.
IRANA *see* IRENE.
IRBY (m) Origin uncertain.
IRELDA (f) A blend of Irene and Kelda.
IRENA (f) Polish form of Irene.
IRENE (f) *Greek* Peace.
IRINA *see* IRENA.
IRIS (f) A flower name of Greek origin, meaning 'play of colours'.
IRISSA (f) A character in the *Sword and Circlet* trilogy of novels by Carole Nelson Douglas.
IRMA (f) *Old German* Whole, universal.
IRMGARD (f) *Old German* Under Irmin's protection (Irmin was a Teutonic god-hero).
IRVING, IRVIN (m) *Gaelic* Handsome, fair.
IRYL (f) Origin uncertain. Possibly a form of Iris.
ISA *see* ISABEL.
ISAAC (m) *Hebrew* He will laugh.
ISABEL (f) Variant form of Elizabeth.
ISADOR, ISADORE (m) *Greek* Gift of Isis.
ISADORA, ISIDORA (f) Feminine forms of Isador.
ISALEE (f) Origin uncertain. Possibly a form of Isabel.
ISAIAH (m) *Hebrew* God is my salvation.
ISIDOR *see* ISADOR.
ISLA (f) Two possible origins: 1. From the Scottish river name; 2. *Old French* Island.
ISLEAN, ISLIEN (f) *Celtic* Sweet voiced.

ISMAY (f) *Old German* Origin uncertain. Possible meaning 'bright'.
ISOBEL *see* ISABEL.
ISOLA (f) *Latin* Alone, solitary.
ISOLDA (f) Two possible origins: 1. *Old German* To rule; 2. *Celtic* The fair one.
ISRAEL (m) Hebrew name of uncertain meaning.
ISSARA (f) Origin uncertain. Possibly a form of Isa.
ISTANA (f) *Malay* Palace.
ITA (f) *Irish* Thirst.
IVA, IVAH (f) Variant of Ivana, the feminine form of Ivan.
IVAN (m) Russian and Slavonic form of John.
IVANNA (f) *Hebrew* God's gracious gift.
IVENA (f) *Hebrew* Grace of the Lord.
IVER *see* IVOR.
IVERNA (f) *Old English* A bank, shore.
IVES, IVE (m) *Middle English* Climbing vine.
IVETTE *see* YVETTE.
IVO (m) *Old German* Yew wood.
IVON (m) French variant of Yves.
IVOR (m) *Latin* Ivory.
IVY (f) *Middle English* A plant name. A vine.
IWONA (f) Origin uncertain.
IZAAK *see* ISAAC.
IZELIA, IZELEA *see* AZALEA.
IZETTA *see* ISABEL.
IZORA (f) *Arabic* Dawn.
IZZY *see* ISIDORE.

Jaala J Jyan

JAALA (f) *Hebrew* Wild she-goat.
JAANA (f) Origin uncertain.
JACADA (f) A blend of Jacinta and Ada.
JACALYN, JACALINE *see* JACQUELINE.
JACANDA (f) A blend of Jacinta and Amanda.
JACANTHA (f) A blend of Jacinta and Samantha.
JACE *see* JASON.
JACENDA (f) A blend of Jacinta and Brenda.
JACINDA (f) A blend of Jacinta and Linda.
JACINE *see* JACINTH.
JACINTA, JACINTH, JACINTHA (f) *Greek* A sapphire.
JACK (m) A form of John.
JACKIE, JACQUI, JAQUI *see* JACQUELINE.
JACKLYN, JACKLINE, JACKLENE *see* JACQUELINE.
JACKSON (m) Son of Jack.
JACKY (m and f) A form of Jack or Jacqueline.
JACOB (m) *Hebrew* One who takes by the heel (hence a supplanter).
JACOBA (f) Feminine form of Jacob.
JACQUELINE, JACQUELYN, JACQUETTA, JAQUETTA (f) French feminine form of Jacques (James).
JADA (f) *Hebrew* Wise.

JADE, JAYDE (f) *Spanish* From the name of the precious stone.
JADEEN (f) A blend of Jade and Doreen.
JADEN (m) Origin uncertain. Possibly a form of Jada.
JAE see JAI.
JAEGER (m) *German* Hunter.
JAEL (f) *Hebrew* Mountain goat.
JAELLE, JAELLA see JAEL.
JAI (f and m) *Sanskrit* Hail, praise, victory.
JAINE see JANE.
JAIRIA (f) *Hebrew* Enlightened by God.
JAGO (m) Cornish form of James.
JAHLIA (f) A blend of Jane and Dahlia.
JAHNA see JANA.
JAHOLA (f) *Hebrew* Dove.
JAKE, JAKO see JACOB.
JALENE (f) A blend of Jane and Lena.
JAMEELA, JAMIL, JAMELLA (f) *Arabic* Beautiful.
JAMES (m) English form of Jacob.
JAMIE (m and f) Scottish form of James or Jamesina.
JAMIESON (m) Son of James.
JAMISINA, JAMESINA (f) Feminine forms of James.
JAN (m) A form of John or James.
JAN (f) A form of Jeanette or Janet.
JANA (f) Two possible origins: 1. A Hungarian form of Jane; 2. *Sanskrit* Knows.
JANAN (m) *Hebrew* Grace of the Lord.
JANCES (f) A blend of Jane and Frances.
JANCIS (f) A character in the novel *Precious Bane* by Mary Webb.

JANCY (f) Variant of Janice.
JANDA (f) A blend of Jane and Amanda.
JANDORA (f) A blend of Jane and Dora.
JANDY (f) A blend of Jane and Mandy.
JANE (f) From the Latin Johanna, a feminine form of John.
JANELLE, JANELLA (f) A blend of Jane and Ella.
JANERETTE, JANERETTA (f) Variants of Jane.
JANET, JANETTE, JANETTA, JANICE, JANIS, JANYCE (f) Forms of Jane.
JANIE, JANY see Jane.
JANINA, JANENE (f) Phonetic forms of the French name Jeannine.
JANITA see JUANITA.
JANN see JAN.
JANNA, JANNAH see JOHANNA.
JANNE (f) A blend of Jane and Anne.
JANORA (f) A blend of Jane and Dora.
JANSEN, JANSON (m) Son of John.
JANSUE (f) A blend of Jane and Susan.
JANTHA (f) A blend of Jane and Samantha.
JANTHEA (f) A blend of Jane and Anthea.
JANTHINA (f) A blend of Jane and Bethina.
JANUARY (f) *Latin* The month name used as a first name.
JAOMI (f) A blend of Jane and Naomi.
JAPHET (m) *Hebrew* Growth, expansion.
JAQUELINE see JACQUELINE.
JAQUETTA see JACQUETTA.
JAQUI see JACQUELINE.
JAQUINDA see JACINDA.
JARA (f) Slavonic form of Gertrude.
JARADO (m) Origin uncertain.
JARDINE (m) *French* A garden.

Jared   Jeannette

JARED (m) *Hebrew* Descendant.
JAREN (m) Origin uncertain. Posibly a form of Jared.
JARETH *see* GARETH.
JARIETTA (f) A blend of Jane and Marietta.
JARITA (f) *Sanskrit* Motherly bird.
JARMAN (m) *Latin* A German.
JARON (m) *Bohemian* Probably 'firm peace'.
JARRAD *see* JARED.
JARRAH (m) From the name of the eucalyptus broadleaved tree.
JARRY (m) Origin uncertain. Possibly a form of Jared.
JARVIS (m) *Old English* Battle spear.
JASA (f) A blend of James and Sara.
JASMEEN *see* JASMIN.
JASMIN, JASMINE (f) *Persian* From the flower name.
JASON (m) *Greek* Healer.
JASPER (m) *Greek* A semi-precious stone.
JAVAN (m) Origin uncertain.
JAY (m) *Latin* From the name of the bird.
JAYA *see* JAI.
JAYE (f) Feminine form of Jay.
JAYELLE (f) A blend of Jay and Ella.
JAYME *see* JAMIE.
JAYNE *see* JANE.
JAYSON *see* JASON.
JEAN, JEANIE (f) Scottish forms of Jane.
JEANELLA (f) A blend of Jane and Ella.
JEANETTE, JEANETTA (f) French form of Jane.
JEANINE *see* JANE.
JEANNE (f) A blend of Jean and Anne.
JEANNETTE *see* JEANETTE.

Jeannine   *Jennet*

JEANNINE see JANE.

JEB see JACOB.

JED (m) *Hebrew* Diminutive of Jedidiah meaning 'friend of the Lord'.

JEFFERSON, JEF (m) Son of Jeffrey.

JEFFERY, JEFFREY, JEF see GEOFFREY.

JEFFIE see JENNIFER.

JELENA (f) *Greek* Light.

JEM (m and f) Two possible origins: 1. A form of James; 2. *Latin* A gem, jewel.

JEMARI (f) A blend of Jem and Mary.

JEMIMA (f) *Hebrew* A dove.

JEMIRA (f) A blend of Jemima and Mira.

JEMITA (f) A blend of Jemima and Rita.

JEMMA see GEMMA.

JEMMY see JEMIMA or JAMES.

JEMONICA (f) A blend of Jem and Monica.

JEN, JENA see JEANNETTE.

JENALYN (f) A blend of Jeanette and Lyn.

JENARIAL (f) Origin uncertain.

JENAVEE see GENEVIEVE.

JENEFER see JENNIFER.

JENELLE, JENELLA (f) A blend of Janet and Ella.

JENET see JANET.

JENETTA, JENELLA see JANET.

JENI, JENIA see JENNIFER.

JENIFER see JENNIFER.

JENILEE (f) A blend of Jennifer and Lee.

JENINE see JANE.

JENISE, JENESSA (f) Variant of Janis.

JENITA see JUANITA.

JENNA, JENA (f) Variants of Jenny.

JENNET see JANET.

Jenetta   Jestine, Jestina

JENETTA *see* JANETTA.
JENNI, JENNIE, JENNEY Variants of Jenny.
JENNIFER (f) *Welsh* White wave.
JENNY *see* JENNIFER.
JENYTH (f) Variant of Jennifer.
JEONY (f) A blend of Jean and Bryony.
JERALD *see* GERALD.
JERALDINE *see* GERALDINE.
JERE, JERI *see* GERALDINE.
JERED *see* JARED.
JEREMIAH (m) *Hebrew* God will uplift.
JEREMY *see* JEREMIAH.
JEREVA (f) A blend of Junior and Reva.
JERI *see* GERALDINE.
JERLENE (f) A blend of Jeri and Marlene.
JERMAINE *see* GERMAINE.
JERMYN (m) A form of Jeremiah.
JEROEN *see* JEROME.
JEROLD *see* GERALD.
JEROME (m) *Greek* Of holy name.
JERROD, JERROLD *see* GERALD.
JERRY, JERRIE *see* GERALD.
JERVIS *see* JARVIS.
JESKA (f) *Hebrew* She who looks out.
JESMOND (m) A blend of Jerry and Desmond.
JESS, JES *see* JESSE.
JESSAMINE, JESSAMYN *see* JASMIN.
JESSAMY, JESSAMIE (f) Blends of Jessie and Amy.
JESSE, JESSEY, JES (m) *Hebrew* Wealthy.
JESSICA (f) Variant of Jessie.
JESSIE (f) *Hebrew* God's grace.
JESTINE, JESTINA *see* IESTIN.

JESTON (m) A form of Justin.
JESWYN, JESWIN (f) A blend of Jessie and Winifred.
JET (f) *Greek* From the name of the precious stone meaning 'hard black stone from Gagai in Asia Minor'.
JET (m) *French* To throw forward.
JETHRO (m) *Hebrew* Riches.
JETTA *see* JET.
JEVAN, JEVON (m) Anglo-Welsh forms of John.
JEVERA (f) *Hebrew* Life.
JEWEL (f) *Old French* Precious stone.
JILL, JILLY, JILLIAN *see* GILLIAN.
JIM, JIMMY, JIMMIE *see* JAMES.
JINJA *see* GINGER.
JINNY *see* VIRGINIA.
JO *see* JOANNA, JOSEPHINE, etc.
JOAN *see* JANE.
JOANN, JOANNE, JOANNA (f) *Hebrew* God is gracious.
JOBETH (f) A blend of Joan and Elizabeth.
JOB (m) *Hebrew* Oppressed.
JOBEY, JOBIE, JOBY *see* JOB.
JOBINA (f) Feminine form of Job.
JOCELYN, JOCELYNE (f) *Old German* Meaning uncertain, but probably linked with the tribal name of the Goths.
JOCK (m) Used as a nickname for Scots called John (and Scots in general). Never used as a first name by Scottish parents.
JODETTE *see* JODIE.
JODIE, JODY (f) Forms of Judith.
JOE *see* JOSEPH.
JOEL (m) *Hebrew* God is willing.

JOELENE see JOLENE.
JOELLA, JOELLE (f) A blend of Jo(anna) and Ella.
JOEY see JOSEPH.
JOHANNA (f) *Hebrew* God is gracious.
JOHN (m) *Hebrew* God is gracious.
JOHNATHON see JONATHON.
JOHNETTE (f) Feminine diminutive of John.
JOHNNIE, JOHNNY see JOHN.
JOI, JOIE, JOIA see JOY.
JOLA (f) A blend of Jo(anna) and Lola.
JOLAINE (f) A blend of Joseph and Elaine.
JOLANDA, JOLANDI see YOLANDE.
JOLANTHA, JOLANTA (f) Blends of Jo(anna) and Samantha.
JOLEA (f) A blend of Joseph and Lea.
JOLENE, JOLEEN see JOLIE.
JOLIE (f) *Middle English* High spirits.
JOLINDA (f) A blend of Jo(anna) and Linda.
JOLYNN, JOLYN see JOLENE.
JOLYON, JOLIAN (m) Northern English form of Julian.
JON see JONATHAN.
JONAH (m) *Hebrew* Dove.
JONAS (m) Greek form of Jonah.
JONATHAN, JONATHON (m) *Hebrew* God has given.
JONCY (f) Variant of Jancy.
JONEDA (f) A blend of Jon and Foneda.
JONELLA, JONELLE (f) A blend of Joni and Ella.
JONI (f) Feminine form of Jon.
JONINA (f) A blend of Joni and Nina.
JONQUIL (f) *Spanish* From the name of the flower in the narcissus family.
JONSY see JONCY.

Jonty   **Judd, Jud**

JONTY (m) Origin uncertain. Perhaps a phonetic form of the word 'jaunty', or a variant of Jon.

JORAH (m) *Hebrew* Autumn rain.

JORAM (m) *Hebrew* The Lord is exalted.

JORDAN (m, rarely f) *Hebrew* To flow down.

JORDANA (f) Feminine form of Jordan.

JOREL (f and m) A blend of Joyce and Reuel.

JORIS (f) A blend of Jo and Doris.

JORY (m) Cornish form of George.

JOSCELYN, JOSCELINE *see* JOCELYN.

JOSELLA (f) A blend of Josie and Ella.

JOSEPH (m) *Hebrew* 'Jehovah will add (or increase)'.

JOSEPHINE (f) French feminine form of Joseph.

JOSETTE (f) Variant of Josephine.

JOSH *see* JOSHUA or JOSIAH.

JOSIAH (m) *Hebrew* Jehovah supports.

JOSIE, JOSY *see* JOSEPHINE.

JOSLIN, JOSLYN *see* JOCELYN.

JOSS, JOS (m) *Celtic* Champion.

JOSSLYN *see* JOCELYN.

JOTHAM (m) *Hebrew* The Lord is perfect.

JOVANNA (f) Variant of Giovanna, an Italian feminine form of John.

JOWAN (m) Cornish form of John.

JOY (f) *Latin* Gladness, delight.

JOYA (f) *Spanish* Treasure.

JOYCE (f) *Latin* Joyful, merry.

JOYCELYN (f) A blend of Joyce and Jocelyn.

JOYLENE (f) A blend of Joy and Helene.

JOYLYN (f) A blend of Joy and Lynda.

JUAN (m) Spanish form of John.

JUANITA (f) Spanish feminine form of Juan.

JUBAL (m) *Hebrew* Ramshorn.

JUDD, JUD *see* JUDE or JORDAN.

JUDE, JUDAS, JUDAH (m) *Hebrew* Praise.
JUDGE (m) *Old French* A magistrate, judge.
JUDI *see* JUDY.
JUDIAN (m) A blend of Jude and Julian.
JUDITH (f) *Hebrew* Praise.
JUDSON (m) A form of Judah (*see* JUDE).
JUDY (f) Variant of Judith.
JULANDA (f) A blend of Julie and Amanda.
JULANTHA (f) A blend of Julie and Samantha.
JULES, JULE (m) French form of Julius.
JULIA, JULIE (f) Latin feminine form of Julius.
JULIAN (m) *Greek* Origin uncertain. Probably 'soft-haired'.
JULIANA (f) Feminine form of Julian.
JULIANNE (f) A blend of Julia and Anne.
JULIENNE (f) French form of Julia.
JULIET, JULIETTE (f) French forms of Julia.
JULINDA (f) A blend of Julie and Linda.
JULITA (f) A blend of Julie and Rita.
JULIUS (m) A form of Julian.
JULY (f and m) *Latin* Name of the month, used as a first name.
JUNE (f) *Latin* Name of the month, used as a first name.
JUNELLA (f) A blend of June and Ella.
JUNIOR (m) *Latin* Young.
JUNIPER (f and m) *Latin* From the name of the evergreen tree.
JUNITA *see* JUANITA.
JUNO (f) Two possible origins: 1. *Irish* Name of uncertain meaning, possibly 'lamb'; 2. *Latin* Queen of heaven (the name of a Roman goddess).
JUSTIN, JUSTYN (m) *Latin* Just.
JUSTINA (f) Latin feminine form of Justin.

JUSTINE (f) French feminine form of Justin.
JYAN (m) A character in the novels of David Wingrove.

Kaarina K Kyrene

KAARINA *see* CARINA.
KACY (f) Two possible origins: 1. Derived from the initials K and C; 2. A blend of Karen and Tracy.
KADE (m) A character in the novel *Kirlian Quest* by Piers Anthony.
KAELA (f) A blend of Kathy and Ella.
KAHLIA (f) A blend of Kathy and Dahlia.
KAHLITA (f) A blend of Kahlia and Rita.
KAI (m) *Japanese* Sea.
KAID *see* CADE.
KAILEIGH *see* KAYLEY.
KAIMANA (f) *Hawaiian* Diamond.
KAIN *see* CAIN.
KAITLYN *see* CAITLIN.
KAIYA (f) Origin uncertain. Perhaps a feminine form of Kai.
KAKI (f) Origin uncertain.
KALA (f) From the novel *Kala* by Nicholas Luard.
KALANDA (f) A blend of Kaley and Amanda.
KALANTHA (f) A blend of Kaley and Samantha.
KALDORA (f) A blend of Kaley and Dora.
KALEY (f) A form of Kelly.
KALILA (f) *Arabic* Beloved.
KALINDA (f) A character in the novel *Neverness* by David Zindell.
KALINKA (f) Russian name linked with Calinda.

KALMAN (m) A form of Kalonymos, a variant of Clement.

KALVIN *see* CALVIN.

KALYA (f) *Sanskrit* Healthy.

KALYANA (f) *Sanskrit* One who is virtuous.

KAMI (f) *Japanese* The divine power of deities in Shintoism.

KAMILLA *see* CAMILLA.

KAMLA (f) Variant of Camilla.

KAN (m) *Japanese* Sense, intuition.

KANA (f) Feminine form of Kane.

KANANI (f) *Hawaiian* A beauty.

KANDI, KANDY *see* CANDY.

KANDORA (f) A blend of Kandy and Dora.

KANDRA (f) *Sanskrit* Bright, lovely.

KANDRIN (m) *Sanskrit* Golden.

KANE (m) *Welsh* Beautiful.

KANGA (f) A character in *Winnie the Pooh* by A. A. Milne.

KANTI (m, rarely f) *Sanskrit* The sun's rays.

KANYA (f) *Sanskrit* Virgin Goddess.

KAORY (m) Origin uncertain.

KARA (f) Two possible origins: 1. *Sanskrit* Doing good; 2. A form of Cara.

KARAN *see* KAREN.

KARANDA (f) A country in the *Malloreon* cycle of novels by David Eddings.

KARANTHA (f) A blend of Kara and Samantha.

KAREL *see* CAROL.

KARELLA (f) A blend of Kara and Ella.

KAREN (f) Danish form of Katarina.

KARENA (f) A blend of Karen and Carina.

KARENZA, KERENZA (f) *Cornish* Love, affection.

KARETTA (f) A blend of Karen and Betty.

KAREY see KARRIE.

KARI (f) *Sanskrit* Doer.

KARIM (m) *Arabic* Generous, noble.

KARIN, KARYN see KAREN.

KARINA see CARINA.

KARIS see CARIS.

KARISSA see CARISSA.

KARITA see CARITA.

KARL see CARL.

KARLA see CARLA.

KARLENE, KARLEEN see CARLENE.

KARLIE, KARLY see CARLY.

KARNA (f) Swedish form of Karina (Carina).

KAROL (m) Slavonic form of Charles.

KAROLA (f) Feminine form of Karol.

KARONA (f) A blend of Karen and Rona.

KARRI (f) From the name of the tree in the eucalyptus family.

KARRIE see KARRI.

KARSTEN (m) Origin uncertain.

KARUNA (f) *Sanskrit* Compassion.

KARYL see CAROL.

KARYN see KAREN.

KASHIMA (f) Possibly a form of Kasmira.

KASIA (f) *Polish* Pure.

KASMIRA (f) *Slavonic* Commander of Peace.

KASOTA (f) *American Indian* Clear sky.

KASSIE see CASSIE.

KASUMI (f) *Japanese* Haze, mist.

KATARINA (f) Slavonic and Scandinavian form of Katherine.

KATARINDA (f) A blend of Katherine and Linda.

KATE see KATHERINE.

Katelin   Kealan

KATELIN see CAITLIN.

KATERINA see KATHERINE.

KATHARINE, KATHERINE, KATHERYN (f) *Greek* Pure.

KATHEVIRA (f) A blend of Kathy and Elvira.

KATHLEEN (f) Irish form of Catherine.

KATHLYN (f) A blend of Kathleen and Kathryn.

KATHRINE, KATHRYN see KATHARINE.

KATHY, KATIE see KATHARINE.

KATINA, KATTINA (f) Slavonic form of Katharine.

KATINKA, KATISHA (f) Russian form of Katharine.

KATONNA (f) A blend of Kathy and Donna.

KATRA (f) A form of Katrina.

KATRINA, KATRINE, KATRIN see KATHARINE.

KATRINKA (f) Slavonic form of Katharine.

KATRUSHKA (f) Russian form of Katharine.

KATY, KATYA see KATHARINE.

KATYANA (f) Russian name linked with Katherine.

KAVINDA (f) Origin uncertain.

KAVITA (f) *Sanskrit* Poetry.

KAY (m) Cornish form of Caius.

KAY (f) A short form of any of the feminine names beginning with the letter 'K'.

KAYA (f) *American Indian* Little elder sister.

KAYE see KAY.

KAYLA, KAYLE, KAILE see KELILA.

KAYLEY see KELLY.

KAYLEIGH (f) A form of Kelly.

KAYNA (f) *Cornish* Beautiful.

KAZ (m) Origin uncertain. Possibly a form of Kazia.

KAZIA see KEZIAH.

KEA see KIA.

KEALAN (m) *Irish* Slender.

KEAN, KEANE see KEENE.
KEBY (m) Cornish name of uncertain meaning. Possibly 'charioteer'.
KECIA (f) Perhaps a form of Cecile.
KEDI (f) *Turkish* Cat.
KEEFE (m) *Irish* Wellbeing.
KEEGAN, KEGAN (m) *Celtic* Son of Egan.
KEELAH see KELLY.
KEELEY, KEELY see KELLY.
KEENA (f) Origin uncertain. Possibly a form of Keene.
KEENAN see KEENE.
KEENE (m) *Old English* Wise, learned.
KEEYAH (f) Origin uncertain.
KEFIRA (f) *Hebrew* Young lioness.
KEIR see KERR.
KEIRA (f) Feminine form of Keiran.
KEIRAN, KAIRAN (m) *Greek* Rays of the sun.
KEIRANNE (f) A blend of Keira and Anne.
KEISHA (f) Variant of Lakeisha.
KEITH (m) *Gaelic* The wind.
KELA (f) Origin uncertain. Possibly a form of Kelda.
KELANA (f) A character in the novel *Isle of Illusion* by Carol Severance.
KELANDA (f) A blend of Kelly and Amanda.
KELANTHA (f) A blend of Kelly and Samantha.
KELBY (m) *Old German* A farm.
KELDA (f) *Scandinavian* Fresh mountain.
KELI see KELLY.
KELILA (f) *Hebrew* A crown.
KELLIE see KELLY.
KELLY, KELLYE (f) *Irish* Strife, warlike one.
KELLEY, KEELY see KELLY.

KELSEY (m) *Old German* From the water.

KELSON (m) A character in the novel *Deryni Rising* by Katherine Kurtz.

KELTON (m) *Old English* Keel town (town where ships are built).

KELVEDON (m) *Old English* Cynelaf's valley.

KELVIN, KELWIN (m) *Old English* Friend of ships.

KEN *see* KENNETH.

KENAN (m) Cornish form of Conan.

KENDAL, KENDALL (m, rarely f) *Celtic* Ruler of the valley.

KENDERN (m) *Cornish* Chief, lord.

KENDRICK (m) *Old English* Royal.

KENLEY (m) *Old English* Headland.

KENNA (f) *Old English* Head.

KENNEDY (m) *Old English* Royal.

KENNET (m) *Celtic* From the river name meaning 'high place'.

KENNETH, KENITH (m) *Gaelic* Handsome.

KENRICK (m) *Old English* Royal.

KENT *see* KENNETT.

KENTON *see* KENT, KENNETH.

KENVER (m) *Cornish* Great chief.

KENWARD (m) *Old English* Brave guard.

KENWYN (m) *Cornish* White chief or white ridge.

KENYON (m) Variant of Kenneth.

KERELLA (f) A blend of Keren and Ella.

KEREN (f) *Hebrew* A form of Kerenhappuch, meaning 'horn of antimony'.

KERETTA, KERET (f) *Hebrew* Settlement.

KERENA (f) A blend of Keren and Rena.

KERENSA, KERENZA (f) *Cornish* Love, affection.

KERI *see* KERRY.

KERMIT (m) Variant of Dermot.

KERN (m) *Irish* A band of soldiers.

KERR (m) *Old Norse* Marshland.

KERRA (f) Feminine form of Kerr.

KERREN see KAREN.

KERRI see KERRY.

KERRICK (m) A character in the *West of Eden* trilogy of novels by Harry Harrison.

KERRY, KERRIE, KERREY (m and f) *Irish* The place of Ciar's people.

KERSTI, KERSTIE see KIRSTY.

KERWIN (m) *Irish* Dark, black.

KERYN, KERRIN (m and f) Variants of Kerry.

KES (m) From the name of a pet kestrel in the novel *A Kestrel for a Knave* by Barry Hines, filmed under the title *Kes*.

KESHA see KESHIA.

KESHET (f) *Hebrew* Rainbow.

KESHIA, KESHISHA (f) *Aramaic* An elder.

KESIRA (f) A character in the novel *The Jade Demons Quarter* by Robert Vardeman.

KESTER (m) Variant of Christopher.

KETA (f) Origin uncertain. Possibly a form of Ketty.

KETTY (f) A blend of Kitty and Betty.

KEVA (f) Feminine form of Kevin.

KEVERN, KEVERNE (m) see KEVIN.

KEVIN (m) *Irish* Handsome at birth.

KEX (m) A blend of Kevin and Rex.

KEYA (f) Feminine form of Keye.

KEYE (m) *Gaelic* Son of the fiery one.

KEZIAH, KEZIA, KETZIA (f) *Hebrew* Fragrant powdered bark.

KIA see KIANA.

KIANA, QUIANA (f) Anna with the Ki- prefix.

KIARA (f) Feminine form of Kiaran.

KIARAN (m) From the name of an Irish saint, meaning uncertain. Often confused with Kieran.

KIBA (f) Origin uncertain. Possibly a form of Keby.

KICHI (f) *Japanese* Fortunate.

KID, KIDD (m) *Old English* Strong.

KIDA (f) Origin uncertain. Perhaps a feminine form of Kid.

KIEL (m) Origin uncertain.

KIERA (f) Feminine form of Kieran.

KIERAN, KIERON, KYRAN (m) *Irish* Dark, black.

KIERSTEN see KIRSTEN.

KIEW (m) Welsh name of uncertain meaning.

KIFFI (f) Origin uncertain.

KIKE (f) Origin uncertain.

KILA, KILAH (f) Possibly a feminine form of Kilian.

KILIAN (m) *Irish* Strife, warlike.

KIM see KIMBERLEY.

KIMBALL see KIM.

KIMBERLEY, KIMBERLY, KYMBERLY (f) *Old English* Land belonging to Cyneburg.

KIMBERLYN (f) A blend of Kimberly and Lynda.

KIMBLE, KYMBLE see KIMBERLEY.

KIMI (f) *Japanese* The best.

KINA (f) Origin uncertain. Possibly a form of Kinetta.

KINETTA, KINETA (f) *Greek* To move.

KING (m) *Old German* Sovereign, king.

KINGSLEY (m) *Old English* King's wood or clearing.

KINGSTON (m) *Old English* King's farm.

KINGSWOOD (m) *Old English* King's wood.

KIONA (f) *American Indian* Brown hills.

KIOWA (f) An ethnic division of Native Americans.

KIRAH see KIRA.

Kira *Kolina*

KIRA (f) A character in the film *The Dark Crystal*.
KIRAN *see* KIERAN.
KIRBY (m, rarely f) *Old English* Church farm.
KIREEN (f) *Old English* A church.
KIRI (f) *Maori* Two possible origins: 1. From *kiritea*, meaning 'fair'; 2. From *kiri*, meaning 'bark, skin'.
KIRIAN *see* KIERAN.
KIRIMA (f) Possibly a variant of Kiri.
KIRIN *see* KAREN.
KIRK (m) *Old Norse* Church.
KIRRELY, KIRRILY (f) Origin uncertain.
KIRSTEN, KERSTEN, KIRSTEEN (f) Scandinavian form of Christine.
KIRSTIE *see* KIRSTY.
KIRSTIN, KIRSTYNE, KIRSTYN *see* KIRSTEN.
KIRSTY (f) Scottish form of Christine.
KIRTON (m) *Old English* Village with a church.
KISANI (f) Origin uncertain.
KISHA (f) *Russian* Pure.
KIT (f) *see* KITTY.
KIT (m) *see* CHRISTOPHER.
KITA (f) *Maori* Fast.
KITAURA (f) Origin uncertain.
KITENA, KETENA (f) Blends of Kitty and Lena.
KITRA (f) *Hebrew* A crown.
KITTY, KETTY, KITTA (f) Forms of Katherine.
KIYA *see* KIA.
KLARA *see* CLARA.
KLEA *see* CLEA.
KOA (f) *Hebrew* Princess.
KODAN (m) Origin uncertain.
KOTHA (f) *Maori* Gift.
KOLINA (f) *Greek* Pure.

Komala — Kushuma

KOMALA (f) *Sanskrit* Charming.
KONRAD, CONRAD (m) *Old German* Wise counsellor.
KONSTANTIN *see* CONSTANTINE.
KOO (f) *Maori* Girl.
KORA *see* CORA.
KOREN, KORE (f) *Greek* Beautiful maiden.
KORENZA (f) An Italian name linked with Koren.
KORI (f) *Maori* To play.
KORINA, KORINNA *see* CORINNE.
KORINDA (f) A blend of Kori and Linda.
KORINTHA (f) A blend of Kori and Samantha.
KORONETTE, KORONET (f) *Hebrew* To shine.
KORUNA (f) *Czech* Crown.
KOS (m) From the name of the Greek island.
KOSHKA (f) *Russian* Cat.
KRAMER (m) *Old English* To cram, fill up.
KRIS, KRISS *see* KRISTIAN.
KRISHA (f) A blend of Kris and Trisha.
KRISTA (f) Slavonic form of Christine.
KRISTEN (f) A blend of Kirsten and Christine.
KRISTIAN (m) Danish form of Christian.
KRISTIN *see* KRISTINA.
KRISTINA (f) Swedish form of Christina.
KRISTINE (f) Scandinavian form of Christine.
KRISTOPHER *see* CHRISTOPHER.
KRISTY (f) A form of Kirsten, Kristina, etc.
KRYSTYNA (f) Polish form of Christine.
KRYSTAL, KRYSTEL, KRYSTLE *see* CRYSTAL.
KUNI (f) *Japanese* Country born.
KURA (f) *Maori* Darling.
KURT *see* KONRAD.
KUSELLA (f) Origin uncertain.
KUSHUMA (f) *Sanskrit* Always be happy.

KYLA (f) Feminine form of Kyle.

KYLANDA (f) A blend of Kylie and Amanda.

KYLANTHA (f) A blend of Kylie and Samantha.

KYLARA (f) A blend of Kyla and Lara.

KYLE (m, rarely f) *Gaelic* Hill where cattle graze.

KYLENE (f) A blend of Kylie and Lena.

KYLER (m) Origin uncertain. Possibly a form of Kyle.

KYLIE (f) *Aborigine* Curved stick or boomerang.

KYLINA (f) A blend of Kylie and Lina.

KYLINDA, KYLYNDA (f) Blends of Kylie and Linda.

KYLORA (f) A blend of Kylie and Lora.

KYM *see* KIM.

KYNA (f) *Gaelic* Great wisdom.

KYRA (f) Feminine form of Cyril.

KYRAN *see* KIERAN.

KYRENE (f) A blend of Kyra and Irene.

Labana L Lythinda

LABANA (f) Origin uncertain.
LABETA (f) Origin uncertain.
LACARA (f) Cara- with the La- prefix.
LACEY, LACI, LACY (f) From the place name Lassy in Calvados.
LACHANA (f) Chana with the La- prefix.
LACHELLE (f) Chelle (Michelle) with the La- prefix.
LACHONDA (f) Chonda with the La- prefix.
LACOLE (f) Cole (Nicole) with the La- prefix.
LACORIA (f) Coria (Cora) with the La- prefix.
LACYNDORA (f) Cyndora with the La- prefix.
LADAISHA (f) Daisha with the La- prefix.
LADENE (f) Dena with the La- prefix.
LADONYA (f) Donya with the La- prefix.
LAFONDRA (f) Fondra with the La- prefix.
LAHELA (f) Origin uncertain.
LAIKA (f) Origin uncertain.
LAILA *see* LEILA.
LAIRD (m) Scottish form of Lord.
LAIS (f) *Greek* Adored.
LAJOIA (f) Joia with the La- prefix.
LAKAIYA (f) Kaiya with the La- prefix.
LAKE (m) *Latin* Pond, lake.
LAKEA (f) Kea with the La- prefix.
LAKECIA (f) Kecia with the La- prefix.
LAKEISHA (f) Keisha with the La- prefix.

LAKESHA (f) Kesha with the La- prefix.
LAKIA (f) Kia with the La- prefix.
LAKIDA (f) Kida with the La- prefix.
LAKILA (f) Kila with the La- prefix.
LAKISHA (f) Kisha with the La- prefix.
LAKITA (f) Kita with the La- prefix.
LAKIYA (f) Kiya with the La- prefix.
LAKRISHA (f) Krisha with the La- prefix.
LAKSHANA (f) Shana with the La- prefix.
LALA (f) Origin uncertain.
LALAKA (f) *Sanskrit* Caressing.
LALANA (f) *Sanskrit* Woman.
LALITA (f) *Sanskrit* Darling.
LALLA, LALAGE, LALLY (f) *Greek* To talk, prattle.
LAMBERT (m) *Old German* Name meaning both 'land' and 'bright'.
LAMBOURN (m) *Old English* Loamy (heavy clay) stream.
LAMINA (f) Origin uncertain.
LAMORNA (f) *Middle English* Morning.
LAMONT (m) *Latin* The mountain.
LANA (f) *Latin* Wool.
LANATA (f) Nata with the La- prefix.
LANCELOT, LAUNCELOT, LANCE (m) Origin uncertain. Possibly from Norman word *Ancel*, meaning 'servant'.
LANDA (f) A blend of Lana and Wanda.
LANDER (m) From the name of the French region of Flanders.
LANDORA (f) A blend of Lana and Dora.
LANDRY (m, rarely f) *Old English* Rough land.
LANE (m) *Old English* To move, go (hence a road or lane).
LANEISHA (f) Neisha with the La- prefix.

LANETTA (f) Netta with the La- prefix.
LANGDON (m) *Old English* Long valley.
LANGFORD (m) *Old English* Long river crossing.
LANGLEY (m) *Old English* Long meadow.
LANGSTON (m) *Old English* Long narrow village.
LANI, LANIE (f) *Hawaiian* Sky.
LANISHA (f) Nisha with the La- prefix.
LANORA (f) Nora with the La- prefix.
LANSON (m) Son of Lance.
LANTANA (f) From the name of the flowering shrub.
LANTHA (f) A blend of Lana and Samantha.
LANTY (m) Irish diminutive of Laurence.
LANY, LANNY (m) Origin uncertain.
LAQUANA (f) Quana with the La- prefix.
LAQUELA (f) Quela with the La- prefix.
LAQUETTA (f) Quetta with the La- prefix.
LAQUINDA (f) Quinda with the La- prefix.
LAQUITA (f) Quita with the La- prefix.
LARA (f) Variant of Larisa or Larissa.
LARAINE (f) Two possible origins: 1. *Latin* Seagull; 2. A form of Lorraine.
LARALYN (f) A blend of Laura and Lyn.
LARCH (m) From the name of the broadleaved tree.
LARELLA (f) A blend of Lara and Ella.
LARENA (f) Rena with the La- prefix.
LARESA (f) Resa with the La- prefix.
LARESHA (f) Resha with the La- prefix.
LARETTA (f) A blend of Lara and Betty.
LARINA (f) *Latin* Seagull.
LARINDA (f) Rinda with the La- prefix.
LARISSA, LARISA (f) *Latin* Cheerful.
LARITA (f) Rita with the La- prefix.
LARKIN (m) Diminutive of Laurence.
LARRAINE *see* LORRAINE.

LARREN, LARRON (m) *French* A thief.
LARRY see LAURENCE.
LARYETTA (f) A blend of Larissa and Marietta.
LASHANA (f) Shana with the La- prefix.
LASHANDA (f) Shanda with the La- prefix.
LASHANNA (f) Shanna with the La- prefix.
LASHAUNA (f) Shauna with the La- prefix.
LASHAWN (f) Shawn with the La- prefix.
LASHEA (f) Shea with the La- prefix.
LASHEBA (f) Sheba with the La- prefix.
LASHEELE (f) Sheele with the La- prefix.
LASHONA (f) Shona with the La- prefix.
LASHONDA (f) Shonda with the La- prefix.
LASONDA (f) Sonda with the La- prefix.
LASONYA (f) Sonya with the La- prefix.
LATA (f) Origin uncertain.
LATAISHA (f) Taisha with the La- prefix.
LATANIA (f) Tania with the La- prefix.
LATANYA (f) Tanya with the La- prefix.
LATARRA (f) Tarra with the La- prefix.
LATASHA (f) Tasha (Natasha) with the La- prefix.
LATASHIA (f) Tashia with the La- prefix.
LATEISHA (f) Teisha with the La- prefix.
LATESHA (f) Tesha with the La- prefix.
LATHAM (m) *Old English* Land that is owned.
LATIMER (m) *Old English* Latin teacher.
LATISHA see LETITIA.
LATONA see LATONIA.
LATONIA, LATONYA (f) Tonia with the La- prefix.
LATORA (f) Tora with the La- prefix.
LATOYA (f) Variant of Latonya.
LATRECIA (f) Trecia with the La- prefix.
LATRICE, LATRICIA (f) Trice (Patrice) with the La- prefix.

Latrisha   *Lavenia*

LATRISHA (f) Trisha with the La- prefix.

LAURA (f) *Latin* Bay, laurel tree.

LAURAINE *see* LORRAINE.

LAURANA (f) A blend of Laura and Anna.

LAURANDA (f) A blend of Laura and Amanda.

LAURANTHA (f) A blend of Laura and Samantha.

LAURANCE *see* LAURENCE.

LAUREEN *see* LAURINA.

LAUREL (f) *Latin* From the name of the evergreen tree.

LAURELIA *see* LAUREL.

LAURELLA, LAURELLE (f) A blend of Laura and Ella.

LAURELLEN, LAURELEN (f) A blend of Laura and Ellen.

LAUREN (f, rarely m) Variant of Laura.

LAURENA, LAUREEN, LAURENE *see* LAURINA.

LAURENCE, LARRY, LAURIE (m) *Latin* Man from Laurentium.

LAURETTA, LAURETTE (f) Diminutive of Laura.

LAURI *see* LORI.

LAURIANE, LAURIANNE (f) French variant of Laura.

LAURICE *see* LORIS.

LAURIE (f) *see* LAURA.

LAURIE (m) *see* LAURENCE.

LAURINA, LORINA (f) Feminine form of Laurence.

LAURINDA (f) Variant of Laura.

LAURINE *see* LAUREEN.

LAURISTON (m) *Old English* Laurie's village.

LAVEDA (f) Veda with the La- prefix.

LAVENDER (f) From the name of the flowering shrub.

LAVENIA *see* LAVINIA.

LAVERNE (f) *Latin* Spring-like, verdant.
LAVETTA (f) Vetta with the La- prefix.
LAVINIA (f) *Latin* Woman of Rome.
LAVONNE (f) Vonne with the La- prefix.
LAWRANCE, LAWRENCE (m) *see* LAURENCE.
LAWRIE *see* LAURIE.
LAWSON (m) Son of Laurence.
LAWTON (m) *Old English* Village on the hill.
LAYA *see* LAYANA.
LAYANA (f) *Sanskrit* Repose.
LAYLA *see* LEILA.
LAYNE *see* LANE.
LAYTON, LEYTON, LEIGHTON (m) *Old English* Place on a waterway.
LAZETTA (f) Zetta with the La- prefix.
LEA, LEIA (f) Variants of Leah.
LEABEL (f) A blend of Leah and Belle.
LEAF (m) *Old English* The botanical term used as a name.
LEAGH *see* LEIGH.
LEAH (f) *Hebrew* To be weary.
LEALA (f) *Middle English* Loyal.
LEANDA (f) Feminine form of Leander.
LEANDER (m) *Greek* Lion man.
LEANDRA (f) A blend of Leah and Sandra.
LEANNE (f) A blend of Leah and Anne.
LEANORA (f) A blend of Leah and Nora.
LEANTHA (f) A blend of Leah and Samantha.
LEANZA, LEANNZA (f) Blends of Leah and Anzil.
LEATRICE (f) A blend of Leah and Beatrice.
LECIA *see* ALECIA.
LEDA, LIDA (f) From the name of the Spartan queen in Greek mythology.
LEE (f and m) *Old English* Wood, clearing.

LEEANN, LEANN, LIANNE (f) A blend of Lee and Anne.

LEEBA (f) *Yiddish* Beloved.

LEELA *see* LEILA.

LEESA, LEEZA *see* LISA.

LEIA (f) *see* LEA. The name of the Princess in the *Star Wars* trilogy of films.

LEIGH (f) Variant of Lee.

LEIGHTON *see* LAYTON.

LEIHINA (f) *Hawaiian* Wreath of the moon.

LEILA (f) *Arabic* Dark beauty.

LEILANI, LEILANE, LELANI (f) *Hawaiian* Heavenly flower.

LEISA *see* LISA.

LEISHA (f) Origin uncertain. Possibly a form of Leisa.

LEITH (m) Origin uncertain.

LELA *see* LEALA.

LELAND, LEELAND, LELAN (m) *Old English* A shelter.

LELANI *see* LEILANI.

LELIA (f) From the Roman name Laelius.

LELINA (f) Lina with the Le- prefix.

LELISA (f) Lisa with the Le- prefix.

LELITA (f) Lita with the Le- prefix.

LELLA (f) Ella with the Le- prefix.

LEMAE (f) Mae with the Le- prefix.

LEMARR, LAMAR (m) *Latin* Of the sea.

LEMMY, LEMY *see* LEMUEL.

LEMUEL (m) *Hebrew* Devoted to God.

LEN *see* LEONARD.

LENA (f) *Sanskrit* Gain.

LENARD, LENNARD *see* LEONARD.

LENDA (f) Feminine form of Leonard.

Lene   *Lettice*

LENE see CHARLENE.
LENETA, LENETTA (f) Neta with the Le- prefix.
LENIS (m) *Latin* Gentle, mild.
LENICE (f) Feminine form of Lenis.
LENNA (f) Feminine form of Leonard.
LENNOX (m) *Old English* Tenant farmer's ox.
LENNY see LEONARD.
LENO (m) A rare variant of Lenis.
LENORE, LENORA, LENOR see ELEANOR.
LEO (m) *Latin* Lion.
LEOLA, LEOLIE (f) *American Indian* Prairie flower.
LEOLINA (f) *Welsh* Little lion.
LEONIA see LEONA.
LEON (m) *Greek* Lion.
LEONA (f) Feminine form of Leon.
LEONARD (m) *Old German* Strong as a lion.
LEONE, LEONIE (f) French feminine form of Leon.
LEONORA (f) From Eleonora, an Italian form of Eleanor.
LEONTICE (f) From the name of the flowering plant.
LEONTINE (f) *Greek* Lion-like.
LEOPOLD (m) *Old German* Bold man.
LEORA (f) *Hebrew* My light.
LERA (f) Variant of French *le roi* meaning 'the king'.
LEROY (m) *French* The king.
LES see LESTER and LESLIE.
LESA see LISA.
LESLEY (f) *Old French* Meadowlands.
LESLIE (f and m) *Old French* Meadowlands.
LESTER (m) *Old English* A camp.
LETA (f) *Latin* Glad.
LETHA see ELIZABETH.
LETITIA, LETTY (f) *Latin* Gladness.
LETTICE see LETITIA.

LEUEEN (f) Origin uncertain.
LEVANA (f) *Hebrew* Moon.
LEVANI (f) *Fijian* Anointed with oil.
LEVENIA (f) *Middle English* To shine.
LEVERNE (m) Origin uncertain.
LEVI (m) *Hebrew* Attached.
LEVIN *see* LEWIN.
LEVINA (f) *Old English* Flash.
LEVINGTON (m) *Old English* Leofa's village.
LEVINIA *see* LAVINIA.
LEVON (m) Origin uncertain. Possibly a variant of Leon.
LEVONA, LEVONNE (f) Origin uncertain. Possibly a variant of Leona.
LEW *see* LEWIS.
LEWIN (m) *Old English* Beloved friend.
LEWIS (m) English form of Louis.
LEX *see* ALEX.
LEXI, LEXIE (f) Two possible origins: 1. Feminine form of Lex; 2. Diminutive of Alexis or Alexandra.
LEYEA (f) Origin uncertain. Possibly a form of Leyla.
LEYLA *see* LEILA.
LEYLAND *see* LELAND.
LEYTON *see* LAYTON.
LIA (f) Italian form of Leah.
LIALA (f) Origin uncertain.
LIAM, LIAN (m) *French* To bind.
LIANA (f) Feminine form of Lian.
LIANE, LIANNE *see* LIANA.
LIBBY *see* ELIZABETH.
LIBERTY (f, rarely m) *Latin* Free.
LICIA *see* ALICIA.
LICHFIELD (m) *Welsh* Gray wood.

LIESA *see* LISA.

LIESL (f) German form of Elizabeth.

LIKA (f) Origin uncertain. Possibly a form of Alika.

LILA (f) *Sanskrit* Playful.

LILAC (f) *Persian* A flower name. Bluish.

LILAH (f) Variant of Lilac.

LILANDA (f) A blend of Lily and Amanda.

LILANTHA (f) A blend of Lily and Samantha.

LILEA, LILIA *see* LILIAN.

LILIAN, LILLIAN (f) *Latin* A lily.

LILLIANA (f) Hawaiian form of Lilian.

LILIANE *see* LILIAN.

LILIMAE (f) A blend of Lily and Mae.

LILINA (f) A blend of Lily and Nina.

LILISA (f) A blend of Lily and Lisa.

LILITA (f) A blend of Lily and Lita.

LILLA *see* LILEA.

LILLETTE (f) A blend of Lilly and Betty.

LILLIA *see* LILEA.

LILLIAN *see* LILIAN.

LILLIE *see* LILLY.

LILLITA (f) A blend of Lilly and Rita.

LILLY, LILY (f) *Old English* The flower name used as a first name.

LILYBETH (f) A blend of Lily and Elizabeth.

LIN *see* LYN.

LINA *see* CAROLINA.

LINARA (f) A blend of Lin and Cara.

LINCOLN (m) *Old English* Lake plus colony, settlement.

LINDA (f) Two possible origins: 1. *Old German* Serpent (hence wisdom); 2. *Spanish* Pretty.

LINDABEL, LINDABELLE (f) Blends of Linda and Belle.

Lindell   Liria

LINDELL (m) *Old English* Lithe, flexible.
LINDO (m) *Old German* Gentle man.
LINDELEY *see* LINDLEY.
LINDEN (m) *Old German* The lime tree.
LINDKA (f) Origin uncertain. Possibly a form of Linda.
LINDLEY (m) *Old English* Meadow near the linden trees.
LINDON, LYNDON (m) *Old English* Lithe, flexible.
LINDSAY, LINDSEY (f and m) *Old English* Linden trees near the water.
LINDSLEY (f and m) Variant of Lindsey.
LINDY *see* LINDSAY, LINDA.
LINET, LINNET, LINETTE (f) *Old French* Flax.
LINFORD, LINDFORD (m) *Old English* Ford near the linden trees.
LINGROVE (m) *Old English* Grove of linden trees.
LINITA (f) A blend of Lin and Rita.
LINKA (f) Origin uncertain.
LINLACE (f) Origin uncertain.
LINLEY *see* LINDLEY.
LINNEA (f) Feminine form of the surname Linnaeus.
LINNEL *see* LYNELL.
LINNIE (f) Form of Lin, Linda, etc.
LINORA (f) A blend of Lin and Nora.
LINORE *see* LEONORE.
LINSAY *see* LINDSAY.
LINTON *see* LYNTON.
LINUS (m) *Greek* Flax.
LINWOOD (m) *Old English* Copse of linden trees.
LINZI *see* LINDSAY.
LIONEL (m) *Latin* Little lion.
LIORA *see* LEORA.
LIRIA (f) *Greek* Lyrical, musical.

LIRONE (f) *Hebrew* The song is mine.
LISA, LIS see ELIZABETH.
LISANNE (f) A blend of Lisa and Anne.
LISABETH, LISBETH (f) Variants of Elizabeth.
LISE see ELIZABETH.
LISELOTTE (f) A blend of Elizabeth and Lotte.
LISETTE see ELIZABETH.
LISLE, LYLE (m) *French* The isle.
LISTER (m) *Old English* Dyer.
LITA (f) Form of Roselita, Lolita, etc.
LITTON, LYTTON (m) *Old English* Little village.
LIVANA see LEVANA.
LIVIA see OLIVIA.
LIVIAN (f) A blend of Livia and Vivian.
LIVINIA see LAVINIA.
LIVONA see LEVONA.
LIZA, LIZZIE, LIZZY, LIZ see ELIZABETH.
LIZANNE (f) A blend of Liza and Anne.
LIZBETH see ELIZABETH.
LLANA see LANA.
LLEWELLYN (m) *Welsh* Like a lion.
LLORET (f) Origin uncertain. Possibly a form of Loretha.
LLOY (f) Origin uncertain. Possibly a form of Lloyd.
LLOYD (m) *Welsh* Grey.
LOCKWOOD (m) *Old English* Enclosed wood.
LOGAN (m) *Middle English* Felled tree.
LOILA see LOLA.
LOIS, LOES (f) *Greek* Good, desirable.
LOLA (f) Variant of Dolores.
LOLANA (f) A blend of Lola and Nana.
LOLANDA (f) A blend of Lola and Amanda.
LOLANTHA (f) A blend of Lola and Samantha.
LOLARA (f) A blend of Lola and Lara.

LOLETA (f) *Spanish* Maiden of sorrows.
LOLITA, LOLLY see LOLA.
LOLORA (f) From the Indian place-name.
LOMAS (m) *Old English* By the pool.
LOMAX (m) Blend of Lomas and Max.
LONA see ILONA.
LONDA (f) A blend of Lona and Wanda.
LONICE (f) A blend of Lona and Patrice.
LONNIE, LONNY, LON see ALONZO.
LONSDALE (m) *Old English* Londe's valley.
LORA see LAURA.
LORAINE, LORANE see LORRAINE.
LORAL see LAUREL.
LORANN, LORANNE see LORRAINE.
LORCAN (m) *Irish* Fierce.
LOREN, LORENE see LAUREEN.
LORELL, LORELLE see LAUREL.
LOREN see LORENZO.
LORENA, LORENE see LAURENA.
LORENZA (f) Feminine form of Lorenzo.
LORENZO (m) Spanish and Italian form of Laurence.
LORETHA (f) A blend of Loretta and Aretha.
LORETTA, LORETTE see LAURETTA.
LOREY, LORI see LAURA.
LORIEN, LORIAN, LORIENNE, LORIANE (f) Names influenced by Lorien, an elf realm in Tolkien's *Lord of the Rings*.
LORIMER (f) *Latin* Slender vine branch.
LORIN see LOREN.
LORINA, LORINE, LORINNE see LORENA.
LORINDA (f) Variant of Laura influenced by Lori.
LORIS, LORISSA (f) Feminine form of Laurence.
LORNA (f) A character in *Lorna Doone*, the novel by

Lorne   Luana

R. D. Blackmore, named after the Scottish place-name Lorn.

LORNE (m) Masculine form of Lorna.

LORRAINE, LORRAYNE (f) From the name of the French region.

LORETTA, LORRETTE *see* LAURETTA.

LORRIE *see* LAURIE.

LOTTIE, LOTTY *see* CHARLOTTE.

LOTUS (f) *Greek* From the name of the flowering plant.

LOU (f) *see* LOUISE.

LOU (m) *see* LOUIS.

LOUANN (f) A blend of Louise and Ann.

LOUANTHA (f) A blend of Louise and Samantha.

LOUELLA (f) A blend of Louise and Ella.

LOUETTA (f) A blend of Louise and Betty.

LOUIE (m) Phonetic form of Louis.

LOUIS (m) *Old German* French form of Ludwig, meaning 'famous in battle'.

LOUISA, LOUISE, LOUIZA (f) Feminine forms of Louis.

LOURANA (f) A blend of Laura and Anna.

LOUVELLA (f) Feminine form of Lovell.

LOVELL (m) *French* Wolf-cub.

LOVINA *see* LAVINIA.

LOVINDA (f) A blend of Lovina and Amanda.

LOWELL (m) *Old English* Beloved.

LOWENNA (f) *Cornish* Joy.

LOWRI (f) Origin uncertain. Possibly a form of Lori.

LOYD *see* LLOYD.

LU *see* LOU.

LUAN (m) Masculine form of Luana.

LUANA (f) *Hawaiian* To be at leisure.

LUCAS (m) Latin form of Luke.
LUCETTA, LUCETTE (f) A blend of Lucy and Betty.
LUCIA (f) *Latin* Feminine form of the Roman name Lucius, meaning 'light'.
LUCIAN (m) *Latin* From the Roman name Lucius.
LUCIE (f) French form of Lucy.
LUCILLA, LUCILLE (f) French forms of Lucia.
LUCINA (f) *Latin* A grove.
LUCINDA (f) Variant of Lucia.
LUCIS (m) *Latin* Light.
LUCIUS (m) *Latin* The Roman clan name, meaning 'light'.
LUCKY (f) *Middle English* Fortunate.
LUCY (f) English form of Lucia.
LUDOVIC, LODOVIC (m) Form of Louis.
LUELLA see LOUELLA.
LUKAS see LUCAS.
LUKE (m) *Greek* Man from Lucania, a district in southern Italy.
LULA (f) Variant of Lulu.
LULU (f) Variant of Lucy.
LURENE, LUREEN (f) *French* To lure, invite.
LUTANZA (f) Origin uncertain.
LUTHER (m) *Old German* Famous people.
LUZINE (f) Variant of Lucille.
LYALL see LYLE.
LYANN see LIANA.
LYDIA (f) *Greek* Woman from Lydia (in Asia Minor).
LYLA, LYLAH see LEILA.
LYLANA (f) Lana with the Ly- prefix.
LYLARA (f) Lara with the Ly- prefix.
LYLE see LISLE.
LYMAN (m) *Old English* One who works with lime.
LYN, LYNN see LYNDA.

LYNDA see LINDA.
LYNDAL (f) A blend of Lyn and Kendal.
LYNDON (m) *Old English* Hill with lime trees.
LYNDORA (f) A blend of Lyn and Dora.
LYNDSAY (f, rarely m) A form of Lindsay.
LYNELL, LYNELLE, LYNETTE (f) Diminutives of Lyn.
LYNETH (f) Welsh form of Lynette.
LYNFORD (m) *Old English* River crossing by lime trees.
LYNIRA (f) A blend of Lyn and Vira (Vera).
LYNITA (f) A blend of Lyn and Anita.
LYNLEY, LYNLEE (m) *Old English* Meadow near the brook.
LYNN, LYNNE see LINDA.
LYNNETTE (f) *French* Idol, icon.
LYNORA (f) A blend of Lyn and Nora.
LYNSAY, LYNSEY see LINDSAY.
LYNTON (m) *Old English* Village near the brook.
LYNWEN (f) *Welsh* Fair image.
LYNWOOD (m) *Old English* Wood near the brook.
LYRA (f) *Greek* Lyre.
LYRICA (f) *Greek* Lyrical, musical.
LYRIS (f) *Greek* Lyrical, musical.
LYSANDRA (f) *Greek* To liberate.
LYSETTE see LISETTE.
LYSSA (f) Origin uncertain. Possibly a form of Alicia.
LYTHANDA (f) A character in a short story by Marion Zimmer Bradley.
LYTHINDA (f) A blend of Lyssa and Lucinda.

M

Maaia — *Mystique*

MAAIA (f) *Maori* Courage.
MABEL (f) *French* My beautiful one.
MABELINE (f) Variant of Mabel.
MABELLE, MAYBELLE, MABLE, MAYBEL (f) Forms of Mabel.
MABYN, MABAN (m) Son of Mab.
MACDONALD (m) Son of Donald.
MACE (m) *Old French* A club.
MACINDA (f) A blend of Mabel and Lucinda.
MACINTHA (f) A blend of Mabel and Hyacinth.
MACY (m) *Old English* Sceptre bearer.
MADALINE, MADDIE *see* MADELEINE.
MADELEINE (f) French form of Magdalen.
MADELIA, MADELIE (f) Blends of Mabel and Delia.
MADELINE, MADOLINE, MADELAIN, MADALAINA, MADELAINE, MADELENE, MADELLEN, MADELINA, MADELON, MADYLON (f) Variants of Madeleine.
MADELYN, MADELYNE, MADILYN, MADLYN (f) Blends of Madeleine and Lynda.
MADGE *see* MARGARET.
MADI, MADY *see* MADDIE.
MADIGAN (m) Origin uncertain. Possibly derived from the Irish word meaning 'a bear'.
MADISON (m) Masculine variant of Maude.

MADLENA (f) Russian form of Madeleine.
MADLIN, MADLINE, MAUDLIN *see* MADELEINE.
MADOC, MADOK (m) *Welsh* Fortunate.
MADRA (f) *Spanish* Mother.
MADRONA *see* MADRA.
MAE *see* MAY.
MAEVE (f) Irish form of Mauve.
MAGDA (f) German form of Magdalene.
MAGDALENE, MAGDALENA, MAGDALEN (f) *Hebrew* High tower.
MAGENTA (f) From the name of the Italian source of the bright magenta dye.
MAGGIE *see* MARGARET.
MAGNOLIA (f) From the tree named after the French botanist P. Magnol.
MAGNUS (m) *Latin* Great.
MAHALA, MAHALIA (f) *Hebrew* Tenderness.
MAHINA (f) Origin uncertain. Possibly a form of Mahira.
MAHIRA (f) *Hebrew* Industrious.
MAHON (m) *Irish* Bear.
MAHRA (f) Possibly a form of Mahira.
MAIA (f) *Latin* Exalted.
MAIDIE, MAIDA (f) *Middle English* Maiden.
MAIMIE *see* MAMIE.
MAIR, MAIRE, MAIRI (f) Irish forms of Mary.
MAIRILENE (f) A blend of Mary and Ilene.
MAIRONA (f) A blend of Mary and Rona.
MAIRWEN (f) A blend of Mary and Wendy.
MAISE (f) *Gaelic* Beauty.
MAISIE (f) *Old English* A field.
MAITLAND (m) *Old French* Unproductive ground.
MAIYA (f) *Sanskrit* An aspect of the Goddess (Gaia).
MAJA (f) *Latin* Exalted.

MAJORIE see MARJORIE.
MAKALA (f) *Hawaiian* Myrtle.
MALA (f) *Old English* Meeting place.
MALANDRA (f) A blend of Mala and Sandra.
MALANTHA (f) A blend of Mala and Samantha.
MALCA (f) *Old German* Active.
MALCOLM (m) *Gaelic* Servant of (St) Columba.
MALDWYN (m) *Welsh* Bold friend.
MALENA (f) Danish form of Magdalene.
MALIA (f) Hawaiian form of Mary.
MALIN (m) Masculine diminutive of Mary.
MALINDA, MALINA (f) Forms of Marcelinda or Melina.
MALISE (f) *Gaelic* Servant of Jesus.
MALITA (f) *American Indian* Salmon.
MALLARD (m) *Old German* Strong in counsel.
MALLORY (m, rarely f) *Old French* A wild duck.
MALLY see MALLORY.
MALU (f) *Hawaiian* Peace.
MALVA (f) *Greek* Tender.
MALVERN (m) *Welsh* Bare hill.
MALVIN see MELVIN.
MALVINA (f) Feminine form of Malvin.
MALVINDA (f) A blend of Malvina and Linda.
MALYN see MALIN.
MAMIE see MARY or MARGARET.
MANDA, MANDY, MANDIE, MANDI (f) Forms of Amanda or Miranda.
MANDER (m) *Old French* Stable lad.
MANDORA (f) A blend of Mandy and Dora.
MANDY see MANDA.
MANEN see MANON.
MANENDA (f) A blend of Manon and Brenda.

MANETTA, MANETTE (f) French feminine form of Marion.
MANFORD (m) *Old English* Small crossing over brook.
MANFRED (m) *Old German* Man of peace.
MANON (f) *Sanskrit* Imagine.
MANNING (m) *Old English* Man.
MANSEL (m) *Old French* Dweller in a manse.
MANSFIELD (m) *Old English* Place by Mam's field.
MANTON (m) *Old French* Farm held in common.
MANVILLE (m) From the French place-name.
MAPLE (m) *Old English* From the name of the broadleaved tree.
MARA (f) *Hebrew* Bitter.
MARAH, MARALA (f) Variant of Mara.
MARALEE (f) A blend of Marala and Lee.
MARAMA (f) *Maori* Moon.
MARANDA (f) A blend of Mara and Miranda.
MARANTHA (f) A blend of Mara and Samantha.
MARAYA (f) A blend of Mara and Maya.
MARC (m) French form of Mark.
MARCEL (m) French form of Marcellus, a diminutive of Marcus.
MARCELINDA (f) Variant of Marcella.
MARCELINE, MARCELYN *see* MARCELLA.
MARCELLA (f) Feminine form of Marcel.
MARCELLE (f) Feminine form of Marcel.
MARCENE, MARCINE (f) Variants of Marcia.
MARCH (m) *Old English* Dweller by a boundary.
MARCHA *see* MARCIA.
MARCI, MARCIE, MARCY (f) Forms of Marcia.
MARCIA (f) Latin feminine form of Marcius a name linked to Marcus and ultimately to Mars.

MARCUS (m) Variant of Mark.

MARDELLA, MARDI (f) *Old English* Meadow near the water.

MARDEN (m) *Old English* Meadow near the water.

MARE (f) *Latin* Sea.

MAREETHA, MARITHA (f) Blends of Mary and Aretha.

MARELLA, MARELLE (f) A blend of Mare and Ella.

MARETTA (f) A blend of Martel and Izetta.

MARGARET, MADGE, MAISIE, PEGGY (f) *Greek* Pearl.

MARGARETA, MARGARETTA (f) Hungarian forms of Margaret.

MARGARIS (f) Origin uncertain. Perhaps derived from the Breton word for 'stallion'.

MARGARITA (f) A form of Margaret.

MARGERY, MARGERIE *see* MARGARET.

MARGHANITA (f) Spanish form of Margaret.

MARGO, MARGOT (f) French form of Margaret.

MARGOLAINE (f) A blend of Margo and Elaine.

MARGUERITE, MARGUERITA (f) *French* A flower name. Daisy.

MARIA (f) The Latin, Italian, French and Spanish form of Mary.

MARIAM (f) A blend of Mary and Miriam.

MARIAMNE (f) An early form of Mary.

MARIAN *see* MARION.

MARIANA (f) Italian form of Marion.

MARIBELLE (f) A blend of Mary and Belle.

MARIBETH (f) A blend of Mary and Elizabeth.

MARIDEL (f) A blend of Mary and Della.

MARIE (f) French form of Mary.

MARIEKE (f) *Dutch* Little Mary.

MARIEL, MARIELLA (f) A blend of Mary and Muriel.
MARIETTA, MARIETTE (f) Diminutive forms of Mary.
MARIGOLD (f) *Middle English* From the flower name.
MARIJA (f) Origin uncertain.
MARIJON (f) A blend of Mary and John.
MARIJUNE (f) A blend of Mary and June.
MARIKE, MARIKA (f) Slavonic forms of Mary.
MARIKO (m) Masculine form of Marike.
MARILANE (f) A blend of Mary and Elane.
MARILLA (f) Variant of Mary.
MARILOU, MARILU (f) Blends of Mary and Louise.
MARILYN (f) A blend of Mary and Lyn.
MARIN, MARRIN, MARYN (m) From Marin County, California, an area noted for its free lifestyle.
MARINA, MERINE (f) *Latin* The sea.
MARINDA (f) A blend of Mary and Linda.
MARINTHA (f) A blend of Mary and Cynthia.
MARION, MARIONNE (f) A form of the French name Marie.
MARIS (f) *Latin* The sea.
MARISA, MARISE (f) Mary influenced by the Dutch form Maryse.
MARISELLA, MARISELA (f) Spanish form of Maris.
MARISKA (f) Russian form of Maris.
MARISSA (f) Variant of Maris.
MARITA (f) A blend of Mary and Rita.
MARITZA (f) Hungarian form of Mary.
MARIUS (m) *Latin* From the Roman name Marius, linked with Mars the god of war.

MARIWIN (f) A blend of Mary and Winifred.
MARJA *see* MARJORIE.
MARJABELLE (f) A blend of Marja and Belle.
MARJALENA (f) A blend of Marja and Elena.
MARJANA (f) A blend of Marja and Jana.
MARJI *see* MARJORIE.
MARJORIE (f) Variant of the French form of Marguerite.
MARK (m) From the Latin name Marcus, linked with Mars, the god of war.
MARKAYA (f) A blend of Mara and Kay.
MARKHAM (m) *Old English* Homestead on the boundary.
MARKUS *see* MARCUS.
MARLA (f) Variant of Marlene.
MARLAINE, MARLANE (f) Phonetic forms of Marlene.
MARLENE, MARLEEN *see* MARLENE.
MARLES (f) A blend of Margaret and Leslie.
MARLEY (m) *Old English* Lake in the meadow.
MARLIN (m) *Latin* Sea.
MARLINE, MARLIN, MARLYN, MARLYNE *see* MARLENE.
MARLO (f) Feminine form of Marlow.
MARLON (m) Probably based on the surname Marlin, linked with Merlin.
MARLOW (m) *see* MARLIN.
MARLY *see* MARLON or MARLIN.
MARLYN, MARLIN *see* MERILYN.
MARMORA (f) *Greek* Radiant.
MARNA (f) Swedish form of Marina.
MARNE (m) *Latin* Sea.
MARNI, MARNIE, MARNEY (f) *Hebrew* To rejoice.

MARNIA (f) A form of Marina.
MARNINA (f) *Hebrew* To rejoice.
MAROLA (f) *Latin* Sea.
MAROSA (f) A blend of Mary and Rosa.
MARSDEN (m) *Old English* Pasture land near the sea.
MARSHA see MARCIA.
MARSHALL (m) *Old English* Horse.
MARSON (m) *Old English* Place by a marsh.
MARSTON (m) *Old English* Village near the sea.
MARTEL (m) Diminutive of Martin.
MARTHA, MARTA, MARTHE (f) *Aramaic* Lady of the house.
MARTIN, MARTYN (m) From the Latin name Martinus, diminutive of Martius, linked with Mars, god of war.
MARTINA, MARTINE (f) Feminine form of Martin.
MARTY see MARTIN or MARTHA.
MARU (f) *Maori* Gentle.
MARVA (f) *Hebrew* The herb sage.
MARVELL, MARVELLE, MARVELLA (f) *Latin* Full of wonder.
MARVIN (m) *Old English* Friend of the sea.
MARY (f) Greek form of Miriam.
MARYA (f) Cornish form of Mary.
MARYAM (f) A blend of Mary and Miriam.
MARYBETH (f) A blend of Mary and Elizabeth.
MARYLOU, MARYLU (f) A blend of Mary and Louise.
MARYLYN, MARYLIN (f) A blend of Mary and Lynda.
MARYSE (f) A blend of Mary and Alyse.
MARZIAN (m) Origin uncertain.

MASADA (f) *Hebrew* Foundation.

MASON (m) *Old French* Craftsman working with stone.

MAT (m) see MATTHEW.

MATALDA see MATILDA.

MATANA (f) *Hebrew* A gift.

MATILDA, MATHILDA, TILLY (f) *Old German* Mighty in battle.

MATTHEW, MATHEW, MAT (m) *Hebrew* Gift of the Lord.

MATYA see MATILDA.

MAUDE, MAUD (f) Variant of Matilda.

MAUDINE (f) Variant of Maude.

MAURA (f) Two possible origins: 1. Phonetic form of Moira; 2. *Celtic* Dark.

MAURAINE see MAUREEN.

MAUREEN (f) Irish form of Mary.

MAURI see MAURA.

MAURICE (m) *Latin* Dark-skinned, Moorish.

MAURILIA (f) *Latin* Woman who sympathizes.

MAURITA (f) A blend of Maureen and Rita.

MAURY see MAURICE.

MAUVE (f) *Latin* The purple-coloured mallow plant.

MAVIS (f) *Old French* Song thrush.

MAX (m) *Latin* A form of Maximillian meaning 'great'.

MAXIMA (f) *Latin* Greatest.

MAXIME (m) *Latin* Greatest.

MAXINE (f) Feminine form of Max.

MAXWELL (m) *Gaelic/Old English* Magnus's stream.

MAY (f) Form of Mary.

MAYA (f) *Sanskrit* Illusion.

MAYDA (f) *Old English* Maiden.

MAYER (m) *Latin* Great.

MAYLOR (m) Origin uncertain.
MAYNARD (m) *Old English* Strength-hard, hence 'robust', 'enduring'.
MAYO (m) *Gaelic* Plain of the yew trees.
MAYRA (f) Origin uncertain.
MAYU (f) *Japanese* True reason.
MAZ see MAZANA.
MAZAL (f) *Hebrew* Star.
MAZALA see MIZELA.
MAZANA (f) Origin uncertain. Perhaps derived from 'amazing'.
MAZELLA, MAZARELLA, MAZERINA (f) Variants of Mizela.
MAZEY, MAZIE see MASIE.
MAZILA see MIZELA.
MCDONALD see MACDONALD.
MEAD (m) *Old English* Meadow.
MEADOW (f) *Old English* Pasture (especially near a river).
MEAGAN see MEGAN.
MEAVE (f) Irish form of Mavis.
MECAH (f) Origin uncertain.
MEDERICK, MEDRIC (m) *Old English* Flourishing meadow.
MEDINA (f) *Arabic* From the name of the Islamic holy city.
MEDORA (f) *Old English* Patient wife.
MEDWENNA (f) A form of Modwenna.
MEDWIN (f) Origin uncertain. Possibly Welsh meaning 'fair mannered, courteous'.
MEENA (f) *Sanskrit* Fish-like enamel work.
MEG, MEGS see MARGARET.
MEGAN, MEGHAN (f) Welsh form of Margaret.
MEGGIE see MARGARET.

Mehala   Meleila

MEHALA *see* MAHALIA.

MEHETABEL, MEHITABEL (f) *Hebrew* Whom God benefits.

MEHIRA (f) *Hebrew* Energetic.

MEIRION, MERION (m) The Welsh name for the county of Merioneth.

MEKA (f) Origin uncertain. Possibly a form of Mika.

MEL, MELL *see* MELVIN.

MELA, MELAH (f) *Latin* Honey. Also the Hawaiian form of Mary.

MELAINA, MELAINE, MELANE (f) Forms of Melanie.

MELANA (f) A blend of Mela and Lana.

MELANDA (f) A blend of Mela and Amanda.

MELANDRA, MELENDRA (f) A blend of Mela and Sandra.

MELANIE, MELANEY, MELONIE, MELONY (f) *Greek* Dark-skinned.

MELANN, MELANNE (f) A blend of Mela and Ann.

MELANTA *see* MELANTHA.

MELANTHA (f) A character in Dryden's play *Marriage à la Mode*.

MELARA (f) A blend of Mela and Lara.

MELATA (f) A blend of Mela and Rita.

MELAURA (f) A blend of Mela and Laura.

MELBA (f) From the Australian city of Melbourne.

MELBOURNE (m) *Old English* Mill (or middle) stream.

MELCENA (f) The name of a island in the *Malloreon* cycle of novels by David Eddings.

MELDA *see* IMELDA.

MELDON (m) *Old English* Master of the mill.

MELEA (f) A blend of Mela and Lea.

MELEILA (f) A blend of Mela and Leila.

Melene *Melton*

MELENA see MELINA.
MELENDIA (f) Origin uncertain.
MELETA (f) A blend of Mela and Rita.
MELFORD (m) *Old English* Ford near the mill.
MELIA see AMELIA.
MELICENT see MILLICENT.
MELIKA (f) A blend of Mela and Annika.
MELINA (f) *Greek* Honey.
MELINDA, MELLINDA, MELYNDA (f) Blends of Melina and Linda.
MELINKA (f) A blend of Melina and Katinka.
MELINTHA (f) A blend of Melina and Samantha.
MELIORA (f) Cornish name of uncertain meaning.
MELIRA (f) A blend of Mela and Mira.
MELISA (f) A blend of Mela and Lisa.
MELISSA, MELISSIA (f) *Greek* Bee.
MELITA (f) Italian form of Melissa.
MELIZA (f) A blend of Melissa and Liza.
MELLAN (m) *Greek* Honey.
MELLANIE, MELONIE see MELANIE.
MELLICENT see MILLICENT.
MELLISSA see MELISSA.
MELLONEY see MELANIE.
MELMAR (m) Origin uncertain.
MELODIA (f) *Italian* Melody.
MELODY, MELODIE (f) *Greek* Song, melody.
MELOLA (f) A blend of Mela and Lola.
MELONA (f) A blend of Mela and Lona.
MELONEY (f) Cornish form of Melanie.
MELORA (f) A blend of Mela and Lora.
MELORNA (f) A blend of Mela and Lorna.
MELOSA (f) A blend of Mela and Rosa.
MELTHA (f) Origin uncertain.
MELTON (m) *Old English* Village near the mill.

MELVA, MELVANA, MELVENE see MELVINA.

MELVILLE (m) *Old English/French* Town near the mill.

MELVIN, MELVYN (m) *Old English* Friendly counsellor.

MELVINA (f) Feminine form of Melvin.

MELWYN (f) *Cornish* Fair as honey.

MELYN (f) A blend of Mela and Lynda.

MELYS (f) *Welsh* Sweet.

MENA (f) *Old German* Strength.

MENORA (f) A blend of Mena and Nora.

MENTHA (f) *Latin* Mint.

MENTY, MENTIE see MINTY.

MERA (f) Two possible origins: 1. From the Indian saint's name of uncertain meaning; 2. Daughter of Praetus in Greek mythology.

MERANDA see MIRANDA.

MERARI (f) *Hebrew* Girl of sadness.

MERCEDES (f) *Spanish* Grace, mercy.

MERCIA (f) From the name of the kingdom in Anglo-Saxon England.

MERCILLE (f) A blend of Mercia and Lucille.

MERCY (f) *Latin* Clemency.

MEREDITH (f and m) *Welsh* Defender of the sea.

MERELINA, MERELYN (f) A blend of Meryl and Lina.

MERETTA (f) A blend of Meryl and Betty.

MERIBETH (f) A blend of Meryl and Elizabeth.

MERIDA see MERITA.

MERIEL see MURIEL.

MERILYN (f) A blend of Meryl and Lynda.

MERINA see MARINA.

MERIS see MERRIE.

MERISSA, MERRISSA (f) Blends of Meryl and Clarissa.
MERITA (f) A blend of Meryl and Rita.
MERLE, MERLA (f) *French* Blackbird.
MERLIN (m) *Welsh* Name meaning sea hill, hence 'cliff'.
MERLYN, MERLINE (f) Feminine forms of Merlin.
MERNA (f) *Gaelic* Beloved.
MEROLA see MERILLA.
MERRELL see MERYL.
MERRIAH (f) A blend of Merrie and Maria.
MERRICK (m) Welsh form of Maurice.
MERRIDEE (f) A blend of Merrie and Dee.
MERRIE (f) *Old English* Joyful, pleasant.
MERRIEL, MERRIELLE see MERRIE.
MERRILL, MERRIL, MERIL (f) Variants of Meryl.
MERRION (f) A blend of Merrie and Marion.
MERRIS see MERRIE.
MERRISSA see MERISSA.
MERRITA (f) A blend of Merrie and Rita.
MERRITT, MERRET (m) *Latin* Valuable.
MERRY (f) *Old English* Joyful, pleasant.
MERRYN (f) Variant of Merry.
MERTA, MERTHIA see MARTHA.
MERTON (m) *Old English* Village near a mere or lake.
MERVILLE (m) *French* Minor town.
MERVYN, MERVIN (m) *Welsh* Sea hill.
MERWIN, MERWYN see MARVIN.
MERYL, MEREL (f) Variants of Meriel.
MERYN (m) Cornish name of uncertain meaning.
MERYNA (f) Feminine form of Meryn.
META, METTA (f) German forms of Margaretta.

MEYER see MAYER.
MEYRICK see MERRICK.
MHAIRI (f) Irish form of Mary.
MHORABELLE (f) A blend of Moyra and Belle.
MIA (f) *Italian/Spanish* Mine.
MICA see MICHAL.
MICAH (m) *Hebrew* Who is like God?
MICHAEL, MICKY, MIKE (m) *Hebrew* Who is like God?
MICHAELA, MIKELA (f) Feminine form of Michael.
MICHAL (m, rarely f) Polish form of Michael or Michaela.
MICHALA see MICHAELA.
MICHELE (f) French feminine form of Michael.
MICHELINE (f) Diminutive of Michele.
MICHELLE, MECHEAL (f) French feminine form of Michael.
MICHONA (f) Modern invention combining the names of two US states, Michigan and Arizona.
MICKY, MICKEY, MICK, MIC see MICHAEL.
MICOLE (f) A blend of Michaela and Nicole.
MIDDLETON (m) *Old English* Village near the meadow.
MIDGE (m) *Old Norse* A form of Midgard, meaning 'midway house'.
MIETTE (f) *French* Small sweet things.
MIGNON (f) *French* Delicate, graceful.
MIKA see MICHAL.
MIKAILA, MIKAELA see MICHAELA.
MIKE see MICHAEL.
MIKI (f) *Japanese* Beautiful tree.
MIKI, MIKKI (f) Feminine form of Michael.
MILA, MILAH (f) Hungarian forms of Mildred.

MILBOROUGH (m) *Old English* Middle town.
MILBURN (m) *Old English* Mill near the brook.
MILDA (f) *Middle English* Mild.
MILDRED (f) *Old English* Mild.
MILENA (f) *Old German* Mild, peaceful.
MILES, MYLES (m) *Old German* Origin uncertain. Possibly 'generous'.
MILIAMA (f) Hawaiian form of Miriam.
MILIRA (f) Origin uncertain.
MILLARD (m) *Old English* Mill-keeper.
MILLEY *see* MILLICENT.
MILLICENT, MILLY, MILLIE (f) *Old German* Noble strength.
MILLIS (f) Origin uncertain. Possibly a form of Millicent.
MILO (m) A form of Miles.
MILORA (f) A blend of Millie and Lora.
MILSON (m) Son of Miles.
MILTON (m) *Old English* Village near the mill.
MIMA *see* JEMIMA.
MIMI (f) A form of Mary.
MIMOSA (f) *Latin* From the name of the flower, meaning sensitive.
MINA (f) A form of Carmina, etc.
MINDA (f) Origin uncertain. Possibly a form of Mindy.
MINDY (f) A form of Melinda or Miranda.
MINERVA (f) *Latin* Roman goddess of wisdom; name linked with 'mind'.
MINETTE (f) A form of Mina.
MINGO (m) *Gaelic* Amiable.
MINIE *see* MINNIE.
MINNA (f) A character in *The Pirate* by Sir Walter Scott.

MINNETTE (f) A form of Minna.

MINNIE (f) A form of Wilhelmina.

MINTY see AMINTA or ARAMINTA.

MIO (f) *Japanese* Waterway.

MIRA, MIRAH (f) Variants of Myra.

MIRABEL, MIRABELLA (f) *Latin* Wonderful.

MIRADA (f) Variant of Miranda.

MIRAGO (f) A blend of Mira and Margo.

MIRAM (f) A blend of Mira and Miriam.

MIRAMER (f) A blend of Mira and Merle.

MIRANDA (f) *Latin* Astonished. Possibly invented by Shakespeare for his play *The Tempest*.

MIRAYA (f) Variant of Mira.

MIRELLA, MIRELLE see MIRABEL.

MIRHAM see MIRIAM.

MIRI see MIRIAM.

MIRIAM (f) *Hebrew* Sea of bitterness.

MIRIAN (f) Possibly a form of Miriam.

MIRIEL see MURIEL.

MIRILYN (f) A blend of Mira and Lyn.

MIRIM (f) Origin uncertain. Possibly a form of Miriam.

MIRJANA (f) A blend of Mira and Jana.

MIROLA (f) A blend of Mira and Lola.

MIROMEL (f) A blend of Mira and Mela.

MIRONEL, MERONEL (f) Modern invention meaning 'lake of the elves'.

MIRORA (f) A blend of Mira and Dora.

MIROSA (f) A blend of Mira and Rosa.

MISA see MISSIE.

MISALYN (f) A blend of Misa and Lyn.

MISHA, MISHKA (m) Russian and Slovak forms of Michael.

MISSIE, MISSY (f) Colloquial American usage for 'young girl'.

MISTRAL (f) *French* Cold Mediterranean wind.
MISTY (f) *Old English* Obscure, misty.
MITA (f) Origin uncertain. Possibly a form of Mitzi.
MITCHELL (m) Variant of Michael.
MITZI (f) German form of Maria.
MIYA *see* MIA.
MIZELA, MIZELLA, MAZELLA (f) Origin uncertain. Possibly variants of Marcella.
MOANA (f) *Maori* Sea.
MOCARA (f) *Gaelic* My friend.
MODESTY (f) *Latin* Chasteness, modesty.
MODWENNA (f) Origin uncertain. Possibly a form of Morwenna.
MO, MOE *see* MAUREEN.
MOHAN (m) *Sanskrit* A name for Krishna.
MOIA *see* MOINA.
MOIDELA (f) Origin uncertain.
MOINA (f) *Celtic* Gentle, soft.
MOIRA, MOYRA, MOIR, MOYR (f) Phonetic Irish forms of Maire (Mary).
MOLANDA (f) A blend of Molly and Amanda.
MOLANTHA (f) A blend of Molly and Samantha.
MOLINA (f) A blend of Molly and Lina.
MOLINDA (f) A blend of Molly and Linda.
MOLISSA (f) A blend of Molly and Alicia.
MOLITA (f) A blend of Molly and Lita.
MOLITHA (f) A blend of Molly and Tabitha.
MOLLEY *see* MOLLIE.
MOLLIE, MOLLY, MOLL (f) Variants of Mary.
MONA (f) *Irish* Noble.
MONDAY (f) *Old English* The day of the week used as a first name.
MONDIALE (f) *French* The world, Gaia.

MONDY (m) A character in the novel *Mercenary* by Piers Anthony.
MONETTE (f) French form of Monday.
MONFORD (m) *Old English* Mountain ford.
MONICA (f) Two possible origins: 1. *Greek* Alone; 2. *Latin* To advise.
MONIQUE (f) French form of Monica.
MONJA (f) Origin uncertain.
MONRO, MONROE (m) *French* One who works with a wheel.
MONTAGUE, MONTAGU, MONTY (m) *Latin* Mountain.
MONTANETTE (f) Woman from Montana.
MONTEL (m) Spanish form of Montague.
MONTGOMERY (m) English form of Montague.
MONTINA (f) *Latin* Of the mountain.
MONTROSE (m) *Gaelic* Place name, literally meaning 'moor on the cape'.
MONTY see MONTAGUE or MONTGOMERY.
MOON (f) *Old French* The moon.
MORAG (f) *Gaelic* Great.
MORANDA (f) A blend of Morag and Amanda.
MORANTHA (f) A blend of Morag and Samantha.
MORAR (f) Feminine form of Moray.
MORASHA (f) *Hebrew* Inheritance.
MORAY, MURRAY (m) *Gaelic* Seaboard settlement.
MORAYNE see MAUREEN.
MOREEN, MORENE see MAUREEN.
MOREL, MORELLE (f) *French* Mulberry colour.
MORELA (f) *Polish* Apricot.
MORELAND (m) *Old English* The moors.
MORENA (f) *Spanish* Brown.
MORENWYN (f) *Cornish* Fair maiden.

MORETTA, MORETA (f) Origin uncertain. Possibly *Hebrew* meaning 'teacher'.

MORFORD (m) *Old English* River crossing on the moor.

MORGAN (m) *Welsh* Great, bright.

MORGANA, MORGANETTA (f) Feminine forms of Morgan.

MORIA (f) *Greek* Simpleton.

MORIANA (f) A character in the *War of Powers* series of novels by Robert E. Vardeman and Victor Milan.

MORIEN (m) *Welsh* Sea-born.

MORINA *see* MARINA.

MORINE *see* MAUREEN.

MORITA (f) A blend of Morag and Rita.

MORITHA (f) A blend of Morag and Tabitha.

MORLAND (m) *Old English* Moor or fen land.

MORLEENA (f) A character in the novel *Nicholas Nickleby* by Charles Dickens.

MORLEY (m) *Old English* Moor clearing.

MORNA (f) *Gaelic* Beloved, gentle.

MORNING (f) *Middle English* Early part of the day.

MOROWA (f) *Akan* Queen.

MORRELL *see* MERRIL.

MORRICE *see* MAURICE.

MORRIGAN *see* MORGAN.

MORRIS *see* MAURICE.

MORRISON (m) Son of Morris.

MORROW (f) *Middle English* Morning.

MORRYS *see* MAURICE.

MORSE *see* MAURICE.

MORT *see* MORTIMER.

MORTIMER, MORTY (m) *French* Dead (stagnant) water.

MORTON (m) *Old English* Moorland village.

MORVEN (f) *Gaelic* Big mountain peak.

MORVOREN, MORVA (f) *Cornish* Maid of the sea, mermaid.

MORWEN, MORWENNA (f) *Welsh* Maiden.

MORYL (f) A blend of Morag and Meryl.

MOSELLE, MOZELLE (f) Feminine form of Moses.

MOSES (m) Old Testament figure. Possibly *Hebrew* meaning 'saviour'.

MOSS (m) *Hebrew* Descendant of Moses.

MOSTYN, MOSTIN (m) *Welsh* Fortress in a field.

MOTIF (f) *French* Dominant feature or theme.

MOULTRIE (m) *Gaelic* Origin uncertain. Possibly 'sea warrior'.

MOUREEN *see* MAUREEN.

MOURILYAN (f) A blend of Moureen, Lynda and Ann.

MOX (m) Colloquial term for courage or daring (derived from the tradename of a drink).

MOYA *see* MOYRA.

MOYNA, MOINA *see* MONA.

MOYA (m) *Ngoni* Good health.

MOYRA *see* MOIRA.

MUIR (m) *Scottish* Dweller by the moor.

MUNA (f) *Maori* Darling.

MUNGO (m) *Gaelic* Amiable.

MUNRO, MUNROE (m) *Irish* Mouth of the river Roe.

MURDO *see* MURDOCH.

MURDOCH, MURTAGH (m) *Gaelic* Two possible origins: 1. Mariner; 2. Sea warrior.

MURIEL, MERIEL, MURIAL (f) *Irish* Sea-bright.

MURPHY (m) *Irish* Of the sea.

MURRAY, MURREY *see* MORAY.

MUSETTE, MUSETTA (f) *Old French* To play music.
MUZ (m) Modern form of Murdoch or Murray.
MYAN, MYANNE (f) A blend of Myra and Ann.
MYCALA, MYKELA *see* MICHAELA.
MYCROFT (m) *Old English* Marsh homestead.
MYDAS *see* MIDAS.
MYER (m) *Old English* Dweller by a marsh.
MYFANWY (f) *Welsh* My fine one.
MYKEL *see* MICHAEL.
MYLYNN (f) A blend of Myra and Lynn.
MYLES *see* MILES.
MYLLE *see* MILLIE.
MYLOR (m) *Celtic* Prince.
MYRA, MIRA (f) Two possible origins: 1. *Greek* Sweet-smelling oil, myrrh; 2. The invention of the seventeenth-century poet Fulke Greville.
MYRETTE (f) Diminutive of Myra.
MYRIAM (f) A blend of Myra and Miriam.
MYRICA (f) From the name of the flowering shrub.
MYRL *see* MERLE.
MYRLIN *see* MERLIN.
MYRLINNE (f) Feminine form of Merlin.
MYRNA (f) *Gaelic* Beloved.
MYRON (m) *Greek* Sweet-smelling oil, myrrh.
MYRREN (m) Origin uncertain.
MYRRH (f) *Greek* The flowering herb Sweet Cicely.
MYRTILLA *see* MYRTLE.
MYRTLE (f) *Latin* An evergreen flowering shrub.
MYRZA (f) Origin uncertain. Possibly a form of Myrrh.
MYSTIQUE (f) *Old French* Atmosphere of mystery.

Naava **N** *Nyssa*

NAAVA (f) *Hebrew* Beautiful, pleasant.
NADA *see* NADIA.
NADENE *see* NADINE.
NADIA, NADYA (f) *Slavonic* Hope.
NADINE (f) *Russian* Hope.
NAIA, NAIIA (f) *Greek* To flow. In Greek mythology Naiad was a water nymph.
NAIMA *see* NAMA.
NAIRN (m) *Celtic* Dweller by the alder tree.
NAJINA, NAJMA (f) *Arabic* Benevolent.
NALANI (f) *Hawaiian* Calmness of the heavens.
NALENE (f) Variant of Nellene.
NALINA (f) *Sanskrit* Lotus flower.
NAMA (f) *Hebrew* Pleasant, beautiful.
NAMIR (m) *Hebrew* Leopard.
NAN, NANA (f) Forms of Nancy, Hannah, Ann etc.
NANCY, NANCE, NANCIE, NANNY (f) Forms of Ann.
NANDA (f) *Sanskrit* Giver of joy.
NANDY, NANDIE (f) Origin uncertain.
NANELLA (f) A blend of Nancy and Ella.
NANETTE (f) Diminutive of Nan.
NANI *see* NANCE.
NANINE *see* NANETTE.
NANITA (f) A blend of Nancy and Anita.
NAOMI (f) *Hebrew* Delight.

NARA (f) Two possible origins: 1.*Celtic* Happy; 2.*Old English* Dear one.

NARA (m) *Sanskrit* Hero, human being.

NARADA (f) Origin uncertain. Possibly a variant of Nara.

NARALIAN (m) Origin uncertain.

NARDA (f) *Greek* A spikenard (aromatic ointment).

NARDI (f) From the name of the Italian sports car.

NARDIA *see* NARDA.

NARELLE (f) A blend of Nara and Ella.

NARISSA (f) A blend of Nara and Larissa.

NARITA (f) A blend of Nana and Rita.

NASIA (f) *Hebrew* Miracle of God.

NAT *see* NATHAN.

NATA, NATACHA *see* NATASHA.

NATALIE, NATALIA, NATALY, NATALYA (f) *Latin* Birthday of the Lord (hence Christmas Day).

NATANIA (f) A blend of Natalie and Tania.

NATASHA (f) Russian form of Natalie.

NATE *see* NATHAN.

NATHALIE (f) French form of Natalie.

NATHAN, NATHANIEL (m) *Hebrew* God has given.

NATHARINA (f) A blend of Natalie and Catherina.

NATRELLE, NATREL (f) Phonetic form of the word 'natural'.

NAUNTON (m) *Old English* New farm.

NAUSHON (f) Origin uncertain.

NAYLAND (m) *Old English* Island inhabitant.

NEAL, NEALE *see* NEIL.

NED (m) Diminutive form of Edward or Edmund.

NEDA (f) *Slavonic* Sunday's child.

NEDRA (f) *Old English* Below the surface of the Earth.

NEDRICK (m) A blend of Ned and Pedrick.
NEIL, NEAL, NIAL, NIALL (m) *Irish* Champion.
NEILA, NEILE (f) Feminine forms of Neil.
NEILSON (m) Son of Neil.
NEISHA (f) Origin uncertain.
NEITH (m) Origin uncertain.
NEKA see ANNEKA.
NELDA (f) Origin uncertain.
NELIA see CORNELIA.
NELITA (f) Origin uncertain.
NELL, NELLIE, NEL see HELEN, ELEANOR etc.
NELLONE (f) Origin uncertain.
NELSON (m) Son of Neil.
NEMA (f) *Hebrew* Thread, hair.
NEMISSA (f) A star maiden in American Indian mythology.
NENA, NENE see NINA.
NENIA see NENA.
NEOLA (f) *Greek* New.
NEOMA (f) *Greek*. Wooded pasture.
NERIDA see NERITA.
NERINE, NERINA (f) The name of a sea nymph in Greek mythology.
NERISSA see NERITA.
NERITA (f) *Greek* Sea snail.
NERYS (f) *Welsh* Lord.
NESHA see NESSA.
NESSA (f) *Old Norse* Headland.
NESTA, NESSIE (f) Welsh forms of Agnes.
NESTOR (m) *Greek* Wise old man.
NETA, NETTA, NETTIE, NETTE (f) *Hebrew* Plant, shrub.
NETANIA (f) *Hebrew* Gift of God.

NETHIS (f) Origin uncertain. Possibly a form of Nerys.

NEULA (f) *Celtic* Champion.

NEVA (f) *Latin* Snow.

NEVADA (f) *Spanish* The name of the American state, meaning 'snowy'.

NEVILLE, NEVIL, NEVYL (m) *French* New town.

NEVIN (m) *Irish* Holy.

NEWBOLD (m) *Old English* Bole or tree trunk.

NEWEL, NEWELL (m) *Latin* New, unusual.

NEWMAN (m) *Old English* New man.

NEWTON (m) *Old English* New village.

NEYLA *see* NILA.

NEYSA (f) *Greek* Pure.

NGAIO (f) *Maori* From the name of an evergreen tree.

NIA (f) Origin uncertain. Possibly a form of Niam.

NIALL *see* NEIL.

NIAM (m) *Irish* Champion.

NICAEL *see* NICHOL.

NICCI *see* NICOLA.

NICHELLE (f) A blend of Nicola and Michelle.

NICHELA (f) A blend of Nicola and Michaela.

NICHOLAS (m) *Greek* Victory people.

NICHOLE *see* NICOLE.

NICHOLSON (m) Son of Nicholas.

NICK *see* NICHOLAS.

NICKI, NICKOLA *see* NICOLA.

NICKOLAS *see* NICHOLAS.

NICKY *see* NICOLA.

NICOL *see* NICHOLAS.

NICOLA, NICOLE, NICOLLE (f) Italian feminine form of Nicholas.

Nicolette   Noeleen

NICOLETTE, NICOLETTA (f) Diminutive of Nicola.
NIEL *see* NEIL.
NIEKA (f) Origin uncertain.
NIGEL (m) Variant of Neil.
NIKA (f) Diminutive of Annika.
NIKKI *see* NICOLA.
NIKOLA *see* NICOLA.
NIKOLAS *see* NICHOLAS.
NILA, NYLA (f) From the name of the river Nile.
NILO *see* NILA.
NIMA *see* NEMA.
NINA (f) Russian form of Annina (Ann).
NINETTE, NINETTA (f) Diminutive of Nina.
NINIAN (m) From the name of the Scottish saint, meaning uncertain.
NINKA (f) Russian variant of Nina.
NIRA (f) A modern invention based on the initials of the National Industrial Recovery Act (USA).
NIREL (f, rarely m) *Hebrew* Light of God.
NISHA *see* NISSA.
NISSA (f) *Hebrew* A sign.
NITA (f) Diminutive of Anita.
NITHA (f) *Scandinavian* An elf.
NIVA (f) Origin uncertain.
NIVEN *see* NEVIN.
NIXIE (f) *Old German* Water sprite.
NIXON (m) *Old English* Son of Nicholas.
NOAH (m) Origin uncertain. Possibly Hebrew meaning 'rest' or 'long-lived'.
NOBLE (m) *Latin* Greatness of character.
NOEL (m) *French* Christmas.
NOELANI (f) *Hawaiian* Beautiful one from heaven.
NOELEEN, NOELINE (f) Diminutives of Noelle.

NOELLA (f) Feminine form of Noel.
NOELLE (f) French feminine form of Noel.
NOEMI (f) Origin uncertain. Possibly a form of Naomi.
NOFIA (f) *Hebrew* Panorama, landscape.
NOIDA (f) Origin uncertain.
NOLA (f) *Irish* Famous.
NOLAN (m) *Irish* Famous.
NOLANA (f) *Italian* Little bell.
NOLEEN *see* NOELEEN.
NOLINA (f) Hawaiian form of Noreen.
NOLL (f) A blend of Nola and Molly.
NOMA (f) Hawaiian form of Norma.
NONA (f) *Latin* The ninth.
NONIE, NONI *see* NONA.
NORA, NORAH (f) Irish forms of Eleanor.
NORANDA (f) A blend of Nora and Amanda.
NORANTHA (f) A blend of Nora and Samantha.
NORBERT (m) *Old German* Famous in the North.
NORDICA (f) *Latin* From the Northern Lands.
NOREEN, NORENE (f) Diminutives of Nora.
NORELLA (f) A blend of Nora and Ella.
NORINE, NORINA *see* NOREEN.
NORISSA (f) A blend of Nora and Clarissa.
NORITA (f) A blend of Nora and Rita.
NORMA (f) *Latin* Pattern, model.
NORMAN (m) *Old English* Man from the North.
NORMAND (m) French form of Norman.
NORNA (f) One of the Fates in Scandinavian mythology.
NOROLA (f) A blend of Norma and Lola.
NORRIE *see* NORMAN.
NORRIS (m) *Old English* Northerner.
NORTON (m) *Old English* Northern village.

NORVAL (m) A character in the play *Douglas* by John Home.
NORVILLE, NORVEL, NORVELL *see* NORVAL.
NORWOOD (m) *Old English* Woods in the North.
NOVA (f) *Latin* New.
NOVANDA (f) A blend of Nova and Amanda.
NOVANTHA (f) A blend of Nova and Samantha.
NOVENDA (f) Modern invention echoing the month of November.
NOWELL *see* NOEL.
NOYA (f) *Hebrew* Beautiful.
NUALA, NULA (f) *Irish* White shoulder.
NUOVA (f) *Italian* News.
NYDIA (f) A character in the novel *The Last Days of Pompeii* by Lord Lytton.
NYE *see* ANEURIN.
NYLA *see* NILA.
NYLANDA (f) A blend of Nyla and Amanda.
NYLANTHA (f) A blend of Nyla and Samantha.
NYLARA (f) A blend of Nyla and Lara.
NYLORA (f) A blend of Nyla and Lora.
NYREE (f) Phonetic form of Maori *ngaire*, possibly derived from *ngare* meaning 'family' or *ngaru* meaning 'wave'.
NYSSA (f) *Greek* The goal.

Oakley  *Oz*

OAKLEY, OAKLEIGH (m) *Old English* Field of oak trees.
OBADIAH (m) *Hebrew* Servant of God.
OBELIA (f) *Greek* A pointer.
OBERON see AUBERON.
OCEA (f) see OCEAN.
OCEAN (f and m) *Greek* Vast sea.
OCEANA see OCEAN.
OCTAVIA (f) *Latin* Eighth.
OCTAVIUS (m) *Latin* Eighth.
ODELIA (f) *Old German* Riches.
ODELL (m) *Old English* Woad hill.
ODESSA (f) From the Russian place-name linked with the Greek *Odyssey* meaning journey or quest, and Homer's epic of that name.
ODETTE (f) *Old German* Riches.
ODILE, ODILLE (f) *Old German* Riches.
ODINA (f) Origin uncertain. Possibly a form of Odile.
OGDEN (m) *Old English* Oak valley.
OHANA (f) *Hawaiian/American Indian* Spiritual family.
OISIN (m) *French* Bird.
OLA (f) Perhaps a diminutive of Lola.
OLAF (m) *Old Norse* Ancestor.
OLATHE (f) *American Indian* Beautiful.
OLAVE (f) *Old Norse* Ancestor.

OLENA (f) *Russian* Cat.

OLETA (f) *Old Norse* Ancestor.

OLGA (f) *Russian/Old Norse* Holy.

OLIN (m) *Old English* The holly tree.

OLINDA, OLYNDA (f) Feminine forms of Olin.

OLIVE (f) *Latin* The olive tree.

OLIVER, OLLIE (m) Two possible origins: 1. *Latin* Olive tree; 2. *Old German* Elf-host.

OLIVETTE (f) Diminutive of Olive.

OLIVIA, OLLIE, LIVIA (f) Italian form of Olive.

OLIVIER (m) French form of Oliver.

OLEANDA (f) From the plant name Oleander.

OLEANTHA (f) From the plant name Oleander.

OLWEN, OLWYN, ALWEN (f) *Welsh* White path.

OMA (f) Feminine form of Omar.

OMAR (m) *Hebrew* Eloquent.

OMEGA (f) Last letter of the Greek alphabet, hence symbolically 'the end, completion'.

ONA (f) Form of Leona, Ilona etc.

ONAWAY (f) *Ojibway* Awake.

ONDINE *see* UNDINE.

ONEIDA (f) *Iroquois* Standing stone.

ONETHA (f) Variant of Oneida.

ONITA, ONI (f) Form of Antonita.

ONORA (f) Irish form of Honorah, a variant of Hannah.

ONYX (f) *Greek* From the name of the decorative stone.

OONAGH (f) Irish form of Una.

OPAL (f) *Sanskrit* From the name of the precious stone.

OPHELIA (f) *Greek* Help.

OPHIRA (f) *Hebrew* Gold.

OPRAH (f) *Latin* Origin uncertain. Perhaps a phonetic form of 'opera', meaning work.

ORA (f) *Maori* Life.

ORABEL (f) *Latin/French* Golden beauty.

ORALIA (f) *Latin* A border.

ORALIE, ORALEE (f) *Hebrew* My light.

ORAM (m) *Old English* Riverbank enclosure.

ORAN (m) *Irish* Green.

ORANDA (f) A blend of Oran and Amanda.

ORANTHA (f) A blend of Oran and Samantha.

ORBAN (m) *Latin* A globe.

ORDE (m) *Old English* Spear.

ORDWAY (m) *Old English* Ridgeway path.

ORELLA (f) *Latin* Listener.

OREN (m) *Hebrew* Pine.

ORENDA (f) *American Indian* Magic power.

ORIANA, ORIANNE (f) *Latin* Dawn.

ORIEL (f) *Latin* Gallery.

ORIEN (m) *Latin* Direction of the sunrise.

ORIENNE (f) Feminine form of Orien.

ORIN, OREN, ORRIN (m) Masculine forms of Orinda.

ORINDA (f) Invented by the poet Cowley.

ORINTHA *see* ORINTHIA.

ORINTHIA (f) A character in the play *The Apple Cart* by Bernard Shaw.

ORIOLE *see* ORIEL.

ORION, ORIEN (m) *Latin* The Orient, the East.

ORLA (f) *Irish* Golden lady.

ORLAN (m) *Old English* From the pointed land.

ORLANA, ORLANE (f) Variants of Orlena.

ORLANDO, ORLAND (m) Italian form of Roland.

ORLENA (f) *Latin* Gold.

ORLENE (f) A character in the novel *Bearing an Hourglass* by Piers Anthony.
ORLIN, ORLON (m) *Latin* Golden.
ORLINA, ORLENA (f) *Latin* Golden.
ORLY (f) From the French place-name.
ORMAR (m) Origin uncertain.
ORMOND, ORMAND (m) *Old Norse* A serpent.
ORMSBY (m) *Old Norse* Orm's farm.
ORNA (f) *Irish* Olive-coloured.
ORRIN *see* ORIN.
ORSON (m) *Latin* Bear.
ORVILLE, ORVIL, ORVAL (m) *French* Golden town.
ORWIN (m) *Old German* Golden friend.
OSBERT (m) *Old German* Famous god.
OSBORN (m) *Old English* Divinely strong.
OSCAR (m) *Old English* Divine strength.
OSELLA (f) *Italian* Bird.
OSMA (f) *Old English* Hero-protection hence 'heroic protector'.
OSMAN (m) *Old English* Servant of God.
OSMANTHA (f) From the name of the Osmanthus tree.
OSMOND, OSMUND (m) *Old English* Protected by God.
OSWALD (m) *Old English* God of the forest.
OSWIN, OSWYN (m) *Old English* Friend of God.
OTIS (m) *Greek* One who hears well.
OTHALIE *see* OTTILIE.
OTTILIE, OTTALIE (f) Swedish feminine form of Otto.
OTTO (m) *Old German* Wealthy.
OTTWAY, OTWAY (m) *Old German* Lucky warrior.
OWEN, OWAIN (m) *Welsh* Well born.

OZELLA (f) *Hebrew* Shadow.
OZORA, OZZIE, OZ (f) *Hebrew* Strength.
OZZIE, OZZY, OZ (m) Diminutive forms of Osmond, Oswald etc.

Paddina P Pryce

PADDINA (f) Feminine form of Paddy.
PADDY, PADDIE see PATRICK.
PADMA, PADME (f) *Sanskrit* Lotus.
PADRAIG (m) Irish form of Patrick.
PAGE see PAIGE.
PAICE (m) *Old French* Peace.
PAIGE (f) *Old English* A servant, page.
PALMER (m) *Old English* Bearer of palm branch, a pilgrim.
PALMIRA (f) *Latin* Palm tree.
PALOMA (f) *Spanish* Dove.
PAM (f) Diminutive form of Pamela.
PAMALA, PAMMALA, PAMMELA see PAMELA.
PAMELA (f) A character in *Arcadi* by Sir Philip Sidney.
PAMELYN (f) A blend of Pamela and Lyn.
PAMINA (f) German variant of Pamela.
PAMIRA (f) A blend of Pamela and Mira.
PAMITA (f) A blend of Pamela and Rita.
PAMOLA (f) A blend of Pamela and Lola.
PAMORA (f) A blend of Pamela and Lora.
PANACHE (f) *French* Plume of feathers (hence confident display, verve).
PANDORA, PANDY (f) *Greek* Very gifted.
PANSY (f) *Latin* From the flower name.
PANTHEA (f) *Greek* She who honours all the gods.

Parilee *Peace*

PARILEE (f) Possibly a form of the Spanish surname Parrilla.
PARIS (f) From the French place-name.
PARK (m) *Middle English* Enclosed land.
PARKER (m) *Old English* One who tends a park.
PARNEL, PARNELL (m) *Greek* Origin uncertain. Possibly derived from 'stone'.
PARR (m) *Old English* Enclosure.
PARRY (m) *Welsh* Son of Harry.
PASCAL (m) *Hebrew* Passover sacrifice.
PASCALE (f) Feminine form of Pascal.
PASCOE (m) *Latin* Connected with Easter.
PAT, PATIA *see* PATRICIA.
PATIENCE, PATTY (f) *Latin* To suffer.
PATRICE *see* PATRICIA.
PATRICIA, PATSY, PAT (f) *Latin* Noble person, patrician.
PATRICK, PAT, PADDY (m) *Latin* Noble person, patrician.
PATRINIA (f) Flowering plant named for the traveller M. Patrin.
PATTI, PATTY, PATSY *see* PATRICIA.
PAUL (m) *Greek* Small.
PAULA (f) *Greek* Small.
PAULETTE, PAULEEN, PAULENE (f) Diminutives of Paula.
PAULINA, PAULINE (f) Spanish form of Paula.
PAVEL (m) Origin uncertain.
PAXTON (m) *Old German* Traveller from a distant land.
PAYN (m) Norman name of uncertain meaning.
PAYTON (m) Scottish form of Patrick.
PAZ (f) *Spanish* Peace.
PEACE (f) *Latin* Freedom from war, hence harmony.

PEARCE see PIERS.
PEARL, PEARLE, PERLE (f) *Middle English* From the name of the precious stone.
PEARLINE (f) A blend of Pearl and Pauline.
PEARSON (m) Son of Piers.
PEDREK, PEDRICK (m) Name linked with Petrok (or Petrock) a Cornish saint's name of uncertain meaning.
PEGGIE, PEGGY, PEGGOTY see MARGARET.
PELHAM (m) *Latin* Tannery town.
PEMBROKE (m) *Old English* Broken hill.
PENDLE (f) To use a pendulum as a divination or diagnostic system.
PENELOPE, PENNY (f) *Greek* Weaver.
PENTA (f) *Latin* Five.
PENTAS (f) *Latin* Five.
PENTHEA (f) *Greek* Fifth.
PEPITA (f) Spanish form of Josephine.
PERAN (m) Cornish saint's name of uncertain meaning.
PERCEVAL, PERCIVAL (m) *French* Valley piercer. Invented by the twelfth century poet Chretien de Troyes.
PERCY, PERZY see PERCEVAL.
PERDITA (f) *Latin* Lost.
PEREGRINE, PERRY (m) *Latin* Wanderer.
PERGOLA (f) *Latin* Covered walk formed by growing plants.
PERONELLE (f) Origin uncertain.
PERPETUA (f) *Latin* Constant.
PERL (f) *Welsh* A pearl.
PERLA see PEARL.
PERRINE (f) Feminine form of Peter.
PERRY see PETER and PEREGRINE.

PETA (f) Two possible origins: 1. *Hebrew* Bread; 2. *Sioux* Fire.
PETER, PETE (m) *Greek* A rock.
PETRA (f) *Greek* A rock.
PETRICE see PATRICE.
PETRINA (f) Russian form of Petra.
PETRONELLA (f) A blend of Petra and Ella.
PETULA (f) *Latin* Impatient.
PETUNIA (f) *French* From the flower name.
PEYTON see PAYTON.
PHELAN (m) *Irish* Wolf.
PHEMIE see EUPHEMIA.
PHENICE (f) *Egyptian* Phoenix.
PHEOBE, PHEBE, PHEOBIE, PHOEBIE see PHOEBE.
PHIL see PHILIP.
PHILA (f) *Greek* Love.
PHILANA (f) A blend of Phila and Lana.
PHILANTHA (f) A blend of Phila and Samantha.
PHILEMON (m) *Greek* Affectionate.
PHILENA, PHILINA (f) *Greek* Lover of mankind.
PHILIP, PHILLIP, PHIL, PIP (m) *Greek* Lover of horses.
PHILIPPA, PHILLIPA, PHILLIPPA (f) Feminine form of Philip.
PHILLIDA see PHYLLIS.
PHILLINA see FELINA.
PHILLIPINA (f) Diminutive of Phillipa.
PHILLIPS see PHILLIP.
PHILLIS see PHYLLIS.
PHILOMENA (f) *Greek* Beloved.
PHINEAS (m) *Hebrew* Oracle.
PHOEBE (f) *Greek* Pure, bright.
PHYLIS see PHYLLIS.

PHYLLIDA (f) A character in *Galathea* by Lyly.
PHYLLIS (f) *Greek* Foliage.
PIA (f) *Latin* Pious.
PIERCE *see* PETER.
PIERS (m) Variant of Peter.
PIP *see* PHILIP.
PIPER (f) *Old English* Pipe player.
PIPPA (f) Italian form of Philippa.
PIRAN, PERRAN (m) Cornish saint's name of uncertain meaning.
PLEASANCE (f) *Old French* Pleasure.
POLLY *see* MARY.
POPLAR (m) *Old French* From the name of the broadleaved tree.
POPPY (f) *Latin* The flower name used as a first name.
PORTER (m) *Old English* Gatekeeper.
PORTIA (f) *Latin* Feminine form of the Roman clan name Porcius.
PRECIOUS (f and m) *Latin* Of great value.
PRENTICE, PRENTIS (m) *Middle English* Beginner, apprentice.
PRESCOTT (m) *Old English* Priest's house.
PRESTON (m) *Old English* Priest's settlement.
PRICE (m) *Welsh* Son of Rhys.
PRICILLA *see* PRISCILLA.
PRIMA (f) *Latin* The first.
PRIMROSE (f) *Latin* A flower name meaning 'the first rose'.
PRIMULA (f) *Latin* A flower name. First.
PRISCILLA, PRECILLA, CILLA (f) *Latin* Ancient.
PROSPER (m) *Latin* Fortunate.
PRUDENCE (f) *Latin* Prudent, cautious.
PRUE, PRU (f) Diminutives of Prudence.

PRUNELLA (f) *Latin* Little plum.
PRYCE *see* PRICE.

Q

Quana — *Quona*

QUANA, QUANAH (f) Origin uncertain.
QUANDA (f) *Old English* Companion.
QUEENIE (f) *Old English* Queen.
QUENBY (f) *Old English* Queen's castle.
QUENTIN (m) *Latin* The fifth.
QUESTA (f) *Latin* Song of the nightingale
QUESTOR (m) *Latin* One who pursues a quest.
QUETTA (f) Origin uncertain. Possibly a form of Questa.
QUIANA *see* KIANA.
QUINBY (f) *Scandinavian* Womanly.
QUINCY (m) Variant of Quentin.
QUINDA *see* QUINTA.
QUINN, QUYNN, QUIN (m) *Irish* Counsel.
QUINTIN, QUINTON *see* QUENTIN.
QUONA (f) Origin uncertain.

Ra R Ryland

RA (m) The sun-god in Egyptian and other mythologies.
RAA (m) *Maori* The sun.
RABBIE *see* ROBERT.
RABIA (f) *Arabic* Fragrant breeze.
RACHEL (f) *Hebrew* Ewe.
RACHELLE, RACHELE (f) Variants of Rachel.
RADCLIFFE, RADCLIFF (m) *Old English* Red cliff.
RADELLA (f) *Old German* Counsel.
RADFORD (m) *Old English* Reedy ford.
RADINKA (f) Russian form of Radella.
RADMAN (m) *Slavonic* Joy.
RAE *see* RACHEL.
RAELAINE (f) A blend of Rae and Elaine.
RAELENE (f) A blend of Rae and Ilene.
RAETHA (f) A blend of Rae and Aretha.
RAF, RAIFE *see* RALPH.
RAFAEL *see* RAPHAEL.
RAFAELA, RAFFAELLA (f) Italian feminine forms of Raphael.
RAHAYA (f) Origin uncertain.
RAINA (f) Possibly a feminine form of Rainer (Rayner).
RAINBOW, RAYNBOW (f) *Old English* Coloured arch seen in the sky.
RAINE *see* RAINA or REINA.

RAINER (m) German form of Rayner.

RAIONA (f) *Maori* Lion.

RAISA (f) *Yiddish* A rose.

RALA (f) Origin uncertain.

RALEIGH, RAWLEY, RAYLEY (m) *Old French* Field of wading birds.

RALPH, RALF (m) *Old Norse* Wolf counsel.

RALPHINA (f) Feminine form of Ralph.

RALSTON (m) *Old English* Farm on red-coloured soil.

RAMAN see RAMON.

RAMON (m) Spanish form of Raymond.

RAMONA (f) Feminine form of Ramon.

RAMOND see RAYMOND.

RAMSDEN (m) *Old English* Valley with rams.

RAMSEY, RAMSAY (m) *Old English* Ram's island.

RANA see RAINA.

RANALD (m) Scottish variant of Ronald.

RANCE (m) *French* Marble.

RANDAL, RANDLE, RANDEL see RANDOLPH.

RANDI, RANDEE see MIRANDA.

RANDOLPH (m) *Old English* Wolf shield.

RANDY (m) Variant of Randolph or Randall.

RANGER (m) *Middle English* Wanderer.

RANI (f) Two possible origins: 1. *Hebrew* Joy; 2. *Hindi* Queen.

RANON, RANEN (m) *Hebrew* Be joyful.

RANSCOMBE (m) *Old English* Valley shield.

RANSOM (m) *Latin* To redeem.

RANULPH (m) Origin uncertain. Possibly a form of Randolph.

RAONA (f) An anagram of Aaron.

RAOUL (m) French form of Ralph.

RAPHAEL (m) *Hebrew* God has healed.

Raphaela — Redford

RAPHAELA (f) Feminine form of Raphael.
RAQUEL (f) Spanish form of Rachel.
RASHANA (f) Origin uncertain. Possibly a form of Rashida.
RASHIDA (f) *Turkish* Rightly guided.
RATHA (f) A character in the novel *Clan Ground* by Clare Bell.
RAVEN (m, rarely f) *Old English* A raven.
RAWDON (m) *Old English* Rough hill.
RAWSON (m) Son of Ralph.
RAY see RAYMOND.
RAYA (f) *Hebrew* Friend.
RAYANNE (f) A blend of Raya and Anne.
RAYE see RAE.
RAYBURN (m) *Old English* The flowered fields.
RAYFORD (m) *Old English* Stream crossing.
RAYLENE (f) Origin uncertain.
RAYMENT see RAYMOND.
RAYMOND, RAYMUND (m) *Old German* Wise protection.
RAYMONDE (f) Feminine form of Raymond.
RAYNER, RAYNOR (m) *Old French* Mighty army.
RAYNOLD, RAYNALD (m) A blend of Raymond and Arnold.
RAZA (f) *Aramaic* My secret.
RAZEEN (f) Origin uncertain. Possibly a form of Raza.
READ see REED.
REAGAN see REEGAN.
REAHAN (m) Origin uncertain. Possibly a form of Reagan.
REBA see REBECCA.
REBECCA, BECKY (f) *Hebrew* To bind.
REDFORD (m) *Old English* Red-stone river crossing.

REDMOND, REDMUND (m) Irish form of Raymond.
REDVERS (m) *Old English* Origin uncertain. Possibly 'counsel-wharf'.
REDWAY (m) *Old English* Reedy road.
REECE, REES see RHYS.
REED (m) *Old English* Red-haired.
REENA, REENIE see RENIE.
REEVER (m) Origin uncertain.
REEVES (m) *Old English* Steward.
REG, REGGIE see REGINALD.
REGAN (f) A character in the play *King Lear* by Shakespeare.
REGAN (m) *Irish* Descendant of the little king.
REGINALD see REYNOLD.
REGINE, REGINA (f) *Latin* Queen.
REGIS (m) *Latin* Kingly.
REI (f) *Maori* Jewel.
REID see REED.
REIKA (f) *Japanese* Beautiful flower.
REIKO (f) *Japanese* Gratitude.
REILLY see RILEY.
REINA, REINE (f) *French* Queen.
REINITA (f) *Spanish* Little queen.
REITA see RITA.
REJA (f) A name invented from the initials of four brothers.
RELDA (f) Origin uncertain.
REMI see REMY.
REMIRA (f) A blend of Remi and Mira.
REMY (f and m) *Latin* An oarsman.
RENA, RINA (f) *Hebrew* Joy.
RENATA see RENEE.
RENDLE see RANDALL.
RENE (f) Diminutive of Irene.

RENE (m) *French* Reborn.
RENEE, RENIE (f) Variants of Irene.
RENISE (f) A blend of Renie and Denise.
RENITA (f) A blend of Rene and Anita.
RENNIE *see* RENEE.
RENNY *see* RENE.
RESA (f) Origin uncertain. Possibly a form of Resha.
RESHA (f) Origin uncertain. Possibly a feminine form of Reshad.
RESHAD (m) Origin uncertain. Possibly from *Sanskrit rishi* meaning 'teacher'.
RETA *see* RITA and MARGARETA.
RETHA *see* ARETHA.
RETTA *see* RETA.
REUBEN (m) *Hebrew* Behold a son.
REUEL (m) *Hebrew* Friend of God.
REVA (f) Anagram of Vera.
REVEL (f) *Old French* To make merry.
REX (m) *Latin* King.
REYLINE (f) Origin uncertain.
REYNARD (m) *Old German* Wise and brave (or strong).
REYNER, REYNOR, RAYNER (m) *Latin* Kingly.
REYNOLD, RAYNOLD (m) *Old Norse* Strong counsel.
RHANNA (f) The name of a Hebridean island in the novels of Christine Marion Fraser.
RHEA (f) Origin uncertain. Possibly a form of Raya.
RHETT, RHET (m) *Old English* Small stream.
RHIAN, RHIANNON (f) *Welsh* Maiden.
RHIANWEN (f) *Welsh* Fair maiden.
RHODA (f) *Greek* A rose.
RHODOS (m) From the name of the Aegean island of Rhodes.

Rhonwen — Rinda

RHONWEN (f) *Welsh* Fair.

RHYLL (f) Origin uncertain.

RHYS (m) *Welsh* Ardour.

RIANE (f) Possibly a feminine form of Ryan.

RIC see RICHARD.

RICA see RICARDA.

RICARDA (f) Feminine form of Ricardo.

RICARDO (m) Spanish form of Richard.

RICHARD, DICK (m) *Old German* Strong ruler.

RICHELLE see RACHELLE.

RICHENDA, RICHANDA (f) Feminine form of Richard.

RICHIE, RITCHIE see RICHARD.

RICHMAL (f) *Old English* A blend of 'ruler' plus an obscure second element.

RICHMOND (m) *Old English* Richly covered hill.

RICK, RICKIE, RICKY, RIK see RICHARD.

RIDDIAN (m) Origin uncertain.

RIDER (m) *Old English* Rider, knight.

RIDLEY (m) *Old English* Cleared wood.

RIESA see THERESA.

RIK see RICK.

RIKA (f) Two possible origins: 1. A variant of Erika; 2. *Japanese* Village flower.

RIKKI, RIKI see ERIKA.

RILEY (m) *Dutch* Small stream.

RILLA (f) A character in the *Canopus in Argos: Archives* novel cycle by Doris Lessing.

RIMA (f) Origin uncertain. Possibly a feminine form of Rimon.

RIMON, RIMMON (m) *Hebrew* Pomegranate.

RIMONA (f) Feminine form of Rimon.

RINA see RENA.

RINDA see LORINDA.

RINGO (m) Two possible origins: 1. *Italian* Ring; 2. *Japanese* Apple.

RIO, REO (f) *Old English* A stream.

RISA (f) A blend of Rita and Lisa.

RISHA (f) *see* RESHAD.

RISHONA (f) *Hebrew* First.

RITA, RETA *see* MARGARETA, DORITA, etc.

RITCHIE *see* RICHIE.

RIVA (f) *Italian* Shore, coast.

RIVANA (f) *Old French* River.

RIVER (m, rarely f) *Old French* Natural flowing waterway.

ROALD (m) *Scandinavian* Famous power.

ROANNA (f) A blend of Roald and Anna.

ROB, ROBBIE, ROBBY, ROBB *see* ROBERT.

ROBANA (f) A blend of Robert and Anna.

ROBARD, ROBART (m) French forms of Robert.

ROBERT (m) *Old English* Bright fame.

ROBERTA (f) Feminine form of Robert.

ROBERTSON (m) Son of Robert.

ROBIN (m) Variant of Robert.

ROBINA (f) Feminine form of Robin.

ROBINSON (m) Son of Robin.

ROBSON (m) Son of Robert.

ROBYN (f) *see* ROBIN or ROBINA.

ROC *see* ROCK.

ROCANA (f) German name of uncertain meaning.

ROCHELLA, ROCHELLE (f) *French* Little rock.

ROCK, ROCKY, ROK (m) *Latin* A stone.

ROCKLIN (m) Variant of Rock.

ROCKNEY (m) *Old English* Rocky island.

ROCKWELL (m) *Old English* Rook stream.

ROD, RODDY *see* RODNEY.

RODELLE (f) Origin uncertain.

Roderick   Romaire

RODERICK (m) *Old German* Famous ruler.
RODGER *see* ROGER.
RODNEY (m) *Old English* Cleared land near water.
RODRICK *see* RODERICK.
ROGAN (m) *Gaelic* Red-haired one.
ROGER (m) *Old English* Famous warrior.
ROGERS (m) Descendant of Roger.
ROHA (f) *Maori* Rose.
ROHAN (m) As use of this name began in the 1960s it is probably traceable to Rohan ('horse land'), a kingdom in Tolkien's *The Lord of the Rings*, first published in 1954–5.
ROHANDA (f) The original name for the planet Shikasta in the *Canopus in Argos: Archives* novel cycle by Doris Lessing.
ROHIN (m) *Sanskrit* One who follows the upward path.
ROIS (f) *Latin* Rose.
ROISIN (f) Irish diminutive of Rosa.
ROLAINE (f) A blend of Rois and Elaine.
ROLAND, ROWLAND, ROLYND (m) *Old German* Famous land.
ROLANDA, ROLANDE (f) Feminine forms of Roland.
ROLANTHA (f) A blend of Roland and Samantha.
ROLARA (f) A blend of Roland and Lara.
ROLENE (f) A blend of Roland and Ilene.
ROLF, ROLFE, ROLPH (m) Scandinavian form of Rudolph.
ROLLAND, ROLLO *see* ROLAND.
ROMA (f) Italian city name used as a first name.
ROMAINE (f) French feminine form of Romain meaning 'Roman'.
ROMAIRE (f) A blend of Roland and Maire (Mary).

188

Roman — Rosabel

ROMAN (m) *see* ROMA.
ROMANA (f) *see* ROMA.
ROMANDA (f) A blend of Roma and Amanda.
ROMANTHA (f) A blend of Roma and Samantha.
ROMARA (f) A blend of Roma and Mara.
ROMELDA (f) A blend of Roma and Imelda.
ROMI, ROMY *see* ROSEMARY.
ROMILY (f) A blend of Roma and Emily.
ROMOLA (f) A character in the novel *Romola* by George Eliot.
ROMONA *see* RAMONA.
ROMY, ROMIE *see* ROSEMARY.
RON *see* RONALD.
RONA *see* RHONA.
RONAELE (f) Eleanor spelt backwards.
RONALD, RON (m) *Old Norse* Strong counsel.
RONALEE (f) A blend of Rona and Lee.
RONAN (m) *Irish* Little seal.
RONDELAINE (f) A blend of Rhonda and Elaine.
RONCEL, RONCIE (f) A blend of Ron and Ancel.
RONEEL (f) Anagram of Lorene.
RONELLE (f) A blend of Ron and Ella.
RONETTE (f) Feminine diminutive of Ron.
RONI (f) *Hebrew* My joy.
RONICA (f) A character in the novel *Orion Shall Rise* by Poul Anderson.
RONNA (f) Feminine form of Ronald.
RONNETTE *see* RONETTE.
RONNIE *see* RONALD.
ROO (f) A character in *Winnie the Pooh* by A. A. Milne.
RORY, RORIE (m) *Gaelic* Red.
ROSA (f) *Latin* Rose.
ROSABEL (f) A blend of Rose and Belle.

ROSALEEN see ROSALINE.
ROSALIE, ROSALEE, ROSALEA, ROSALIA (f) *Latin* Garland of roses.
ROSALIN (f) A blend of Rose and Lin.
ROSALINA (f) A blend of Rosa and Lina (Lena).
ROSALIND (f) A character in *The Shepherd's Calendar* by Edmund Spenser.
ROSALINDA, ROSALYN, ROSALINE, ROSALYND, ROSALYNNE see ROSALIND.
ROSAMOND, ROSAMUND (f) *Old German* Protector of fame.
ROSAN, ROSANN, ROSANNA, ROSANNE (f) A blend of Rose and Ann.
ROSANDA (f) A blend of Rose and Wanda.
ROSANTHA (f) A blend of Rose and Samantha.
ROSARIA (f) A blend of Rose and Maria.
ROSCOE (m) *Old German* Sea horse.
ROSE, ROSA, ROSIE (f) *Latin* From the flower name.
ROSEAN, ROSEANN (f) A blend of Rose and Ann.
ROSEDALE (m) *Old Norse* Valley of horses.
ROSEHANNA, ROSEHANNAH (f) A blend of Rose and Hannah.
ROSELIA, ROSELLA see ROSALIA (ROSALIE).
ROSELIND, ROSELINE see ROSALIND.
ROSELLE, ROSELLA (f) A blend of Rose and Ella.
ROSELTHA (f) A blend of Rose and Meltha.
ROSELYN (f) A blend of Rose and Lynda.
ROSEMARY, ROSEMAIRIE, ROSIE (f) *Latin* From the flower name meaning 'dew of the sea'.
ROSEN (f) *Cornish* Rose.
ROSENA see ROSINA.
ROSETTA (f) Diminutive of Rose.
ROSHEEN (f) Phonetic form of Roisin.

ROSHELLE see ROCHELLE.
ROSIA see ROSE.
ROSIE, ROSEY, ROSI see ROSE.
ROSILYN see ROSALIND.
ROSINA (f) Italian diminutive of Rose.
ROSINDA (f) A blend of Rose and Linda.
ROSINTHA (f) A blend of Rose and Cynthia.
ROSIRA (f) A blend of Rose and Mira.
ROSITA (f) A blend of Rose and Rita.
ROSLYN see ROSALIND.
ROSS (m) *Gaelic* Cape.
ROSSALYN, ROSSLYN see ROSALIND.
ROSY see ROSE.
ROUANE see ROWENA.
ROWAN (m) A Scandinavian tree name: the mountain ash.
ROWANDA (f) A blend of Rowena and Wanda.
ROWANTHA (f) A blend of Rowena and Samantha.
ROWENA (f) Variant of Rowan.
ROWLAND see ROLAND.
ROWLEY (m) *Old English* Rough clearing.
ROXANNA, ROXANNE, ROXY, ROXI (f) *Latin/Persian* Dawn.
ROXOLANA (f) A blend of Roxanna and Lana.
ROY (m) *Gaelic* Red.
ROYCE (m) *Old German* Origin uncertain. Probably 'kind fame'.
ROYDEN (m) *Old English* Hill where rye grows.
ROYSTON, ROYSTAN (m) *German/Old French* Rohesia's cross.
ROZA, ROZ see ROSE.
ROZAN (f) A blend of Rose and Ann.
ROZELLA (f) A blend of Rose and Ella.
ROZENA, ROZINA see ROSINA.

ROZLYN (f) A blend of Rose and Lyn.
RUBEN see REUBEN.
RUBINA (f) Diminutive of Ruby.
RUBY, RUBI, RUBIE (f) *Latin* From the jewel name. Red.
RUDGE (m) *Old French* Red-haired.
RUDOLF, RUDY, RUDI (m) *Old German* Fame-wolf.
RUDYARD (m) *Old English* Red pole.
RUE (f) *Old German* A plant name. Also 'fame'.
RUEBEN see REUBEN.
RUFUS (m) *Latin* Red-haired.
RULA (f) *Latin* Ruler.
RUMER (f) A name of uncertain origin meaning 'gypsy'.
RUNA (f) *Old Norse* To flow.
RUNIA (f) Origin uncertain.
RUPERT (m) German form of Robert.
RUPERTA (f) Feminine form of Rupert.
RUSHEEN see ROSHEEN.
RUSS see RUSSELL.
RUSSELL, RUSSEL (m) *French* Red-haired.
RUSSET (f and m) *Latin* Reddish brown.
RUSTY (m, rarely f) Nickname (sometimes first name) for a red-haired person.
RUTH (f) *Hebrew* Companion.
RUTHAN (f) A blend of Ruth and Ann.
RUTHENA (f) A blend of Ruth and Athena.
RUTHERFORD (m) *Old English* Ford for oxen.
RUTHVEN (m) *Gaelic* Red earth place.
RUY, RY see RYAN.
RYAN (m) *Gaelic* Little king.
RYDER see RIDER.
RYDON (m) *Old English* Rye valley.

RYE *see* RYAN.
RYFORD (m) *Old English* Ford near the rye field.
RYLAN, RYLAND (m) *Old English* Land where rye grows.

Saada **S** *Symon*

SAADA, SAANA (f) *Hebrew* Support.
SABELLA (f) *Latin* Wise.
SABINA, SABENA (f) *Latin* Woman from the Sabine region of Italy.
SABLE (f) *Old French* Black (in heraldry).
SABRA (f) *Hebrew* Cactus.
SABRINA (f) *Latin* The river Severn.
SACHA (f) Russian form of Alexandra.
SACHA (m) Russian form of Alexander.
SACHEVERELL (m) Origin uncertain. Possibly *French* 'without leather'.
SADIE *see* SARAH
SADIRA (f) *Arabic* Ostrich returning from water.
SAETHYDD (m) *Welsh* Archer.
SAFFRON (f) *Arabic* Crocus.
SAFIRE *see* SAPHIRE.
SAGINA, SAGUNA (f) *Latin* Wise one.
SAHRA, SAHRAH *see* SARAH.
SAI (f) *Japanese* Intelligence.
SAISHA *see* SACHA.
SAITH (m) *Welsh* Seven.
SAKETA (f) *Sanskrit* Single-pointed (hence integrity).
SAKIMA (m) *American Indian* King.
SAKURA (f) *Japanese* Cherry blossom.
SAL *see* SARAH.

Salema — Samuela

SALEMA (f) *Hebrew* Peace.
SALEN *see* SALEMA.
SALENA *see* SELINA.
SALENE (f) A blend of Salvatore and Irene.
SALIM (m) *Arabic* Flawless, whole.
SALIMA (f) Feminine form of Salim.
SALLEY, SALLIE *see* SARAH.
SALLIANNE (f) A blend of Sally and Anne.
SALLY *see* SARAH.
SALMA (f) Origin uncertain. Possibly a form of Salome.
SALOME (f) *Hebrew* Peace.
SALONA (f) A blend of Salome and Rona.
SALONE *see* SOLOMON.
SALVIA (f) *Latin* Sage herb.
SALVIN (m) *Latin* Saviour.
SAM *see* SAMUEL or SAMANTHA.
SAMALA (f) *Hebrew* Prayed for.
SAMANA (f) A blend of Samantha and Lana.
SAMANDA (f) A blend of Samantha and Amanda.
SAMANTHA (f) *Aramaic* Listener.
SAMARA (f) *Latin* Seed of the elm.
SAMARRA (f) From the place-name in Iraq.
SAMILLA (f) A blend of Samantha and Camilla.
SAMINA (f) A blend of Samantha and Nina.
SAMIRA (f) *Arabic* Entertainer.
SAMMI, SAMMIE, SAMMY *see* SAMUEL.
SAMORA (f) A blend of Samantha and Nora.
SAMPHIRE (f) *French* From the name of the cliff-growing plant.
SAMPSON, SAMSON (m) *Hebrew* The sun.
SAMUEL, SAM (m) *Hebrew* Two possible origins: 1. Heard of God; 2. Name of God.
SAMUELA (f) Feminine form of Samuel.

Sanaya *Sarella*

SANAYA (f) Origin uncertain.
SANCHIA (f) *Spanish* Holy.
SANDEREL, SANDERELLE (f) A blend of Sandra and Elle.
SANDERS (m) Variant of Alexander.
SANDFORD, SANFORD (m) *Old English* Sandy river crossing.
SANDI, SANDIE see ALEXANDER.
SANDINA (f) A blend of Sandra and Nina.
SANDOR (m) Slavonic form of Alexander.
SANDORA (f) Feminine form of Sandor.
SANDRA (f) Variant of Alessandra, the Italian form of Alexandra.
SANDREENA (f) A blend of Sandra and Reena (Rena).
SANDRIANA (f) A blend of Sandra and Diana.
SANDY see ALEXANDER or ALEXANDRA.
SANTANA (f) A shortened version of Santa Anna, a Spanish form of Saint Anne.
SAPPHIRE, SAPPHIRA, SAPPHYRE (f) From the Hebrew jewel name for lapis lazuli.
SARA (f) Two possible origins: 1. A form of Sarah; 2. *Sanskrit* Essence.
SARADA (f) *Sanskrit* Goddess of wisdom.
SARAH (f) *Hebrew* Princess.
SARAI, SARAY (f) *Hebrew* Quarrelsome.
SARAIN see SARAYN.
SARALA (f) A blend of Sarah and Mala.
SARAM (f) Variant of Sarah.
SARANA (f) *Sanskrit* Protecting, guarding.
SARANN, SARANNE (f) A blend of Sarah and Ann.
SARANTHA (f) A blend of Sarah and Samantha.
SARAYN (f) A blend of Sarah and Ann.
SARELLA (f) A blend of Sarah and Ella.

Sarenne · Scarlett

SARENNE (f) A blend of Sarah and Vivienne.
SARETTA, SARETTE (f) Diminutives of Sarah.
SARGENT (m) *Old English* Law officer.
SARI *see* SARAH.
SARIDA *see* SARITA.
SARINA, SARINE (f) Diminutives of Sarah.
SARINDA (f) *Sanskrit* A musical instrument.
SARINKA (f) A blend of Sarah and Katinka.
SARITA, ZARITA (f) Spanish diminutive of Sarah.
SARITIA *see* SARITA.
SAROBI (f) Origin uncertain.
SAROLA (f) A blend of Sarah and Lola.
SARRA *see* SARA.
SARUK (f) *Arabic* East wind.
SASHA, SASCHA *see* SACHA.
SASKIA (f) *Dutch* Saxon.
SASSY (f) *Middle English* Saucy, cheeky.
SATI (f) *Sanskrit* Virtuous wife.
SATYA (f) Origin uncertain. Possibly a form of Sati.
SAUL (m) *Hebrew* Asked for.
SAUNDERS *see* SANDERS.
SAUNDRA *see* SANDRA.
SAVILLA (m) From the French place-name.
SAVINA (f) Variant of Sabina.
SAWARD (m) *Old English* Fort where the sallows (willows) grow.
SAWYER (m) *Middle English* Woodworker.
SAXON (m) *Old German* Short sword (as carried by the Anglo-Saxons).
SAYER (m) *Old German* Victory.
SAYRE (f) Origin uncertain. Possibly a form of Sayer.
SCANLON (m) *Old English* Descendant of Scannal.
SCARLET *see* SCARLETT.
SCARLETT (f) A character in the novel *Gone With*

The Wind by Margaret Mitchell. The name means a dealer in scarlet (a type of cloth).

SCHERRI *see* SHERRY.
SCILLA *see* CILLA.
SCIROCCO, SIROCCO (f) *Arabic* Warm sultry wind in Southern Europe.
SCOT, SCOTT (m) *Old English* Man from Scotland.
SEABROOKE (m) *Old English* Stream by the sea.
SEAMON (m) *Old English* Seaman.
SEAMORE *see* SEYMOUR.
SEAMUS, SEAMAS, SHAMUS (m) Irish form of James.
SEAN (m) Irish form of John.
SEARLE, SEAR (m) *Old English* Battle.
SEATON (m) *Old English* Place by the sea.
SEBASTIAN (m) *Greek* Venerable.
SEBASTIANA (f) Feminine form of Sebastian.
SEBERT (m) *Old English* Bright victory.
SEBINA *see* SABINA.
SEBRA (f) Origin uncertain. Possibly a form of Sebina.
SECUNDA (f) *Latin* Second.
SEDGWICK (m) *Old English* Farm with reeds (sedges).
SEELIA *see* CELIA.
SEENA *see* SHEENA.
SEETHA (f) *Sanskrit* The wife of Rama in Hindu mythology; literally 'furrow or track'.
SEFTON (m) *Old German* Place in the reeds (sedges).
SEIKO (m and f) *Japanese* Success.
SELA, SELAH (f) *Hebrew* Rock.
SELANDA (f) A blend of Selina and Amanda.
SELANTHA (f) A blend of Selina and Samantha.
SELARA (f) A blend of Selina and Lara.

SELBY (m) *Old English* Willow barn.
SELDEN, SELDON (m) *Old English* New valley.
SELIA *see* CELIA.
SELINA, SELENA, SELENE, CELENE (f) *Greek* The moon. The goddess of the moon in Greek mythology.
SELINDA (f) A blend of Selina and Linda.
SELINKA (f) A blend of Selina and Katinka.
SELITA (f) A blend of Selina and Lita.
SELMA (f) Diminutive of Anselma (*see* ANSELL).
SELORA (f) A blend of Selma and Lora.
SELVA (f) Spanish form of the Latin *silva* meaning 'a wood'.
SELVIN (m) Masculine form of Selva.
SELWYN, SELWIN (m) *Old English* Holy friend.
SEMIRA (f) *Hebrew* Height of the heavens.
SENARA (f) Latinized form of the Cornish saint's name Zennor.
SENGA (f) Backspelling of Agnes.
SEONAID (f) Gaelic form of Janet.
SEPTA (f) *Latin* Seven.
SEPTEMBER (f) *Latin* The name of the month used as a first name.
SEPTIMUS (m) *Latin* Seventh.
SEQUIN (f) *Arabic* Shining decoration on a costume.
SEQUOIA (f) *Cherokee* From the name of the tall Californian coniferous tree.
SERA (f) *Italian* What will be (hence destiny).
SERAPHINA, SERAFINE (f) *Hebrew* To burn.
SEREN (f) *Welsh* Starlight.
SERENA, SERENATA (f) *Latin* Peaceful.
SERGEANT (m) *Old English* Law officer.
SERILDA (f) *Old German* Girl of war.
SERINA *see* SERENA.

SERINDA (f) A blend of Serina and Linda.
SERINTHA (f) A blend of Serina and Samantha.
SERLE (m) *Old German* Armour.
SETA (f) Origin uncertain.
SETH (m) *Hebrew* To set.
SEUMA (f) Feminine form of Seumas.
SEUMAS *see* SEAMUS.
SEVERINE (f) *French* Severe.
SEVERN (m) *Latin* The river name used as a first name (*see also* SABRINA).
SEWARD (m) *Old English* Sea victory or sea guardian.
SEWELL, SEWAL (m) *Old German* Victorious at sea.
SEYMOUR (m) *Old English* Moor by the sea.
SHAE *see* SHAY.
SHAFAYE (f) Faye with the Sha- prefix.
SHAFIKA (f) Fika with the Sha- prefix.
SHAHEENA (f) Hena with the Sha- prefix.
SHAINA (f) *Yiddish* Beautiful.
SHAIRA (f) Origin uncertain.
SHAKEENA (f) Keena with the Sha- prefix.
SHAKELA (f) Kela with the Sha- prefix.
SHAKETA (f) Keta with the Sha- prefix.
SHAKEYA (f) Keya with the Sha- prefix.
SHAKIA (f) Kia with the Sha- prefix.
SHAKILAH (f) Kilah with the Sha- prefix.
SHAKINA (f) Kina with the Sha- prefix.
SHAKIRA (f) Kira with the Sha- prefix.
SHAKIRAH, SHAKARA (f) *Arabic* Be grateful.
SHALANDA (f) Landa with the Sha- prefix.
SHALANTHA (f) Lantha with the Sha- prefix.
SHALAYA (f) Laya with the Sha- prefix.
SHALENA (f) Lena with the Sha- prefix.

SHALETA (f) Leta with the Sha- prefix.
SHALIKA (f) Lika with the Sha- prefix.
SHALINDA (f) Linda with the Sha- prefix.
SHALISA (f) Lisa with the Sha- prefix.
SHALOM (f) *Hebrew* Peace, wholeness.
SHALONDA (f) Londa with the Sha- prefix.
SHALYN (f) Lyn with the Sha- prefix.
SHAMA, SHARMA (f) Probably forms of Sharon.
SHAMARI (f) Mary with the Sha- prefix.
SHAMEKA (f) Meka with the Sha- prefix.
SHAMICA (f) Mica with the Sha- prefix.
SHAMIKA (f) Mika with the Sha- prefix.
SHAMITA (f) Mita with the Sha- prefix.
SHAMUS (m) Phonetic form of Seamus.
SHAN (f) Phonetic form of Welsh Sian.
SHANA, CHANA (f) Variants of Shan.
SHANALEE (f) A blend of Shan and Lee.
SHANAY (f) Variant of Shan.
SHANDA (f) A blend of Shan and Wanda.
SHANDI, SHANDY (f) Blends of Shan and Wendy.
SHANE (m) Anglicised form of Sean.
SHANEA *see* SHAN.
SHANEEN, SHANENE *see* SHAN.
SHANEKA (f) Neka with the Sha- prefix.
SHANEL, SHANELL *see* CHANEL.
SHANETHA *see* SHAN.
SHANETHIS (f) Nethis with the Sha- prefix.
SHANETTA, SHANETTE (f) Netta with the Sha- prefix.
SHANI (f) *Swahili* Wonderful.
SHANIKA (f) Nika with the Sha- prefix.
SHANITA (f) Nita with the Sha- prefix.
SHANITHA (f) Nitha (Nissa) with the Sha- prefix.

SHANNA (f) A blend of Shan and Anna.
SHANNARA (f) A character in the *Shannara* trilogy of novels by Terry Brooks.
SHANNON, SHANNAN (f and m) *Celtic* Old one.
SHANTA, CHANTA see CHANTAL.
SHANTEKA (f) Variant of Shanti.
SHANTELLE, SHANTELLA, SHANTEL, SHANTALE (f) Variants of Chantal.
SHANTI (f) *Sanskrit* Peace.
SHANTINA (f) A blend of Shanti and Tina.
SHANTRICE (f) A blend of Shanti and Beatrice.
SHARA, SHARAN, SHARANE see SHARON.
SHARANA (f) *Sanskrit* Take refuge.
SHAREEN, SHARENE see SHARON.
SHARELDA (f) A blend of Shara and Imelda.
SHARELLA (f) A blend of Shara and Ella.
SHAREN see SHARON.
SHARETTA (f) Diminutive of Shara.
SHARI, SHARIA, SHARIE, SHAREE (f) Forms of Sharon.
SHARIN, SHARYN see SHARON.
SHARLA see CHARLA.
SHARLENE see CHARLEEN.
SHARMA (f) Origin uncertain. Possibly a variant of Sharon or Charmain.
SHARMAIN, SHARMAINE see CHARMAIN.
SHARMALEE (f) A blend of Sharon and Lee.
SHARMANKA (f) Origin uncertain.
SHARNI (f) Origin uncertain.
SHAROLYN (f) A blend of Sharon and Lyn.
SHARON, SHAARON (f) *Hebrew* The plain.
SHARONA (f) A blend of Sharon and Rona.
SHARONE, SHARONNE see SHARON.
SHARONDA (f) A blend of Sharon and Rhonda.

SHARRA see SHARA.
SHARRED see JARED.
SHARROL see CHERYL.
SHARRON, SHARY, SHARRY see SHARON.
SHARLY (f) A blend of Shara and Carly.
SHARYN (f) A blend of Shara and Lyn.
SHASTA (f) From the name of the mountain in California.
SHAUN, SHAWN (m) Phonetic forms of the Irish name Sean.
SHAUNA, SHAUNNA (f) Feminine forms of Shaun.
SHAUNE, SHAUNIE see SHAUNA.
SHAVONNE, SHAVON (f) Phonetic forms of Siobhan.
SHAW (m) *Old English* Wood, copse.
SHAWN see SEAN.
SHAWNEE (f) Origin uncertain. Possibly a form of Shawn.
SHAY, SHAYA, SHAYNA (f) Variants of Shaina.
SHAYLA see SHEILA.
SHAYLIH (f) Origin uncertain.
SHAYNE see SHANE.
SHEA (f) From the name of the tropical tree.
SHEANDA (f) A blend of Shea and Amanda.
SHEANTHA (f) A blend of Shea and Samantha.
SHEBA (f) Diminutive form of Bathsheba.
SHEEANA (f) A character in the *Dune* sequence of novels by Frank Herbert.
SHEELAGH, SHEELE see SHEILA.
SHEENA (f) Phonetic version of Gaelic Sine, a Scottish form of Jean.
SHEILA, SHIELA, SHEELAH, SHELAGH (f) An English version of the Irish name Sile, a form of Celia.

SHELAH *see* SHEILA.

SHELBY (m) *Old English* Sheltered settlement.

SHELDON (m) *Old English* Sheltered hill.

SHELIA (f) A blend of Sheila and Celia.

SHELL (f) *Old Norse* The outer case of a seed or animal.

SHELLEY, SHELLIE, SHELLY, SHELLI (f and m) *Old English* Meadow on a slope.

SHELTON (m) *Old English* High place.

SHENA *see* SHEENA.

SHENDY (f) A blend of Shan and Wendy.

SHEONA *see* SHEENA.

SHEPHERD (m) *Old English* Keeper of sheep.

SHER (f and m) Diminutive of Sheryl or Sherwood.

SHERALA (f) A blend of Shera and Lala.

SHERALYN (f) Variant of Cheryl.

SHERBAN (m) Origin uncertain.

SHEREE, SHERIE *see* CHERIE.

SHEREEN, SHERENE (f) Variants of CHERIE.

SHERELLA (f) A blend of Sher and Ella.

SHERI, SHERIE, SHERRY *see* CHERIE.

SHERIDAN (m) *Old English* Master of the shire.

SHERIE *see* CHERIE.

SHERILYN (f) A blend of Sherie and Lyn.

SHERLEEN (f) Diminutive of Sherley.

SHERLEY *see* SHIRLEY.

SHERLOCK (m) *Old English* Sheltered area.

SHERMAN, SHERMON (m) *Old English* Dweller in the shire.

SHERON *see* SHARON.

SHERRALYN (f) A blend of Sherry and Lyn.

SHEREE, SHERRI, SHERRIE *see* CHERIE.

SHERRIL, SHERRYL *see* CHERYL.

SHERRILL (m) *Old English* Hill on the shire.

Sherry · Shivon

SHERRY (f) Phonetic form of Cherie.
SHERRYN (f) Variant of SHERRY.
SHERWELL see SHERRILL.
SHERWIN, SHERWYN (m) *Old English* Friend of the shire.
SHERWOOD (m) *Old English* Wood in the shire.
SHERYL see CHERYL.
SHERYN (f) A blend of Sheryl and Sharon.
SHEVAUN, SHEVONNE, SHEVON (f) Variants of Siobhan.
SHIBUI (f) *Japanese* Exquisite severity.
SHIEL, SHIELA see SHEILA.
SHIFRA (f) *Hebrew* Beautiful.
SHIKASTA (f) The name of a planet in the *Canopus in Argos: Archives* novel cycle by Doris Lessing.
SHILO (f) Feminine form of Shiloh.
SHILOH (m) From the Biblical place-name of uncertain meaning.
SHIMA (f) *Japanese* Island.
SHIMAKO (f) *Japanese* Island child.
SHIMIAH (f) *Hebrew* To guard.
SHIMONA (f) *Hebrew* Little princess.
SHIMONEL (f) A modern invention meaning 'peace of the elves'.
SHIONA (f) A blend of Sheila and Fiona.
SHIRA (f) *Hebrew* Strong.
SHIREEN, SHIRENE, SHIRIN (f) Diminutives of Shirley.
SHIRI (f) *Hebrew* My song.
SHIRL see SHIRLEY.
SHIRLEEN, SHIRLENE (f) Diminutives of Shirley.
SHIRLEY, SHIRLIE (f) *Old English* Bright clearing.
SHIVON see SHAVONNE.

SHIZU (f) *Japanese* Quiet, clear.

SHOBANA (f) Origin uncertain. Possibly a form of Sioban.

SHOLOHA (f) Origin uncertain. Possibly a form of Shilo.

SHOLTO (m) *Gaelic* Sower.

SHONA (f) Phonetic form of Gaelic Seonaid (Joan).

SHONDA (f) A blend of Shona and Rhonda.

SHONET (f) Origin uncertain. Possibly 'sower': *Celtic*.

SHOSHANA (f) Hebrew form of Susannah.

SHREELA (f) Origin uncertain. Possibly a form of Shiela.

SHUBUTA (f) *Choctaw* Smokey.

SHUKA (f) Origin uncertain. Possibly a form of Shula.

SHULA, SULA, SHULIE (f) Origin uncertain. Probably from Arabic root *sul* or *sal* meaning 'peace'.

SHUNA, SHUNE see SHULA.

SHURA (m) Origin uncertain. Possibly a phonetic form of 'surer'.

SI see SIMON.

SIAN (f) Welsh form of Jane.

SIARI, SIARA (f) Origin uncertain. Possibly a form of Sian.

SIBBY, SIBELLE, SIBELLA see SIBYL.

SIBYL, CYBIL (f) *Greek* Prophetess.

SID see SIDNEY.

SIDNEY, SYDNEY, SIDNE (m, rarely f) Two possible origins: 1. From the *French* place-name Saint Dennis; 2 *Old English* Wide, well-watered land.

SIDONY, SIDONIA (f) Woman from Sidon.
SIDRA (f) *Latin* Starlike.
SIDWELL (m) *Old English* Broad stream.
SIEGFRIED (m) *Old German* Victory-peace.
SIERRA (f) From the name of the Spanish mountain range.
SIG, SIGGY *see* SIGMUND or SIGBERT.
SIGBERT (m) *Old German* Famous victory.
SIGMA (f) Eighteenth letter in Greek alphabet.
SIGMUND, SIGMOND (m) *Old German* Victory-shield.
SIGOURNEY (f) Variant of Sagina.
SIGRID (f) Feminine form of Siegfried.
SIKA (f) Two possible origins: 1. *Japanese* From the name of the sika deer; 2. Phonetic form of 'seeker'.
SILAS, SI (m) *Latin* Wood.
SILE (f) Irish form of Celia.
SILENE, SILEEN (f) Origin uncertain.
SILKY (f) *Old Norse* Smooth like silk.
SILVA (f) *Latin* Wood.
SILVAN (m) *Latin* Wood.
SILVANA (f) Feminine form of Silvan.
SILVER, SYLVER (m) *Old Norse* Precious metal name used as a first name.
SILVESTER, SYLVESTER (m) *Latin* Woody, rural.
SILVIA, SYLVIA, SILVIE (f) *Latin* Wood.
SIMA (f) *Arabic* Treasure.
SIMEON, SIM (m) *Hebrew* Listen attentively.
SIMBA (m) *Swahili* Lion.
SIMON, SI, CY (m) Two possible origins: 1. A form of Simeon; 2. *Greek* Snub-nosed.
SIMONE, SIMONA (f) French feminine form of Simon.

SIMPSON (m) Son of Simon.
SINA, SINAH (f) Forms of the *Gaelic* name Sine (Sheena).
SINCLAIR (m) From the *French* place-name St Clair.
SINDY *see* CINDY.
SINEAD (f) Irish form of Janet.
SIOBAN, SIOBHAN, SIOBHANA, CHAVONNE (f) Irish form of Joan.
SION (m) Welsh form of John.
SIOR (m) *Greek* Farmer.
SIRAN (m) Irish form of the Latin name Sigiranus.
SIRENA *see* SERENA.
SIRI (f) *Norman French* Conquering impulse.
SIRIOL (f) From the name of the star Sirius.
SIRION (m) A river in the Tolkien novel cycle.
SIS, SISSIE, SISSY (f) Diminutive forms of Cecilia (Cecile).
SITA (f) *Sanskrit* The wife of Rama in Hindu mythology.
SIVANA (f) *Assyrian* The ninth month of the Jewish calendar.
SIVIA (f) *Hebrew* A deer.
SKEETER (m) *Old English* The swift.
SKELLY (m) *Gaelic* Storyteller.
SKIPPER, SKIP (m) *Dutch* Captain of a ship.
SKY (f, rarely m) *Old Norse* The heavens.
SKY (m) *Old Norse* A form of Skee, meaning 'a projectile'.
SKYE (f) The Scottish island name used as a first name.
SLADE (m) *Old English* Valley or dell between woods.
SLIM (m) *Old English* Slime, mud.

SLOANE, SLOAN (m) *Celtic* Warrior.
SNOWDEN (m) *Old English* Place sheltered from snow.
SOFIA *see* SOPHIA.
SOL, SOLLY *see* SOLOMON.
SOLA (f) *Latin* The sun.
SOLACE (f) *Latin* To comfort.
SOLAIRE, SOLAYRE (f) A modern invention combining 'the sun' (Latin) with 'air', hence 'sunshine and air', implying good health.
SOLANA (f) A blend of Sola and Lana.
SOLANDA (f) A blend of Sola and Amanda.
SOLANDRA (f) A blend of Sola and Sandra.
SOLANE (f) A blend of Sola and Jane.
SOLANGE (f) *Italian* Alone, special.
SOLANN, SOLANNE (f) A blend of Sola and Anne.
SOLANTHA (f) A blend of Sola and Samantha.
SOLARA (f) A blend of Sola and Lara.
SOLAS *see* SOLACE.
SOLATA (f) A blend of Sola and Lata.
SOLEA (f) A blend of Sola and Lea.
SOLEILA (f) Two possible origins: 1. A blend of Sola and Leila; 2. *French* Sun.
SOLELLA, SOLEIL (f) *French* Sun.
SOLENA, SOLINA (f) Blends of Sola and Lena.
SOLINDA, SOLYNDA (f) Blends of Sola and Linda.
SOLITA (f) *Latin* Standard setter.
SOLITAIRE (f) *Latin* Alone.
SOLIZA (f) A blend of Sola and Liza.
SOLOLA (f) A blend of Sola and Lola.
SOLOMON, SOLOMAN (m) *Hebrew* Peace.
SOLORNA (f) A blend of Sola and Lorna.
SOLYN, SOLYNNE (f) A blend of Sola and Lyn.

SOMERBY (m) *Middle English* Village over there.

SOMERSET (m) *Old English* Dweller at Somerton (settlement used in summer).

SONA (f) *Gaelic* Happy.

SONDA (f) A blend of Sonia and Wanda.

SONDRA (f) A blend of Sonia and Sandra.

SONESTA (f) A blend of Sonia and Vesta.

SONGAN (m) *American Indian* Strong.

SONIA, SONYA, SONJA (f) Russian and Slavonic forms of Sophia.

SONNY, SONNIE (m) Colloquial name for a boy.

SONORA (f) From Gila-Sonora, an ethnic division of American Indians.

SONTARA (f) A blend of Sonia and Tara.

SONYA *see* SONIA.

SOOZI *see* SUSIE.

SOPHIA, SOPHIE (f) *Greek* Wisdom.

SOPHORA (f) From the name of the broadleaved tree.

SOPHRONIA (f) *Greek* Prudent.

SOPHY, SOPHIE *see* SOPHIA.

SORAYA (f) Persian name of uncertain origin.

SORCHA, SORSHA (f) *Irish* Bright.

SOREL, SORREL, SORELLE (f) *Old French* From the name of the herb sorrel.

SORKINA (f) A blend of Sorcha and Kina.

SPANGLE (f) *Dutch* Ornament.

SPECTRA (f) *Latin* Rainbow of colours, spectrum.

SPENCER (m) *Old English* Dispenser of provisions.

SPERLING (m) Origin uncertain.

SPIKE (m) *Middle English* Ear of grain.

SPINEL, SPINELLE (f) *French* From the jewel name.

Spring, Spryng   Stedman, Steadman

SPRING, SPRYNG (f) *Old English* The season name used as a first name.

SPRINGFIELD (m) *Old English* Pasture of dwellers by a spring.

SPRUCE (m) From the name of the coniferous tree.

SQUIRE (m) *Old French* Shield bearer.

STACI, STACY, STACIE (f) Diminutives of Anastasia.

STACY, STACEY (m) Diminutives of Eustace.

STACIA *see* STACI.

STAFFORD (m) *Old English* Ford near a landing place.

STAMFORD (m) Variant of Stanford.

STANDFORD, STANFORD (m) *Old English* Stony ford.

STANDISH (m) *Old English* Stony pasture.

STANFIELD (m) *Old English* Stony meadow.

STANHOPE (m) *Old English* Stony valley.

STANLEY, STAN (m) *Old English* Stony meadow.

STANNARD (m) *Old English* Stone hard.

STANTON (m) *Old English* Village near a stony field.

STANZI, STANSI (f) Origin uncertain.

STAR, STARR (f) *Old Norse* Celestial body, star.

STARCHILD (f) A modern invention combining 'star' and 'child'.

STARKIE (m) *Old English* Diminutive of Stark, meaning 'tough, harsh'.

STARLA (f) A blend of Star and Carla.

STARLYTE, STARLIGHT (f) *Old Norse* Light of the stars.

STASIA, STASSIA *see* ANASTASIA.

STEDMAN, STEADMAN (m) *Old English* Groom (steed-man).

STEFAN (m) Russian form of Stephen.
STEFANELLE (f) A blend of Stefanie and Ella.
STEFANIE, STEFFI (f) Feminine form of Stefan.
STELLA (f) *Latin* Star.
STELLAN (m) *Latin* Star.
STELLANDA (f) A blend of Stella and Amanda.
STELLANTHA (f) A blend of Stella and Samantha.
STELLARA (f) A blend of Stella and Lara.
STELLINA (f) A blend of Stella and Lina.
STELLINDA, STELLYNDA (f) Blends of Stella and Linda.
STELLISE (f) A blend of Stella and Elise.
STEPHAN (m) Hungarian form of Stephen.
STEPHANIE, STEFFI, STEVE (f) French feminine forms of Stephen.
STEPHEN, STEVEN (m) *Greek* Crown.
STEPHENE, STEPHENA (f) Feminine forms of Stephen.
STERLING (m) *Old English* Excellent quality.
STEVEN, STEVE, STEVIE, STEVENS, STEPHENS *see* STEPHEN.
STEWART *see* STUART.
STIRLING *see* STERLING.
ST JOHN, SINJON (m) The name of the saint used as a first name.
STORM (f) *Old Norse* Tempest, storm.
STRATFORD (m) *Old English* Ford on a Roman road.
STRATTON (m) *Old English* Place on a Roman road.
STROTHER (m) *Gaelic* Stream.
STRUAN (m) *Gaelic* Origin uncertain. Possibly 'stream'.
STUART (m) *Old English* A steward.

SUE *see* SUSAN.

SUDI, SUDY, SUDIE (f) *Old English* From the south.

SUELLA (f) A blend of Sue and Ella.

SUELLEN (f) A blend of Sue and Ellen.

SUGDEN (m) *Old English* Valley where sows are kept.

SUKEY, SUKIE, SUKY *see* SUSAN.

SUKINA (f) A blend of Suky and Kina.

SULA *see* SHULA.

SULAIKA (f) A blend of Sue and Laika.

SULLIVAN (m) *Irish* Black-eyed or hawk-eyed.

SULU (f) A blend of Sue and Lu.

SUMMER (f) *Old English* The season name used as a first name.

SUMNER, SUMNOR (m) *Latin* One who summons.

SUMMERTON (m) *Old English* Summer settlement.

SUNA (f) Origin uncertain.

SUNDANCE (f) The name of the American Indian dance used as a first name.

SUNDARAH (f) A blend of Suna and Darah.

SUNDEW (f) From the name of the flowering plant.

SUNEETHA (f) A blend of Suna and Aretha.

SUNITA (f) A blend of Suna and Nita.

SUNNY, SUNNIE (f) Usually a nickname for someone with a happy and 'sunny' disposition, but sometimes found as a first name.

SUNREY (m) Ray of sun.

SUNSHINE (f and m) Light of the sun.

SUNYA, SUNIA (f) Origin uncertain. Possibly a form of Sanaya.

SUPERBA (f) *Latin* Exquisite, superb.

SURAH (f) *French* Twilled silk.

Susan, Sue, Susie, Suzy — Symon

SUSAN, SUE, SUSIE, SUZY (f) *Hebrew* Lily.
SUSANA, SUSANNA, SUSANNAH, SUSANNE *see* SUSAN.
SUSANDA (f) A blend of Susan and Amanda.
SUSANTHA (f) A blend of Susan and Samantha.
SUSETTE (f) German form of the French diminutive of Susan.
SUSIE, SUSEY, SOOZI, SUSY *see* SUSAN.
SUSITA, SUZITA (f) Blends of Susan and Zita.
SUTA (m) *American Indian* Tough.
SUTCLIFFE (m) *Old English* Southern cliff.
SUZAN *see* SUSAN.
SUZANNA, SUZANNE, SUZANA (f) Blends of Susan and Anna.
SUZELLA, SUZELLE (f) Blends of Susan and Ella.
SUZETTA, SUZETTE *see* SUSETTE.
SUZY, SUZI *see* SUSAN.
SWITHIN (m) *Old English* Strong man.
SYBEL, SYBELLA, SYBIL, SYBILLE *see* SIBYL.
SYD *see* SYDNEY.
SYDNEY (m, rarely f) *see* SIDNEY.
SYDONIA *see* SIDONIA.
SYKIE (f) *Greek* Phonetic form of 'psyche' meaning 'soul, mind'.
SYLVESTER *see* SILVESTER.
SYLVETTE (f) Diminutive of Sylvia.
SYLVI, SYLVIE (f) Variants of Sylvia.
SYLVIA *see* SILVIA.
SYLVONIA (f) Variant of Silvia.
SYMON *see* SIMON.

T

Tab — Tyson

TAB (m) A short form of David.
TABATHA *see* TABITHA.
TABITHA, TABETHA, TABOTHA (f) *Aramaic* Gazelle.
TABOR, TABORI (m) *Persian* A drum.
TACE, TACEY, TACITA (f) *Latin* Silent.
TAD *see* THADDEUS.
TAFFI, TAFFY (m) Welsh nickname for David.
TAHUNA (f) *Maori* Beach.
TAI (m) *Chinese* Peace.
TAIMANA (f) *Maori* Diamond.
TAISHA (f) Variant of Tai.
TAKARA (f) *Japanese* Treasure.
TAL *see* TALIA.
TALAN (m) *Breton* Forehead.
TALANDA (f) A blend of Talia and Amanda.
TALANTHA (f) A blend of Talia and Samantha.
TALARA (f) A blend of Talia and Lara.
TALBOT (m) *Old English* Botolph's river.
TALCOTT (m) *Old English* Lakeside cottage.
TALDON (m) *Celtic/Old English* Lake near the hill.
TALFRYN (m) *Welsh* Brow of the hill.
TALI *see* TALIA.
TALIA (f, rarely m) Two possible origins. 1. *Aramaic* Young lamb; 2. *Hebrew* Dew.
TALIESIN (m) *Welsh* Radiant brow.

Talina   *Tamasin, Tamasine*

TALINA (f) A blend of Talia and Lina.

TALINDA (f) A blend of Talia and Linda.

TALIRA (f) A blend of Talia and Lira.

TALISA (f) A blend of Talia and Lisa.

TALISHA, TALICIA *see* TALITHA.

TALITA (f) A blend of Talia and Lita.

TALITHA (f) *Aramaic* Little girl.

TALLIS (f) A character in the novel *Lavondyss* by Robert Holdstock.

TALLULAH (f) *American Indian* Running water.

TALLY (f, rarely m) *see* TALIA.

TALMA (f) *Hebrew* Mound, hill.

TALMAN (m) *Aramaic* Deprive.

TALONA (f) A blend of Talia and Lona.

TALORA, TALOR (f) *Hebrew* Dew of the morning.

TALTRYN (m) Origin uncertain.

TALWYN (f) *Cornish* Fair brow.

TALYA *see* TALIA.

TAM *see* TAMSIN.

TAMANA (f) A blend of Tamsin and Lana.

TAMANDA (f) A blend of Tamsin and Amanda.

TAMANDRA, TAMANDRIA (f) Blends of Tamsin and Sandra.

TAMANTHA (f) A blend of Tamsin and Samantha.

TAMAR, THAMAR (f and m) *Hebrew* Date palm.

TAMARA (f) Feminine form of Tamar.

TAMARANTHA (f) A blend of Tamar and Samantha.

TAMARIN (f) *French* Small monkey.

TAMARIS *see* DAMARIS.

TAMARISK, TAMARIX (f) *Latin* From the name of the evergreen flowering shrub.

TAMAS *see* THOMAS.

TAMASIN, TAMASINE *see* TAMSIN.

TAMATH *see* TAMATHA.

TAMATHA, TAMASHA (f) *Arabic* To walk around.

TAMELDA (f) A blend of Tamsin and Imelda.

TAMELLA, TAMELLE (f) Blends of Tamsin and Ella.

TAMIA (f) A blend of Tam and Mia.

TAMILA (f) A blend of Tam and Mila.

TAMINA (f) A blend of Tam and Mina.

TAMLAN (m) *Scottish* Twin.

TAMLIN, TAMBLIN (m) Variants of Thomas.

TAMMY, TAMMIE, TAMME, TAMMI *see* TAMSIN.

TAMON (m) Guardian of the North in Japanese mythology.

TAMOR *see* TAMAR.

TAMORA (f) Feminine form of Tamor.

TAMSIN, TAMSYN, TAMASIN, TAMASINE (f) Variants of Thomasin.

TAMSON (f) Feminine form of Tamson, meaning 'Son of Thomas'.

TAMZYN, TAMZIN, TAMZINE *see* TAMSIN.

TANA *see* DANA.

TANAMARA (f) A blend of Tana and Mary.

TANDY (m) Diminutive of Andrew.

TANGA (f) A blend of the dances tango and rumba.

TANGERINE, TANGERENE, TANGERYNE (f) A deep orange colour, named from the fruit associated with Tangier.

TANGINA (f) Origin uncertain.

TANIA *see* TANYA.

TANIS, TANNIS, TANYS (f) Two possible origins: 1. Variant of Tanya; 2. From the biblical place name.

TANISHA (f) Possibly linked with a Hausa day name.

TANITA *see* TANITH.

TANITH, TANITHA (f) The goddess of love in Carthage.

TANJA *see* TANYA.

TANSY (f) *Greek* From the flower name. Immortality.

TANYA (f) Diminutive of Russian Tatiana, a feminine form of Tatius, the name of a Sabine king.

TAO (f and m) *Chinese* Life-force or life-essence.

TARA (f) Four possible origins: 1. *Irish* Hill; 2. *Sanskrit* Sparkling, star; 3. *Aramaic* To carry; 4. *Maori* Courage.

TARALYN, TARALYNDA (f) Blends of Tara and Lynda.

TARAN *see* TARYN.

TARAS (f) Variant of Tara.

TARATI (f) Maori form of Dorothy.

TARAZA (f) A character in the *Dune* sequence of novels by Frank Herbert.

TARETH (m) Origin uncertain. Possibly influenced by Gareth.

TARIKA (f) A blend of Tara and Rika.

TARIN, TARINA *see* TARYN.

TARNIA, TARNYA *see* TANYA.

TARO (m) *Japanese* Big boy.

TARQUIN *see* TORQUIL.

TARRA *see* TARA.

TARRAGON (m) *Greek* From the name of the herb.

TARU (f and m) *Sanskrit* Tree.

TARUM (f) *Sanskrit* Maiden.

TARUNA (m) *Sanskrit* Youth.

TARRY *see* TERRY.

TARYN, TARRYN, TARYNA (f) Blends of Tara and Lyn.

Tasha, Tashia, Tacha — Tenea

TASHA, TASHIA, TACHA *see* NATASHA.

TASMIN (f) A form of Tamsin.

TATIANA (f) Russian name based on that of a saint (*see* TANYA).

TATTANIA, TATANYA *see* TITANIA and TATIANA.

TATE (m) *Old English* Two possible origins: 1. A tenth, a tithing; 2. To be cheerful.

TATUM, TATHUM (m and f) Variants of Tate.

TAVIS (m) *Celtic* Son of David.

TAVITA, TEVITA, TAV (f) Feminine variants of David.

TAWANA (f) American Indian name of unknown meaning.

TAYLOR, TAY (m) *Old English* Worker with cloth, a tailor.

TAZ (m) *Arabic* Shallow cup.

TAZARA (f) A blend of Taz and Zara.

TEAGUE (m) *Celtic* Poet.

TEAL (m) *Middle English* Waterfowl, teal.

TEASDALE (m) *Old English* Valley of the river Tees.

TECCA (f) *Cornish* Fairer.

TED, TEDDY *see* EDWARD.

TEENA *see* TINA.

TEHYA (f) Origin uncertain.

TEISHA (f) Origin uncertain. Possibly a form of Tessa.

TELFORD (m) *Latin* Shallow stream.

TEMBA (f) *Zulu* Hope.

TEMIRA (f) *Hebrew* Tall.

TEMPEST (m) *Latin* Violent storm.

TEMPLE (m) *Latin* Holy sanctuary.

TENA *see* TINA.

TENEA (f) Origin uncertain. Possibly a form of Tena.

TENISHA (f) A blend of Tena and Trisha.

TENNESSEE (m) The name of the US State used as a first name.

TENNIEL (m) Origin uncertain. Perhaps a variant of Daniel.

TENNYSON, TENNY (m) Son of Dennis.

TERAH, TERA (f and m) *Latin* The Earth.

TERALL, TERREL, TERANCE *see* TERENCE.

TERANDA (f) A blend of Tera and Amanda.

TERANTHA (f) A blend of Tera and Samantha.

TEREE *see* TERRY.

TERELLA (f) A blend of Terri and Ella.

TERENA (f) A blend of Terri and Irene.

TERENCE, TERRY, TERRANCE (m) *Latin* A Roman clan name, meaning 'gracious'.

TERESA, THERESA, TESSA, TESS (f) *Greek* Summer.

TERESITA (f) Spanish diminutive of Teresa.

TERESSA (f) A blend of Teresa and Tessa.

TERETTA (f) Diminutive of Teresa.

TEREZA (f) Spanish form of Teresa.

TERICE (f) A blend of Terri and Patrice.

TERINA (f) A blend of Terri and Rina.

TERRAN, TERRON (m) Origin uncertain.

TERRANDA (f) A blend of Terri and Amanda.

TERRANTHA (f) A blend of Terri and Samantha.

TERRIE, TERRY, TERRI (f and m) *see* TERENCE or TERESA.

TERRYL, TERRIL (f) Variants of Terry.

TESHA (f) Origin uncertain. Possibly a form of Tessa.

TESMOND (m) *Old German* Protector.

TESS, TESSA, TESSIE *see* TERESA.

TETTY (f) A pet form of Elizabeth.

TEVITA (f) Fijian feminine form of David.
TEX (m, rarely f) Person from Texas.
TEXA (f) From Texas.
TEYA (f) Origin uncertain.
THADDEUS, THAD (m) Aramaic name of uncertain meaning. Possibly 'gift of God', derived from Greek.
THAISA (f) Origin uncertain. *Greek* Possibly a diminutive of Thalassa, meaning 'the sea'.
THALIA (f) *Greek* Blossom, plenty.
THANA, THANE (f) *Greek* Death.
THANIA see THANA.
THAYER (m) *Old German* The nation's army.
THEA (f) Two possible origins: 1. Form of Dorothea; 2. *Greek* Of God.
THECLA, THEKLA (f) *Greek* God-famed.
THEDA (f) A blend of Thea and Heda (Hedy).
THELMA (f) A character in the novel *Thelma* by Marie Corelli. Probably from Greek word meaning 'will'.
THEMA (f) *Greek* Subject or theme, melody.
THEO see THEODORE.
THEOBALD (m) *Old German* People-bold.
THEODORA (f) Feminine form of Theodore.
THEODORE (m) *Greek* God's gift.
THEODORIC (m) *Old German* Ruler of the people.
THEOLA (f) *Greek* Divine.
THEONE, THEONI (f) *Greek* Godly.
THEOPHILUS (m) *Greek* God-loved.
THEORA (f) *Greek* Watcher for God.
THERESA, TREZA, THERESSA see TERESA.
THERON (m) *Greek* A hunter.
THERSA see THIRZA.
THETIS (f) *Greek* To dispose.

THEYDON (m) *Old English* Valley where thatch is found.

THION (m) Origin uncertain. Perhaps a variant of Theron.

THIRZA (f) *Hebrew* Two possible origins: 1. Pleasantness; 2. Cypress tree.

THOM *see* THOMAS.

THOMAS, TAMAS, TOMOS, TOM, TOMMY (m) *Aramaic* A twin.

THOMASIN, THOMASINA, THOMASENA (f) Feminine forms of Thomas.

THOMAZIN, THOMASINE (f) Feminine forms of Thomas.

THOMPSON, THOMASON (m) Son of Thomas.

THOR (m) *Old Norse* The god of war in Norse mythology.

THORA (f) Two possible origins: 1. *Old Norse* Feminine form of Thor; 2. Variant of Thyra.

THOREN, THORIN (m) Variants of Thor.

THORLEY (m) *Old English* Thorn clearing.

THORNE (m) *Old English* Thorn, hawthorn.

THORNTON (m) *Old English* Village amongst thorns.

THORSTON *see* THURSTAN.

THURSDAY (f and m) *Old English* The day name used as a first name.

THURSTAN, THURSTON, THURSTYN (m) *Old English* Thor's stone.

THYRA, TYRA (f) *Old Norse* Thor's battle.

THYRZA *see* THIRZA.

TIA (f) *Spanish* Aunt.

TIARELLA (f) A blend of Tia and Ella.

TIBBY, TIBBIE (f) Origin uncertain.

Tiffany, Tiffanie — Tolan

TIFFANY, TIFFANIE (f) *Greek* Manifestation of God.

TIKA (f) *Maori* Just.

TILDA see MATILDA.

TILDEN (m) *Old English* Fertile valley.

TILLY, TILLA see MATILDA.

TILMAN (m) Two possible origins: 1. *Old English* Tile maker; 2. *Old English* Farmer, tiller of the land.

TIM, TIMMY see TIMOTHY.

TIMA, TIMI, see TIMORA.

TIMOLYN, TIMOLIN (f) A blend of Timi and Lyn.

TIMON (m) A character in Shakespeare's play *Timon of Athens*.

TIMORA (f) *Hebrew* Tall.

TIMOTHY, TIM (m) *Greek* Honouring God.

TINA, TEENA, TINAH see CHRISTINA or MARTINA.

TINESSE (f) A blend of Tina and Jesse.

TIRA (f) *Hebrew* Encampment.

TIRZAH see THIRZAH.

TISA (f) Origin uncertain.

TISHA see LETITIA.

TITANIA, TITANYA (f) *Greek* Great one.

TITUS (m) Roman name of uncertain meaning.

TIVIAN, TIVON, TIBON (m) *Hebrew* Lover of nature.

TIVONA, TIVONI (f) Feminine form of Tivian.

TOBE see TOBY.

TOBIAS (m) *Hebrew* God is good.

TOBIRA (f) From the plant name.

TOBY, TOBI see TOBIAS.

TODD (m) *Old English* Fox hunter.

TOLAN (m) *Old French* Land on the river Tone.

TOLMAN (m) *Old English* Collector of tolls.
TOM, TOMMY, TOMMIE see THOMAS.
TOMASINA see THOMASINA.
TOMMINA (f) Feminine form of Thomas.
TONDA (f) A blend of Toni and Wanda.
TONEY see TONI.
TONI, TONIA, TONINA, TONJA see ANTOINETTE or ANTONIA.
TONY see ANTHONY.
TONYA, TONIA see ANTONIA.
TOORA (f) Origin uncertain.
TOPAZ (f) *Greek* From the name of the precious stone.
TOPSY, TOPSEY, TOPSIE (f) A character in the novel *Uncle Tom's Cabin* by Harriet Beecher Stowe.
TORA (f) *Japanese* Tiger.
TORAN, TORN, TORRANCE (m) Irish forms of Terrance.
TORANDA (f) A blend of Tora and Amanda.
TORANTHA (f) A blend of Tora and Samantha.
TORBEN, TORBAN (m) *Old English* Bean hill.
TORI (f) *Maori* Cat.
TORIA (f) *Old English* Hill.
TORIN (m) *Italian* From Torino (Turin) in Italy.
TORINA, TORINE (f) Feminine form of Torin.
TORQUIL (m) *Old Norse* Thor's cauldron.
TORREYA (f) From the name of the nutmeg tree.
TOTTIE, TOTTY, TOTI (f) Diminutive forms of Charlotte.
TOVA, TOVAH (f) *Hebrew* Good.
TOWNSEND (m) *Old English* End of the town.
TOYA (f) *Sioux* Green.

TOYAH (f) A Scottish name for a type of woman's headdress.

TRACY, TRACEY, TRACI (f) Forms of Teresa.

TRACY (m) *Norman French* From the Norman place-name.

TRAFFORD (m) *Old English* Ford in a valley.

TRAHERN (m) *Welsh* Strong as iron.

TRANCER (f) Origin uncertain. Perhaps a form of 'entrancer'.

TRAVERS (m) *Old English* Tollbridge keeper.

TRAVIS *see* TRAVERS.

TRAYTON (m) *Old English* Village near trees.

TREASA (f) *Irish* Strength.

TREBOR (m) Welsh form of Robert which is also a backspelling of the name.

TRECIA *see* PATRICIA.

TREENA *see* KATRINA.

TREFOR *see* TREVOR.

TRELAWNEY (m) *Cornish* Church village.

TRELLA (f) Variant of Estrella, the Spanish form of Esther.

TRENA, TRENNA *see* KATRINA.

TRENT (m) *Welsh/Irish* River name meaning 'journey through'.

TRENTON (m) *French* Thirty.

TRESA *see* TERESA.

TRESSA (f) *Cornish* Third.

TREVOR, TREFOR (m) *Welsh* Great or sea homestead.

TREVYN (m) A blend of Trevor and Mervyn.

TREYA (f) Origin uncertain.

TREZA *see* TERESA.

TRICIA, TRYCIA, TRISH *see* PATRICIA.

TRILBY (f) A character in the novel *Trilby* by George Du Maurier.

TRILLOW (f) *Old English* From the Devon place-name.

TRINA *see* KATRINA.

TRINETTE (f) *Greek* Purity.

TRINITA (f) *Latin* Threefold, the Trinity.

TRINITY *see* TRINITA.

TRIONA *see* KATRIONA.

TRISHA, TRISH, TRISSIE *see* PATRICIA.

TRISTA (f) *Latin* Woman of sadness.

TRISTAN, TRYSTAN (m) Cornish name of uncertain meaning.

TRISTRAM (m) Form of Tristan.

TRIUNE (f) *Latin* Threefold.

TRIX, TRIXIE, TRIXY *see* BEATRIX.

TROY (m) Two possible origins: 1. *Irish* Foot soldier; 2. From the name of the ancient city.

TRUGAREDD (f) *Welsh* Loving kindness.

TRUDY, TRUDIE, TRUDI, TRUDA *see* GERTRUDE.

TRULA (f) Probably a variant of Gertrude.

TRUMAN (m) *Old English* Faithful man.

TRUVY (f) Origin uncertain. Possibly a diminutive of Tryphena.

TRYPHENA (f) *Greek* Delicacy.

TUDOR (m) Welsh form of Theodore.

TUELLA (f) Origin uncertain.

TUESDAY (f) *Old English* The day name used as a first name.

TULEDA (f) A blend of Tully and Leda.

TULIP (f) *Persian* From the flower name.

TULLY (m, rarely f) *Latin* A diminutive of Tullis, meaning 'a title'.

TURAS (m) Origin uncertain.

Turlough   Tyson

TURLOUGH (m) Origin uncertain. *Old English* Perhaps 'warriors' burial mound'.

TURNER (m) *Latin* Craftsman working with a lathe.

TURQUOISE (f) A jewel name. *Old French* Gem from Turkey.

TUSHKA (f) Origin uncertain.

TUSSOCK (m) *Old English* From the name of the moth.

TWILA (f) *Middle English* A modern invention echoing 'twilight'.

TY *see* TYRONE, TYLER or TYSON.

TYANN (f) A blend of Tyrus and Ann.

TYLER (m) *Middle English* Roof builder.

TYM *see* TIMOTHY.

TYMON *see* TIMON.

TYNA (f) *Gaelic* Dark grey.

TYNDALL (m) *Old English* Everlasting light.

TYNE (f) *Welsh* River name meaning 'to flow'.

TYRONE, TYRON (m) The Irish county name used as a first name.

TYSON (m) Son of Ty.

Udele U Uta

UDELE (f) *Old English* Great wealth.
UFFA, ULFA (m) Forms of Ulrich.
ULA (f) *Celtic* Sea jewel.
ULANI (f) *Hawaiian* Merry.
ULEMA (f) *Arabic* To know.
ULLA (f) *Middle English* To fill (a cask etc).
ULRICH, ULRICK (m) *Danish* Wolf.
ULYSSES (m) Origin uncertain. *Greek* Possibly 'the angry one'.
UMA (f) Origin uncertain. Possibly a form of Una.
UNA, OONA (f) *Latin* One.
UNDINE, UNDINA (f) *Latin* A wave. In mythology, a female water spirit.
UNI (f) *Latin* One.
UNICE see EUNICE.
UNITA (f) *Italian* Unity.
UNITY (f) *Latin* Unity.
UPTON (m) *Old English* Upper village.
URBAN (m) *Latin* Of the city.
URIAH (m) *Hebrew* My light is the Lord.
URSA (f) *Latin* She-bear.
URSULA, URSALA (f) Diminutives of Ursa.
USHA (f) Origin uncertain.
UTA, YUTTA (f) *Spanish* Mountain dwellers.

Vail **V** *Vyvyan*

VAIL (m) *Latin* Valley.
VAL see Valerie, Valentine, etc.
VALARIE see Valerie.
VALDA, VELDA (f) *Old German* Battle heroine.
VALDIS (m) *Old German* Lively in battle.
VALE (f) *Old English* Valley.
VALEDA (f) *Old German* Wholesome.
VALENCE (m) *Latin* Vigorous.
VALENE (f) Perhaps a diminutive of Valerie.
VALENTIA, VALENCIA (f) *Latin* Vigorous.
VALENTINA (f) Feminine form of Valentine.
VALENTINE (m) *Latin* Vigorous.
VALERIA (f) Feminine form of Valerian.
VALERIAN (m) *Latin* To be strong.
VALERIE, VAL (f) French form of Latin name Valeria.
VALETTA (f) From the Maltese place-name.
VALI (f) Origin uncertain.
VALMA, VALMAY, VALMAI (f) *Welsh* May-flower.
VALMOND (m) *Old German* Strong protection.
VALONIA (f) *Latin* Acorn.
VALORA (f) *Latin* To be strong.
VALORIE see Valerie.
VAN (m) *Old English* Two possible origins:
    1. A boundary; 2. High.
VANCE (m) *Old English* High places.

VANDA *see* WANDA.

VANECIA *see* VANESSA.

VANESSA (f) Two possible origins: 1. *Greek* Butterfly; 2. The invention of Jonathan Swift from the elements of the surname 'Van Homrigh' and the first name 'Esther' of a woman friend.

VANETTA, VANETTE, VANNETA (f) Diminutives of Vanessa.

VANIA (f) Feminine form of Ivan (John).

VANINA (f) A blend of Vania and Nina.

VANNA (f) A character in the novel *Orion Shall Rise* by Poul Anderson.

VANORA (f) *Celtic* White wave.

VANTON (m) *Old English* Vane's settlement.

VANYA (m) Russian form of John.

VARDA (f) *Hebrew* Rose.

VARDON, VARDEN (m) *Old English* Green hill.

VARELLA (f) A blend of Varda and Ella.

VARENA *see* VARINA.

VARETTA (f) Diminutive of Varda.

VARINA (f) A blend of Varda and Rina.

VARUNA (f) A blend of Varda and Una.

VAS (m) Origin uncertain.

VASARA (f) *Sanskrit* Morning.

VARSHA (f) *Sanskrit* Rain.

VASHTI, VASSY (f) *Persian* Beautiful.

VAUGHAN, VAUGHN (m) *Welsh* Little.

VAY (f) Diminutive of Veigh.

VEDA (f) *Sanskrit* Knowledge.

VEDETTE (f) *Italian* Sentinel.

VEENA (f) *Sanskrit* A sitar (Indian stringed instrument).

VEIGH (f) Origin uncertain.

VELA (f) *Greek* Sails.
VELANDA (f) A blend of Vela and Amanda.
VELANTHA (f) A blend of Vela and Samantha.
VELDA *see* VALDA.
VELIA (f) From the Greek place-name.
VELINDA (f) A blend of Vela and Linda.
VELINTHA (f) A blend of Vela and Melintha.
VELMA *see* WILHELMINA.
VELVET (f) *Middle English* The fabric name used as a first name.
VENA, VENEA (f) *Latin* A vein.
VENESSA *see* VANESSA.
VENETA, VENETIA, VENITA, VENETTA (f) *Latin* Woman of Venice.
VENTURA (f) *Spanish* Good fortune.
VENUS (f) *Greek* To love. The goddess of love in Greek mythology.
VERA (f) *Latin* Truth.
VERADA (f) *Latin* Truthful, forthright.
VERDA (f) *Old French* Green, springlike.
VERDANT (m) *Latin* Green, springlike.
VERDUN, VERDON (m) From the French place-name.
VERE (m) *Latin* Truth.
VERELLA (f) A blend of Vera and Ella.
VERENA, VERINA, VERITY, VERITA (f) *Latin* Truth.
VERLIE, VERLEY (m) From the French place-name.
VERLIN (m) *Latin* Spring.
VERNA (f) *Latin* Truth.
VERNETTA (f) Diminutive of Verna.
VERNON (m) *Old French* Alder tree.

VERON, VERONA *see* VERONICA.
VERONICA, VERONYKA (f) Two possible origins: 1. Form of Berenice; 2. *Latin* True image.
VESTA (f) Goddess of fire in Roman mythology.
VETA, VETTA (f) Slavonic form of Elizabeth.
VEVINA (f) *Gaelic* Sweet woman.
VIAN *see* VIVIAN or OCTAVIAN.
VIANNEY (f) Origin uncertain.
VICKI, VIKI *see* VICTORIA.
VICTOR (m) *Latin* Victory.
VICTORIA, VICKY, VICKIE, VIKI (f) *Latin* Victory.
VICTORINE (f) French diminutive of Victoria.
VIDA (f) Two possible origins: 1. *Spanish* Life; 2. Variant of Davida.
VIDAL (m) *Latin* Variant of Vitas, meaning 'life'.
VIDETTE (f) Diminutive of Vida.
VIJAY (m) *Sanskrit* Victory.
VIKKI *see* VICTORIA.
VIKRAM (m) *Sanskrit* Record-breaker.
VILA (f) *Latin* A farm.
VILETTE (f) *Latin* Diminutive of Vila, meaning 'a farm'.
VILMA *see* VELMA.
VINA *see* LAVINA or DAVINA.
VINCE *see* VINCENT.
VINCENT (m) *Latin* To conquer.
VINNA (f) *Old English* The vine.
VINSON (m) Son of Vincent.
VIOLA, VI (f) A flower name. *Latin* Violet.
VIOLET, VI (f) *Middle English* From the flower name.
VIOLETTE, VIOLETTA (f) Diminutives of Violet or Viola.

VIRENDA (f) Origin uncertain.
VIRGIL (m) *Latin* Strong.
VIRGINIA (f) Two possible origins: 1. The Roman clan name Verginius, linked with Virgil; 2. *Latin* Untouched, pure.
VITA (f) *Latin* Life.
VITARA (f) A blend of Vita and Tara.
VITESSE (f) *French* Swiftness.
VIV see VIVIAN or VIVIEN.
VIVEKA (f) *Sanskrit* Discrimination.
VIVIAN (m) *Latin* Alive.
VIVIAN, VYVIAN, VYVYAN, VIV (f) *Latin* Alive.
VIVIANA (f) Russian form of Vivienne.
VIVIEN, VIVIENNE, VIV (f) *Latin* Alive, lively.
VOLANTA, VOLANTE (f) *Italian* Flying.
VOLETTA see VIOLETTA.
VONA, VONDA see WANDA.
VONNE see YVONNE.
VONORA (f) A blend of Vona and Nora.
VYNDRA (f) Origin uncertain. Possibly a form of Vinna.
VYVIAN, VYVYAN see VIVIAN.

Wade **W** *Wystan*

WADE (m) *Old English* River crossing.

WADHAM (m) *Old English* Homestead with a shallow lake.

WADSWORTH (m) *Old English* Farm with a shallow lake.

WAINWRIGHT (m) *Old English* Wagon maker.

WAKEFIELD (m) *Old English* Field for the yearly wake (festival).

WALCOTT (m) *Old English* Cottage of the Welsh.

WALDEN (m) *Old French* Woods.

WALDO, WALDRON (m) *Old English* Ruler.

WALFORD (m) *Old English* Stream ford.

WALKER (m) *Old English* One who cleans and thickens cloth.

WALLACE, WALLIS (m) *Old French* Stranger.

WALLY *see* WALTER or WALLACE.

WALT *see* WALTER.

WALTER, WALT, WAT (m) *Old German* Ruling people.

WALTON (m) *Old English* Walled village.

WANAKA, WANIKA (f) Hawaiian forms of Wanda.

WANDA, WENDA (f) Two possible origins: 1. *Slavonic* Traveller, wanderer; 2. *Old Norse* A young tree.

WANETTA (f) *Old English* Young pale one.

WARD (m) *Old English* Watchman.

WARNER (m) *Old French* Park-keeper.

WARREN (m) *Middle English* To preserve.

WARRENE (f) Feminine form of Warren.

WARWICK (m) *Welsh* Hero.

WASHINGTON (m) *Old English* Watery site.

WAT, WATS *see* WALTER.

WATKIN (m) *Celtic* A ford.

WATSON (m) Son of Wat.

WAYLAND, WAYLON (m) *Old English* Land near the highway.

WAYNE (m) *Welsh* A meadow.

WEBSTER (m) *Old English* Weaver.

WELBY (m) *Old English* Village near willow trees.

WELDON (m) *Old English* Willow trees on the hill.

WENDA (f) *Welsh* Fair and good.

WENDELL (m) *Welsh* Good valley.

WENDELIN, WENDELINE (f) *Old English* The Wanderer.

WENDIE, WENDI *see* WENDY.

WENDY (f) Invented by J. M. Barrie for the play *Peter Pan*, and based on the phrase 'friendy-wendy'.

WENNA (f) Latinized form of Gwen used in Cornwall.

WENONA, WENONAH (f) Two possible origins: 1. *Old English* Joy; 2. *American Indian* First-born daughter.

WENSLEY (m) *Old English* Clearing sacred to Woden.

WENTWORTH (m) *Old English* Homestead occupied in winter.

WERNER *see* WARREN.

WES *see* WESLEY.

WESLEY (m) *Old English* West meadow.

WESTBOURNE, WESTBROOK (m) *Old English* West stream.
WESTLEIGH (m) *Old English* West meadow.
WESTON (m) *Old English* Western village.
WEXEL (m) Origin uncertain.
WHALLEY (m) *Old English* Wood on a hill.
WHARTON (m) *Old English* Farm near the shore.
WHEATLEY, WHITLEY, WHIT (m) *Old English* Wheat field.
WHITNEY (m only in UK; m and f in USA) *Old English* Land near the water.
WHITTAKER (m) *Old English* Small acreage.
WILBER, WILBUR (m) *Old English* Willow town.
WILBERT (m) *Old English* Bright willows.
WILBY *see* WILBER.
WILDON (m) *Old English* Curving valley.
WILEY (m) *Old English* Willow field.
WILFORD (m) *Old English* Willow trees near a ford.
WILFRID, WILFRED, WILFRYD (m) *Old English* Hope for peace.
WILHELMINA, MINA (f) German feminine form of Wilhelm.
WILKINSON (m) Surname linked to William.
WILL, WILLY, WILLIE *see* WILLIAM.
WILLA (f) *Old English* Desirable.
WILLARD (m) *Old English* Willow yard.
WILLIAM, WILLIE, BILL (m) *Old German* Will-helmet, hence 'resolute protector'.
WILLIS (m) Surname linked to William.
WILLOUGHBY (m) *Old English* Farm near the willows.
WILLOW (f, rarely m) *Old English* From the tree name. The name of the hero in the film *Willow*.

Wilma   Wyatt

WILMA see WILHELMINA.
WILMOT (m) Surname linked to William.
WILONA (f) *Old English* Desired.
WILSON (m) Son of Will.
WILTON (m) *Old English* Farm near the willow trees.
WIM, WIN (m) *Old French* Victory.
WINDSOR (m) *Old English* River bank with a winch.
WINEFRED see WINIFRED.
WINFIELD (m) *Old English* Successful field (of battle).
WINFRED, WINFORD (m) *Old English* Peaceful friend.
WINGATE (m) *Old English* Victory gate.
WINIFRED, FREDA, WINNIE, WIN, WYN (f) *Welsh* Blessed reconciliation.
WINMER (m) *Old English* Famous friend.
WINOLA (f) *Old German* Gracious friend.
WINONA, WINONAH (f) *American Indian* First-born daughter.
WINSLADE (m) *Old English* Friend's stream.
WINSLOW (m) *Old English* Friend's hill.
WINSTON (m) *Old English* Wine's (or Friend's) farm.
WINTHROP (m) *Old English* Friendly village.
WINWOOD (m) *Old English* Friend's wood.
WIRA (f) *Celtic* Lady of the castle.
WOLFGANG (m) *German* 'Wolf strife'.
WOODROW (m) *Old English* Row of cottages in a wood.
WOODSTOCK (m) *Old English* Place in the woods.
WOODY see WOODROW.
WRIGHT (m) *Old English* An artisan.
WYATT (m) Norman form of Guy.

WYBERT (m) *Old German* Battle bright.
WYLIF (m) Origin uncertain. Possibly a form of Wilfrid.
WYMAN, WYMOND (m) *Old English* Battle protector.
WYNDHAM (m) *Old English* Wyman's farm.
WYNFORD, WENFORD (m) *Welsh* White torrent.
WYNN (f) *Welsh* White, pure.
WYNNE, WYN (m and f) *Welsh* White, pure.
WYNTON (m) *Welsh/Old English* White farm.
WYNYARD (m) *Old English* Vineyard.
WYONA (f) Origin uncertain.
WYSTAN (m) *Old English* Battle stone.

Xanthe  Xylvia

XANTHE, XAN (f) *Greek* Yellow.
XAVIER (m) *Spanish* New house.
XENA, CENA, XENIA (f) *Greek* Hospitable.
XYLLA, XYLVIA *see* SYLVIA.

Yakira **Y** *Yvonne*

YAKIRA (f) Origin uncertain.
YALE (m) *Old English* Fertile upland.
YALONDA *see* YOLANDE.
YAMA (f) *Sanskrit* Path, way.
YAN *see* JOHN.
YANCY (m) *French* Englishman.
YAPHET *see* JAPHET.
YARDLEY (m) *Old English* A yard.
YARROW (f) *Old English* From the name of the flowering plant.
YASMIN *see* JASMINE.
YASNA (f) Origin uncertain.
YAVIN (m) *Hebrew* God will understand.
YAZ (f) Origin uncertain. Possibly a form of Yasna.
YEDA (f) *Hebrew* Heart's ease.
YEHUDI (m) Hebrew form of Judah.
YELENA (f) *Latin* Lily blossom.
YEO (m) *Old English* River stream.
YESSICA *see* JESSICA.
YESTEN, YESTIN (m) Cornish form of the Latin name Justus, linked to Justin.
YETTA *see* HENRIETTA.
YOKO (f) *Japanese* Ocean child or sun child.
YOLANA (f) Variant of Yolanda.
YOLANDA, YOLANDE, YOLA (f) *Greek* Violet flower.

Yolandra   Yvonne

YOLANDRA (f) A blend of Yolanda and Sandra.
YOLANTA (f) Variant of Yolanda.
YOLANTHA (f) A blend of Yolanda and Samantha.
YOLARA (f) A blend of Yolanda and Lara.
YOLINA (f) A blend of Yolanda and Lina.
YOLITHA (f) A blend of Yolanda and Talitha.
YOLONDA (f) A blend of Yolanda and Londa.
YONA (f) Feminine form of Jonah.
YOOTHA (f) Phonetic form of 'youth'.
YORATH (m) English form of the Welsh name Iorwerth, meaning 'worthy lord'.
YORICK (m) From Shakespeare's *Hamlet*. Probably a phonetic version of the Danish form of George.
YORK (m) *Celtic* Yew tree estate.
YSABELLE *see* ISABEL.
YUL (m) *Mongolian* Beyond the horizon.
YULAN (f) *Chinese* Jade orchid.
YURI *see* URIAH.
YUTA *see* JUDITH.
YVELDA (f) A blend of Yvette and Velda.
YVELLA (f) A blend of Yvette and Ella.
YVES (m) *Scandinavian* An archer.
YVETTE, EVETTE (f) *Old French* Feminine form of Ivo, meaning 'archer'.
YVINA (f) Origin uncertain. Possibly a variant of Yvonne.
YVIKA (f) Origin uncertain.
YVONNE (f) *Scandinavian* An archer.

Zabrina Z Zilpah

ZABRINA see SABRINA.

ZACCHAEUS (m) Two possible origins: 1. *Hebrew* A form of Zachariah; 2. *Aramaic* Pure.

ZACHARIAH, ZACHARIAS, ZACKERY, ZACK, ZAK (m) *Hebrew* Jehovah has remembered.

ZACHARY, ZACHERY see ZACHARIAH.

ZADAH (f) *Arabic* Prosperous.

ZADE (m) *Yiddish* Grandfather.

ZADIA (f) Feminine form of Zade.

ZADH, ZADHA see ZADAH.

ZADINA (f) A blend of Zade and Dina.

ZADOK, ZADOC (m) *Hebrew* Righteous.

ZADORA see ISADORA.

ZAHEERA, ZEHAVA (f) *Hebrew* Golden.

ZAHRA see SARAH.

ZAHRINA (f) Perhaps a form of Zarina.

ZAIDA, ZAIGA (f) Two possible origins: 1. *Yiddish* Grandfather; 2. *Spanish* Heron.

ZAHARI (m) Origin uncertain. Possibly a form of Zahri.

ZAKA (f) *Hebrew* Bright, clear.

ZAKINA, ZAKIRA (f) A blend of Zala and Kina or Kira.

ZAKIYA, ZAKYA (f) *Arabic* Intelligent.

ZALA (f) *Spanish* Greeting.

ZALINA (f) A blend of Zala and Lina.

ZALORA (f) A blend of Zala and Lora.
ZAMIA (f) The Jamaica sago tree.
ZAMIR (m) *Hebrew* Song.
ZAMORA *see* SAMORA.
ZAN (f) Origin uncertain. Possibly a form of Zanna.
ZANA (f) A character in the novel *Unbalanced Earth* by Jonathan Wylie.
ZANDER *see* ALEXANDER.
ZANDOR *see* SANDOR.
ZANDORA (f) Feminine form of Zandor.
ZANDRA *see* SANDRA.
ZANE (m) *Italian* A clown.
ZANETA, ZANETTA (f) A blend of Zane and Netta.
ZANNA (f) A blend of Zane and Anna.
ZARA, ZARAH (f) *Arabic* Splendour.
ZARALA (f) A blend of Zara and Rala.
ZARANDA (f) A blend of Zara and Amanda.
ZARANNA (f) A blend of Zara and Anna.
ZARANTHA (f) A blend of Zara and Samantha.
ZAREBA (f) An enclosure. Sudanese name of uncertain origin.
ZARED (m) *Hebrew* Ambush.
ZARELLA (f) A blend of Zara and Ella.
ZARETTA (f) Diminutive of Zara.
ZARIA (f) Dawn in Slavonic mythology.
ZARINA (f) Spanish form of Tsarina, meaning 'Empress'.
ZARISA, ZARISSA (f) Blends of Zara and Lisa or Clarissa.
ZARISHA (f) A blend of Zara and Risha.
ZARITA (f) A blend of Zara and Rita.
ZAROLA (f) A blend of Zara and Lola.
ZARONA (f) A blend of Zara and Rona.
ZASU *see* ZAZA.

Zathara   Zenaide

ZATHARA (f) Invented for an American radio soap opera in the 1930s.
ZAVIER *see* XAVIER.
ZAZA (f) *Hebrew* Movement.
ZAZIE (f) A character in the novel *Zazie* by Raymond Quen.
ZAZILIE *see* CECILY.
ZEA (f) *Latin* The herb rosemary.
ZEBA (f) Origin uncertain. Possibly a form of Zebrina.
ZEBEDEE (m) *Hebrew* Gift of God.
ZEBRINA (f) From the name of the flowering herb.
ZECHARIAH *see* ZACHARIAH.
ZEDEKIAH (m) *Hebrew* God is righteous.
ZEDRIC *see* CEDRIC.
ZEENA *see* ZINA.
ZEFIRA (f) *Italian* Breeze, zephyr.
ZEHARA (f) *Hebrew* Light.
ZEKE, ZEEK *see* ZECHARIAH.
ZELAH (f) Origin uncertain.
ZELDA *see* GRISELDA.
ZELIA (f) *Latin* Zealous.
ZELICK, ZELIG, SELIG (m) *Old English* Blessed, holy.
ZELIE (f) *Greek* Ardent.
ZELINDA, ZERLINDA (f) *Hebrew/Latin* Beautiful dawn.
ZELINKA (f) A blend of Zelia and Linka.
ZELLA, ZELLY *see* ZELIA.
ZELMA (f) A blend of Zaida, Ella and Mark.
ZEMA, ZEMIRA, ZEMORA (f) *Hebrew* A branch.
ZEN (m) *Japanese* Meditation.
ZENA (f) *Persian* Woman.
ZENAIDE (f) Variant of Zena.

Zenana   Zinevra

ZENANA (f) *Sanskrit* Women's quarters.
ZENDA (f) *Persian* Sacred.
ZENNA *see* ZENA.
ZENO (m) *Greek* Sign, symbol.
ZENKA (f) *Slavonic* Ice glade.
ZENOBIA (f) *Greek* Power of Zeus.
ZENON (m) *Greek* Gift of Zeus.
ZEONA *see* ZIONA.
ZEPHANIAH (m) Hebrew name of uncertain meaning.
ZEPHIRA (f) *Hebrew* Morning.
ZEQUINA, ZEQUINHA (f) Origin uncertain.
ZERELDA (f) A blend of Zephira and Imelda.
ZERLINA, ZELINA (f) Forms of Zelia.
ZERLINDA *see* ZELINDA.
ZETA (f) *Hebrew* An olive.
ZETAN (m) Masculine form of Zeta.
ZETTA, ZETTE *see* ZETA.
ZEVA (f) *Hebrew* Wolf.
ZEVAN, ZIVAN (m) *Slavonic* Lively.
ZEZIA (f) Origin uncertain. Possibly a form of Zaza.
ZHENYA (f) Origin uncertain. Possibly a form of Zena.
ZIA (f) *Hebrew* To tremble.
ZIGENA (f) *Italian* Moth.
ZIGGY *see* SIGMUND.
ZILAH, ZILLAH (f) *Hebrew* Shadow.
ZILIA (f) *Hebrew* My shadow.
ZILPAH (f) *Hebrew* Sprinkling.
ZILVIA *see* SILVIA.
ZIMARRA (f) *Italian* Long coat.
ZIMRA, ZIMRI, ZIMRIA (f) *Hebrew* A song.
ZINA *see* ZINNIA.
ZINEVRA (f) *Celtic* White wave.

Zingara — Zowie

ZINGARA (f) *Italian* Gypsy.
ZINNIA (f) A flowering plant named after the German botanist J. G. Zinn.
ZION, ZIO (m) From the Hebrew *siyon*, the name of the hill on which Jerusalem was built.
ZIONA (f) *Hebrew* Excellent.
ZIPPORAH (f) *Hebrew* A bird.
ZIRA (f) *Hebrew* An arena.
ZITA *see* THERESA.
ZITO (m) *Greek* To seek.
ZIVA (f) *Greek* To seek.
ZIVANA (f) *Slavonic* Lively.
ZOANNA (f) A blend of Zoe and Anna.
ZOBA (f) *Old German* Daughter of the ruler.
ZOE (f) *Greek* Life.
ZOHAR (m) *Hebrew* Radiant light.
ZOHARA (f) *Hebrew* Light.
ZOLA (f) *Greek* Duty.
ZOLLY *see* SOLOMON.
ZOLTAN (m) *Arabic* Variant of Sultan, meaning 'ruler'.
ZONA (f) *Latin* Sound.
ZONIA *see* SONIA.
ZORA, ZORAH (f) *Arabic* Dawn.
ZORAN, ZORIN (m) Origin uncertain.
ZORANA (f) Feminine form of Zoran.
ZORELLA (f) A blend of Zora and Ella.
ZORINDA (f) A blend of Zora and Lorinda.
ZORITA (f) *Spanish* Wood pigeon.
ZORNA (f) A blend of Zora and Lorna.
ZORYA *see* ZARIA.
ZOSIMA (f) *Greek* Riches.
ZOWIE (f) Variant of Zoe.
ZOWIE (m) Origin uncertain.

ZSA ZSA (f) *Hebrew* Princess.
ZUBA, AZUBA, AZUBAH (f) *Hebrew* Biblical name of uncertain meaning.
ZULEIKA (f) *Arabic* Beautiful.
ZULEMA (f) *Arabic* Peace.
ZUMA see ZUMAYA.
ZUMAYA (f) *Spanish* Barn owl.
ZWANDA see WANDA.
ZYLA, ZYLLA see ZYLPHA.
ZYLPHA, ZILPAH (f) *Hebrew* Sprinkling.

Concept Index

This index is restricted to names that have a direct link to an idea or concept. Proper names, patronymics and place-names are *not* given here. (*See also* the Special Category Index on page 312).

ABBEY Abbot
ACTIVE Disa, Malca (*see also* LIVELY)
ADORED Gertrude, Lais (*see also* BELOVED)
ADVISE, ADVISER Eldridge, Monica (*see also* COUNSELLOR)
AFFECTION, AFFECTIONATE Charity, Philemon (*see also* LOVE)
AIR Solaire
ALDER TREE Alder, Aldridge, Alford, Delaney, Ellery, Nairn
ALIVE Vernon, Vivian, Vivienne (*see also* LIVE, LIVELY)
ALL Ella
ALMOND Almon
ALONE Isola, Monica, Solange, Solitaire
ALWAYS Aina, Kushuma
AMAZING Mazana
AMBUSH Zared
AMIABLE Craddock, Mingo, Mungo
AMOROUS Delilah
ANCESTOR Olaf, Olave, Oleta

The Pan Guide to Babies' Names

ANCIENT Priscilla
ANGEL Aingeal, Anahera, Angela, Arella, Deva, Ingram
ANGRY Ulysses
ANIMAL LOVER Derwin
ANNOUNCE Delmelda
ANOINTED Levani
ANVIL Anyon
APRIL Ebrel
ARCHER *see* BOWMAN
ARDENT, ARDOUR Idris, Rhys, Zelie
AREA Sherlock
ARENA Zira
ARMOUR Byrne, Serle
ARMY Alvar, Harcourt, Harold, Harva, Harvey, Herbert, Hereward, Rayner, Thayer (*see also* BATTLE, SOLDIER, WARRIOR)
ARROW Alvira, Flann, Fletcher
ARTISAN Wright
ASCEND Aliya
ASH TREE Ashby, Ashcroft, Ashford, Ashton, Astley, Aston, Dasha, Dashiel, Dashwood
ASKED FOR Saul
ASPEN TREE Aethnen
ASS Farrah
ASSEMBLY Daley, Doyle
ATTACHED Levi
AUNT Tia
AUSPICIOUS Euphemia
AUTUMN Aki, Elfed, Jorah
AWAKE Ara, Effro, Onaway

BADGER Brock
BANK Clive, Glanna

Concept Index

BARK Keziah, Kiri
BARLEY Barden, Barton, Berwick
BATTLE Aloysia, Audley, Averil, Baden, Cade, Chad, Clotilda, Harva, Harvey, Hildegarde, Hildreth, Imelda, Jarvis, Louis, Louisa, Matilda, Searle, Thyra, Valda, Valdis, Winfield, Wybert, Wyman, Wymond, Wystan (*see also* ARMY, SOLDIER, STRIFE, VICTORY, WAR, WARRIOR)
BAUBLE Bibi
BAY COLOUR Bayard
BAY TREE Daphne
BEACH Tahuna
BEAR Arthur, Barnes, Barrett, Berenger, Bernadette, Bernard, Madigan, Mahon, Orson, Ursa, Ursula
BEAUTIFUL Angwen, Arabella, Bo, Calla, Fairfield, Iorwen, Jameela, Kane, Kayna, Koren, Mabel, Miki, Naava, Nama, Noelani, Noya, Olathe, Reika, Shaina, Shifra, Vashti, Zelinda, Zuleika (*see also* BEAUTY, FAIR)
BEAUTY Alika, Astrid, Belinda, Kanani, Leila, Orabel
BEAVER Beresford
BEE Deborah, Melissa
BEECH TREE Buckley
BEGINNER Prentice
BEHOLD Reuben
BELL Nolani
BELOVED Amelinda, Darel, Darlene, David, Haviva, Kalila, Leeba, Lewin, Lowell, Merna, Morna, Myrna, Philomena (*see also* LOVED, ADORED)
BENEFITS Mehetabel
BENEVOLENT Ambika, Najina

The Pan Guide to Babies' Names

BENT Coman
BERRY Aelita, Afina, Berry, Bramble, Geneva (*see also* FRUIT)
BEST, THE Ila, Kimi (*see also* GOOD)
BIND Liam, Lian, Liana, Rebecca
BIRCH TREE Barclay, Barker, Birch
BIRD Aderyn, Ava, Birdie, Bryden, Daya, Deryn, Efrona, Jarita, Oisin, Osella, Raleigh, Zipporah
BIRTH Cavan, Kevern, Kevin
BIRTHDAY Natalie
BITTER, BITTERNESS Mara, Miriam
BLACK Duane, Kerwin, Kiera, Kieran, Sable (*see also* DARK)
BLACKBIRD Merle
BLACK-EYED Sullivan
BLACKSMITH Caird, Farrar
BLAME Dempsey
BLESS, BLESSED Benedict, Benedicta, Zelick
BLIND Cecil, Cecile
BLISS Ananda, Bliss, Dechen
BLITHE Blythe
BLOOMING Chloe, Chloris, Florence
BLOSSOM Blossom, Calantha, Flower, Thalia, Zhara
BLUE Blue, Cyan, Hyacinth, Lilac
BOAR Averill, Everard, Everton
BOATMAN Derman
BOLD Archibald, Baldwin, Bernadette, Bernard, Cavendish, Gordon, Leopold, Maldwyn, Theobald
BOLDNESS Ferdinand (*see also* BRAVE, COURAGE)
BOND Desma
BOOMERANG Kylie
BORDER Oralia
BORN Eugene, Kuni
BOUNDARY Clayton, March, Markham, Van

Concept Index

BOUNTIFUL Dorena
BOUNTY Cedric
BOWMAN Archer, Saethydd, Yves, Yvette, Yvonne
BOY Aki, Sonny, Taro
BRAMBLE Bramwell
BRANCH Lorimer, Zema
BRAVE Andra, Andrea, Andrew, Andriana, Conrad, Gaylord, Gerard, Kenward, Reynard (*see also* BOLD, COURAGE)
BREATH Abel, Aura, Hawa
BREEZE Rabia, Zefira (*see also* WIND)
BREWER Brewster
BRIGHT Albert, Bertha, Bertram, Elian, Gilbert, Gisela, Herbert, Hubert, Humbert, Ismay, Kandra, Lambert, Morgan, Morgana, Muriel, Phoebe, Robert, Roberta, Sebert, Shirley, Sorcha, Wilbert, Wybert, Zaka (*see also* CLEAR, INTELLIGENCE)
BRITON Brett
BROAD Braden, Sidwell
BROKEN Pembroke
BROOK *see* Stream
BROTHER Broderick
BROW Taliesin, Talwyn
BROWN Bron, Bruna, Burnett, Donnan, Kiona, Morena, Russet
BUD Germaine
BURN Seraphina
BUTTERFLY Vanessa
BYRE Byram, Byron

CALMNESS Nalani
CAMP Chesley, Lester, Tira
CANDLE Chandelle, Chandler

The Pan Guide to Babies' Names

CAPE Montrose, Ross
CARE Carel
CARESSING Lalaka
CARRY, CARRIAGE Gig, Tara
CASK Cooper
CASTLE Bailey, Burke, Quency, Wira (*see also* FORT)
CASTLE MOAT Dermot
CAT Felina, Kedi, Koshka, Olena, Tori
CATTLE Kyla, Kyle
CEDAR TREE Cedar
CENTRE Centa
CHAFFINCH Asgell
CHALICE Chalconel, Challis
CHAMPION Carlin, Joss, Neil, Neila, Neula, Niam
CHARACTER Noble
CHARCOAL Fraser
CHARIOTEER Keby
CHARITY Carita
CHARMING Komala
CHEERFUL Hilary, Ilaria, Larissa, Tate
CHERISH Cherith
CHERRY BLOSSOM Sakura
CHIEF Einar, Kendern, Kenver, Kenwyn (*see also* LEADER)
CHILD Chel, Dalta, Erda, Fairburn, Neda, Shimako, Starchild, Yoko
CHOICE Angus, Fergus
CHRIST Christabel, Christmas, Christopher
CHRISTIAN Christian, Christine
CHRISTMAS Noel, Noeleen, Noella
CHUBBY Gifford
CHURCH Churston, Kirby, Kireen, Kirk, Kirton, Trelawney

Concept Index

CITY Medina, Urban (*see also* TOWN, VILLAGE)
CLAY Clay, Clayton, Lambourn
CLEAN Glendale, Glenford
CLEAR Chiara, Clara, Clarence, Clarity, Cleone, Shizu, Zaka
CLEARED, CLEARED LAND Ridley, Rodney
CLEARING Bentley, Bramley, Fernley, Glade, Hedley, Henly, Hewitt, Morley, Rowley, Shirley, Thorley, Wensley (*see also* GLADE)
CLERK Clark
CLIFF Clifford, Clifton, Radcliffe, Samphire, Sutcliffe
CLOAK Domino
CLOTH, FABRIC Fuller, Lister, Scarlett, Taylor, Velvet, Walker
CLOUD Anan, Aolani, Cirra, Iola
CLOWN Zane
CLUB Mace
COAL Colby, Coleman, Colville, Colvin
COLONY Lincoln
COLOURS, PLAY OF Iris
COMB, TO Carden
COMFORT Solace
COMMAND Kasmira
COMPANION Cronan, Quanda, Ruth
COMPASSION Karuna
COMPLETE Gomer
COMPLETION Omega
COMPLEXION Bruna
CONFIDENCE Panache
CONQUER, CONQUERING Siri, Vincent (*see also* VICTORY)
CONSIDERATION Adara
CONSOLATION Barnabus, Comfort
CONSTANT Perpetua

The Pan Guide to Babies' Names

COPSE Linwood (*see also* WOOD, FOREST)
COSTUME Sequin
COTTAGE Borden, Talcott, Walcott, Woodrow (*see also* HOUSE)
COUNSEL Alfred, Conrad, Goddard, Hildreth, Mallard, Quinn, Radella, Ralph, Redvers, Reynold, Ronald, Ronna
COUNSELLOR Alura, Konrad, Melvin (*see also* ADVISER)
COUNTRY Erland, Kuni
COURAGE Ferdinand, Maaia, Mox, Tara (*see also* BRAVE)
COURTEOUS Gawain, Medwin
COURTYARD Curtis, Harcourt
CRAG Craig
CRANE Cranford, Cranleigh, Cranston
CRIB Binnie
CRIPPLED Blaise
CROSS Avelanne, Royston
CROSSING *see* Ford
CROW Crawford
CROWN Adeola, Atara, Coromel, Corona, Kelila, Kitra, Koruna, Stephen, Stephene
CUP Taz (*see also* CHALICE)
CURVING Wildon

DAISY Caja
DANCE Calinda, Sundance, Tanga
DANE Daine, Danby, Dane, Denby, Denholm
DARE Dara, Denning
DARK Ciara, Leila, Kerwin, Maura, Maurice, Melanie
DARLING Kura, Lalita, Muna

Concept Index

DAUGHTER Bethia, Canace, Cordelia, Sheba, Wenona, Winona, Zoba

DAWN, SUNRISE Alaula, Aostra, Aruna, Aurora, Dagan, Dawn, Eola, Eolande, Iola, Izora, Oriana, Orien, Orienne, Roxanna, Zaria, Zelinda, Zora

DAY Dayton

DAY OF WEEK *see* WEEKDAY

DEAR Annwyl, Bevis, Caromel, Cher, Cherie, Nara

DEATH Thana

DEDICATED Enoch

DEEP Holden

DEER Aphra, Buck, Civia, Darley, Fawn, Sika, Sivia

DEFENCE Hereward

DEFENDER Aleka, Alexis, Meredith (*see also* PROTECTOR)

DELICACY Tryphena

DELIGHT Delicia, Edna, Naomi

DELL Ardell, Dell

DEPRIVE Talman

DESCEND Ira

DESCENDANT Jared, Regan, Scanlon

DESIRE, DESIRABLE, DESIRED Adina, Connor, Desi, Desiree, Lois, Willa, Wilona

DESTINY Sera

DEVOTED Lemuel

DEW Rosemary, Talia, Talora

DIKE Digby, Diggory

DIRECT, TO Diretta

DISCRIMINATION Viveka

DISPOSE Thetis

DIVINE, DIVINELY Ansell, Astrid, Diana, Dianora, Diantha, Geta, Osborn, Oscar, Theola (*see also* GOD, HOLY)

257

The Pan Guide to Babies' Names

DIVINE POWER Kami
DOER Kari
DOG Caleb
DOLPHIN Delpha, Delvin
DOVE Colman, Colum, Columba, Culver, Jahola,
    Jemima, Jonah, Paloma
DOWN Elingdon
DRAGON Drake
DREAM Aisling, Hyone (*see also* VISION)
DUCK Mallory, Teal
DUTY Zola

EAGER Arita, Emile
EAGLE Ahren, Akilina, Aleria, Aquila, Arabella,
    Arlin, Arney, Arnold
EARTH Abra, Adam, Adamina, Eartha, Earthan,
    Erda, Hertha (*see also* PLANET EARTH)
EARTH MOTHER Hertha (*see also* THE GODDESS)
EASE Yeda
EAST, EASTERN Easton, Orion, Saruk
EASTER Pascoe
EDGE Brink
EIGHTH Octavia, Octavius
ELDER Keshia
ELDER TREE Elden, Elingdon
ELEGANT Finesse
ELEMENT Elfen
ELF, ELVES Alden, Aldrich, Alford, Alfred, Algar,
    Alnod, Alstone, Alton, Alvar, Alvaston, Alvey,
    Alvira, Auberon, Aubrey, Chalconel, Crystonel,
    Damarel, Dashiel, Denerel, Elber, Elbourne,
    Eldon, Elendil, Elenya, Elford, Elingdon, Elmore,
    Elmstone, Elra, Elsdun, Elstead, Elston, Elvaston,

Concept Index

Elvedon, Elvina, Erlina, Harmonel, Ilva, Mironel, Nitha, Oliver, Shimonel
ELFIN Druella, Elfin
ELM TREE Elmstone, Elowen, Samara
ELOQUENT Omar
EMINENT Hywel
EMPRESS Zahrina, Zarina
ENCLOSED LAND Courtenay, Lockwood, Park, Parker
ENCLOSURE Dinsdale, Garth, Oram, Parr, Zareba
END Omega, Townsend
ENDURING Allard, Durand, Durrant
ENERGETIC Mehira
ENGLISHMAN Yancy
ENLIGHTENED Jairia
ENTERTAINER Samira
ENTHUSIASTIC Ardelle, Arden
ENTRANCER Trancer
ESSENCE Sara
ESTATE Ainsworth, Alonzo, Bosworth, York
ESTEEM Esma, Esme
EVERLASTING Tyndall
EWE Rachel
EXALTED Joram, Maia, Maja
EXCELLENCE, EXCELLENT Flair, Ziona
EXQUISITE Shibui, Superba
EXULTATION Gilana
EYE Sullivan

FAIR, FAIRER Andris, Anwen, Aubin, Bellamy, Feya, Finbar, Finlay, Finn, Finnian, Fintan, Fiona, Fynn, Glenda, Gwyn, Isolda, Kiri, Lynwen, Melwyn, Morenwyn, Rhianwen, Rhonwen,

The Pan Guide to Babies' Names

Talwyn, Tecca, Wenda (*see also* BEAUTY, BEAUTIFUL)
FAITHFUL Amina, Fidel, Truman
FAME Cleopatra, Elmer, Elmira, Robert, Roberta, Rosamond, Royce, Rudolf, Rue
FAMILY Nyree, Ohana
FAMOUS Aylmer, Clairmond, Cleodel, Clotilda, Derek, Dirk, Hodgson, Louis, Louisa, Luther, Nola, Nolan, Norbert, Osbert, Roald, Roderick, Roger, Roland, Rolanda, Sigbert, Thecla, Winmer
FAR Dacia
FARM Ashby, Ashcroft, Berwick, Dalby, Everton, Grainger, Kelby, Kingston, Kirby, Manton, Naunton, Ormsby, Ralston, Sedgwick, Selby, Vilette, Wadsworth, Wharton, Willoughby, Wilton, Winston, Wyndham, Wynton
FARMER Fabia, Fabian, George, Georgia, Hillman, Lennox, Sior, Tilman
FATHER Abbot, Abigail, Abner, Abraham, Abram, Absalom, Cleopatra
FAST Kita
FAVOURITE Dalta
FAWN Elain
FEATHERS Panache
FENCE Haymon (*see also* HEDGE)
FERTILE Yale
FESTIVITY, FESTIVAL Gala, Wakefield
FIDELITY Fay
FIELD Ardath, Bancroft, Blair, Fairfield, Felda, Fielding, Fulton, Garfield, Harley, Maisie, Mansfield, Mostyn, Oakley, Raleigh, Rayburn, Stanton, Wakefield, Wheatley, Wiley (*see also* LAND, MEADOW)
FIELD OF BATTLE Winfield

Concept Index

FIERCE Lorcan
FIERY Keye
FIGHT Boris
FIGHTER Carney (*see also* WARRIOR)
FILL Ulla
FINE Myfanwy
FIRE Aidan, Aideen, Aine, Aithne, Ethne, Peta, Vesta
FIRM Jaron
FIRST Prima, Primrose, Primula, Rishona
FIRST-BORN Wenona, Winona
FISH Grayling
FISHERMAN Fisher
FIVE, FIFTH Penta, Pentas, Penthea, Quentin
FLAME Celosia
FLASH Levina
FLATTERING Blandon
FLAX Linet, Linus
FLOW Naia, Runa, Tyne
FLOW DOWN Jordan, Jordana
FLOWER Blodwen, Cliantha, Diandra, Diantha, Elodie, Fleur, Flora, Florimel, Floris, Flower, Garland, Leilani, Leola, Rayburn, Reika, Rika, Zhara
FLOWERING PLANT Aloma, Azalea, Azami, Bluebell, Calendula, Caltha, Camelia, Celandine, Chirita, Cleome, Coris, Dahlia, Daisy, Elestren, Elisena, Erantha, Forbes, Heliantha, Hyacinth, Ianthe, Iris, Jasmin, Jonquil, Lantana, Leontice, Lilac, Lilian, Lily, Lotus, Marguerita, Marigold, Mimosa, Myrica, Myrtle, Nalina, Padma, Pansy, Patrinia, Petunia, Poppy, Primrose, Primula, Raisa, Rhoda, Rois, Roha, Rosa, Rosalie, Rose, Rosemary, Rosen, Saffron, Sundew, Susan,

The Pan Guide to Babies' Names

Tamarisk, Tansy, Tulip, Valma, Varda, Viola, Violet, Yelena, Yolanda, Yulan, Zinnia (*see also* HERB, PLANT, TREE)

FLOWERY Anthea

FLYING Volanta

FOLIAGE Leaf, Phyllis

FORD Adair, Alford, Ashford, Blanford, Bradford, Burnford, Cranford, Elford, Glenford, Halford, Hanford, Harford, Hayford, Langford, Linford, Lynford, Manford, Melford, Monford, Morford, Rayford, Redford, Rutherford, Ryford, Sandford, Stafford, Stanford, Stratford, Trafford, Wade, Walford, Watkin, Wilford (*see also* CROSSING)

FOREHEAD Talan

FOREST Forrest, Garwood, Oswald (*see also* COPSE, WOOD)

FORT, FORTRESS Burchard, Burgess, Carlile, Chester, Demelza, Garrison, Glendon, Mostyn, Saward (*see also* CASTLE)

FORTUNATE Kichi, Lucky, Madoc, Prosper (*see also* LUCKY)

FORTUNE, GOOD Evadne

FOUNDATION Eben, Masada

FOX Todd

FRAGRANT Levani, Narda, Rabia

FREE Frances, Francis, Freeman, Freemont, Liberty, Lysandra

FREEDOM Freemont

FREE LIFESTYLE Marin

FRIEND Aldwin, Alvan, Alvina, Amica, Baldwin, Bellamy, Buddy, Caromy, Edina, Edwin, Edwina, Elvina, Garvin, Gladwin, Godwin, Goodwin, Jed, Kelvin, Lewin, Maldwyn, Marvin, Mocara, Orwin,

Concept Index

Oswin, Raya, Reuel, Selwyn, Sherwin, Winfred, Winmer, Winola
FRIENDLY Farquhar, Melvin, Winthrop
FRUIT Aeron, Anzu, Berry, Bramble, Cerise, Cherry, Damson, Geneva, Prunella, Rimmon, Ringo (*see also* BERRY)
FRUITFUL Cerelia, Ephraim, Eustace, Morela
FURROW Seetha

GAIN Lena
GALLERY Oriel
GARDEN Felton, Gardner, Hortense, Horton, Jardine
GARLAND Rosalie
GATE Wingate
GATEKEEPER Porter
GAZELLE Dorcas, Tabitha
GENEROUS Karim, Miles
GENTLE Bonar, Clemence, Clement, Delinda, Duma, Lewis, Lenice, Lindo, Maru, Moina
GENUINE Dillys
GIFT Aldora, Caldora, Darshan, Denning, Doran, Dorea, Dorian, Dorothy, Geoffrey, Isador, Isadora, Ivanna, Koha, Matana, Matthew, Netania, Thaddeus, Theodora, Theodore, Zebedee, Zenon
GIFTED Pandora
GIRL Arletta, Cailin, Cinderella, Colleen, Deirdre, Diella, Geneth, Koo, Merari, Missie, Serilda, Talitha
GIVE, GIVER Grant, Nanda
GIVEN Jonathan, Nathan, Nathaniel
GLAD, GLADNESS Gladwin, Joy, Leta, Letitia
GLADE Astley, Glade, Zenka

The Pan Guide to Babies' Names

GLASS Crystal
GLEN Belden, Gilmore, Glendon (*see also* VALLEY)
GLOBE Orban
GLORY Gloria, Hercules
GOAL Nyssa
GOAT Giles, Harrington, Jaala, Jael
GOD Amaris, Ancel, Ariella, Athalia, Babette, Bethia, Danice, Daniel, Danielle, Darshan, David, Dominic, Dominique, Dorothy, Eliana, Elijah, Eliora, Elisha, Elizabeth, Ellendea, Emanuel, Gabriel, Gabriella, Gilda, Godfrey, Godwin, Harel, Isaiah, Ivanna, Jairia, Jeremiah, Jessie, Joann, Joel, Johanna, John, Jonathan, Lemuel, Mehetabel, Michah, Michael, Michaela, Miki, Nasia, Nathan, Nathaniel, Netania, Nirel, Obadiah, Osbert, Osman, Osmond, Oswald, Oswin, Raphael, Raphaela, Reuel, Samuel, Samuela, Thaddeus, Thea, Thecla, Theodora, Theodore, Theophilus, Theora, Tiffany, Timothy, Tobias, Yavin, Zebedee, Zedekiah (*see also* THE LORD, DIVINE)
GODDESS, THE Ceridwen, Dee, Gaia, Maiya (*see also* PLANET EARTH)
GODDESS Juno, Kanya, Sarada
GODLY Theone
GODS Panthea
GOLD, GOLDEN Aurea, Aurelia, Cressida, Eldora, Golda, Goldwin, Iora, Kandrin, Ophira, Orabel, Orla, Orlena, Orlin, Orlina, Orville, Orwin, Zaheera
GOOD Agatha, Bonnie, Boone, Gita, Glenda, Goodwin, Gwynfor, Gwynfa, Lois, Tobias, Tova, Wenda, Wendell

Concept Index

GOOD, DOING Kara
GOOD FORTUNE Ventura
GRACE Annora, Blessing, Caris, Carisma, Charis, Eastman, Esmond, Girvan, Grace, Ivena, Janan, Jessie, Mercedes
GRACEFUL Anita, Ann, Mignon
GRACIOUS Hannah, Ivanna, Joann, Johanna, John, Terence, Winola
GRAIN Garnet, Spike (*see also* SEED)
GRANARY Garner
GRANDFATHER Zade, Zaida
GRANDMOTHER Amma, Emma
GRATITUDE Reiko, Shakira
GRAVELLY Graham
GRAY Ferrant, Grayling, Lichfield, Lloyd, Tynan
GREAT Magnus, Max, Maxine, Mayer, Morag, Morgan, Morgana, Titania, Trevor
GREATEST Maxima
GREATNESS Noble
GREEN Greendale, Greenwood, Oran, Toya, Vardon, Verda, Verdant
GREETING Zala
GRIFFIN Griffith
GROOM Stedman
GROUND Maitland (*see also* LAND)
GROVE Chesney, Delaney, Elber, Greville, Lingrove, Lucina
GROW Cyma, Grover
GROWTH Japhet
GUARD Kenward, Shimiah (*see also* PROTECTOR)
GUARDIAN Edward, Greer, Howard, Seward
GUIDE, GUIDED Guy, Rashida
GYPSY Rumer, Zingara

The Pan Guide to Babies' Names

HAIR Burl, Caprice, Ciara, Crispin, Dolan, Ginger, Julian, Nema

HAIRY Esau

HANDSOME Alan, Beau, Fairburn, Irving, Kenneth, Kevern, Kevin

HAPPINESS Beatrice, Felicia, Gwyneth

HAPPY Ada, Asher, Edlyn, Edward, Edwin, Edwina, Elora, Felix, Kushuma, Nara, Sona

HARBOUR Haven, Hazena

HARD Allard, Everard, Maynard, Stannard

HARE Harford, Harwood

HARMONY Accord, Alan, Alana, Concord, Cosina, Harmonel, Harmonia, Harmony, Harman

HARPOON Harper

HAWK Gavin, Hawk

HAWK-EYED Sullivan

HAWTHORN Hawthorne

HAY Hayden, Hayford

HAZEL TREE Avelina, Haslam, Hazel, Hazelwood, Hyssop

HEAD Finbar, Kenna

HEADDRESS Toyah

HEADLAND Kenley, Nessa

HEALED, HEALS Raphael, Raphaela

HEALER Asa, Gallen, Jason

HEALTH, HEALTHY Kalya, Moyo, Solaire

HEARS, HEARD Clyde, Otis, Samuel, Samuela

HEART Yeda

HEARTH Hestia

HEATH Haddon, Hadley, Heath (*see also* MOOR)

HEAVEN, HEAVENS Juno, Nalani, Noelani, Semira, Sky

HEAVENLY Celeste, Leilani

Concept Index

HEDGE, HEDGED Hawley, Hay, Hayward, Haywood
HEIGHT Erskine
HEIR Aeres, Aerin, Aerion
HELM *see* RUDDER
HELMET Ansell, William
HELP, HELPER Orphelia, Alexis
HEMP Harland, Harley
HERB Coriander, Fennel, Marva, Mentha, Myrrh, Rue, Lavender, Salvia, Sorel, Tarragon, Yarrow, Zea, Zebrina (*see also* FLOWERING PLANT, PLANT, TREE)
HERDSMAN Booth, Calvert
HERO Finlay, Haley, Halley, Hally, Nara, Osma, Warwick
HEROIC Osma
HEROINE Arwen, Valda
HERON Zaida
HIDDEN Cachel
HIGH Abram, Bridget, Eli, Hampton, Heaton, Henly, Heywood, Hiam, Hyman, Kennet, Shelton, Van, Vance
HIGH SPIRITS Jolie
HILL, HILLS Alden, Barlow, Bowden, Branden, Bryn, Clarendon, Clinton, Crichton, Darren, Donnell, Elfyn, Elphin, Elphine, Geva, Hamilton, Hanford, Haymon, Hillman, Hilmer, Hilton, Hobart, Howell, Howland, Hurst, Kiona, Kyla, Kyle, Lawton, Lyndon, Malvern, Merlin, Merlyn, Odell, Pembroke, Rawdon, Richmond, Royden, Sheldon, Sherrill, Taldon, Talfryn, Talma, Tara, Torben, Toria, Vardon, Whalley, Winslow (*see also* MOUNTAIN)

The Pan Guide to Babies' Names

HOLD, HOLDING Hector
HOLLOW Holbrook, Holman
HOLLY Olin, Olinda
HOLY Ariadne, Ariane, Diella, Glenys, Heron, Jerome, Nevin, Olga, Sanchia, Selwyn, Zelick, Zenda
HOME Darby, Emery, Graham, Hamlin, Harriet, Henry, Howard, Humbert
HOMESTEAD Hiam, Ingham, Markham, Mycroft, Trevor, Wadham, Wentworth
HONEY Caromel, Coromel, Florimel, Honey, Mela, Melina, Mellan, Melwyn
HONOUR, HONOURING Adeola, Honor, Panthea, Timothy
HONOURABLE Eric, Erica, Erland
HOPE Hope, Nadia, Nadine, Temba, Wilfrid
HORIZON Yul
HORN Keren
HORSE Hesketh, Margaris, Marshall, Philip, Philippa, Rohan, Rosedale, Stedman
HOSPITABLE Xenia
HOST (MULTITUDE) Oliver
HOUND Conroy
HOUSE Bethany, Mansel, Martha, Midge, Prescott, Xavier (*see also* COTTAGE)
HUMAN BEING Nara
HUNT, HUNTING, HUNTER Hunt, Hunter, Huntley, Jaeger, Theron, Todd

ICE Zenka
IDOL Eluned, Lynnette
ILLUSION Maya
ILLUSTRIOUS Albert, Grady (*see also* FAMOUS)
IMAGE Lynwen, Veronica

Concept Index

IMAGINE Manon
IMMORTAL Amara, Ambrose, Ambrosine, Tansy
IMPATIENT Petula
INCREASE Joseph
INDUSTRIOUS Amelia, Emily, Mahira
INGENIOUS Cassady, Cassidy
INHERITANCE Morasha
INNOCENT Acacia, Imogen
INTEGRITY Saketa
INTELLIGENCE, INTELLIGENT Akira, Conn, Sai, Zakiya (*see also* BRIGHT, CLEAR)
INTUITION Kan
INVITE Lurene
IRON Ferrant, Ferris, Trahern
ISLAND Ailsa, Avalon, Brady, Carlile, Elan, Holm, Holmes, Innes, Innis, Isla, Kos, Lisle, Nayland, Ramsey, Rockney, Shima, Shimako, Skye
IVORY Ivor

JAUNTY Jonty
JAY Jay
JEHOVAH Joseph, Josiah, Zachariah (*see also* GOD)
JEWEL Amber, Amethyst, Beryl, Cameo, Coral, Diamond, Emerald, Esmeralda, Garnet, Gem, Gemma, Glain, Hyacinth, Iona, Jacinta, Jade, Jasper, Jem, Jet, Jewel, Kaimana, Margaret, Onyx, Opal, Pearl, Perl, Rei, Ruby, Sapphire, Solange, Spinel, Taimana, Topaz, Turquoise, Ula, Yulan
JOURNEY Faramond, Farrant, Trent
JOY Abigail, Charmian, Farah, Gila, Lowenna, Nanda, Radman, Rani, Rena, Roni (*see also* BLISS, HAPPINESS)
JOYFUL Faine, Joy, Joyce, Merrie, Merry, Ramon

The Pan Guide to Babies' Names

JUDGE Dana, Danice, Daniel, Danielle, Judge
JUDGEMENT Dinah
JUST Justin, Justina, Tika

KEEL Carina, Kelton
KESTREL Kes
KIND, KINDNESS Royce, Trugaredd
KING Darius, Fitzroy, King, Kingsley, Kingston, Kingswood, Lera, Leroy, Regan, Rex, Ryan, Sakina
KINGLY Basil, Darian, Regis, Reyner
KNIGHT Rider
KNOW Jana, Ulema
KNOWING Alvis
KNOWLEDGE Veda

LABOUR Idona
LADY Damita, Donna, Gevira, Martha, Orla, Wira
LAKE Emlyn, Hilmer, Lincoln, Marley, Merton, Mironel, Taldon, Wadham, Wadsworth
LAKESIDE Talcott
LAMB Juno, Talia
LAME Claud, Claudette, Claudia, Gladys
LAND Arval, Cleveland, Farland, Grantley, Haviland, Holland, Howland, Kimberley, Lambert, Landry, Latham, Orlan, Roland, Rolanda, Ryland, Sidney, Wayland, Whitney (*see also* GROUND)
LANDING PLACE Chelsea, Stafford
LANDSCAPE Nofia
LARK Calandra
LAUGH Isaac
LAUREL TREE Daphne

Concept Index

LEADER Ariki, Dean, Duke, Harold (*see also* CHIEF)
LEATHER Sacheverell
LED Homer
LEISURE Luana
LEOPARD Namir
LIFE Chaya, Eva, Eve, Hawa, Hilora, Jevera, Ora, Vida, Vidal, Vita, Zoe
LIFE-FORCE Tao
LIGHT Abner, Alienor, Eilan, Elena, Eliora, Ellendea, Gayora, Helen, Jelena, Leora, Lucia, Lucian, Lucis, Lucius, Nirel, Oralie, Tyndall, Uriah, Zehara, Zohar, Zohara
LIME Lyman
LIME TREE *see* LINDEN
LINDEN TREE Linden, Lindley, Lindsay, Linford, Lingrove, Linwood, Lyndon, Lynford
LION Leander, Lenna, Leo, Leolina, Leon, Leona, Leonard, Leontine, Lionel, Llewellyn, Raiona, Simba
LIONESS Ariella, Kefira
LISTENER, LISTEN Harker, Orella, Samantha, Simeon
LITHE Lindell, Vaughan
LIVELY Erlinda, Hauora, Valdis, Zevan, Zivana
LONG-LIVED Amarinda, Noah
LOOK Jeska
LORD Gwynfor, Gwynfa, Idris, Ifor, Inca, Iole, Kendern, Nerys, Yorath
LORD, THE Acima, Elijah, Gavra, Girvan, Ivena, Janan, Jed, Joram, Jotham, Malise, Matthew, Natalie, Uriah
LOST Perdita
LOVABLE Amabel, Amanda, Annabel

The Pan Guide to Babies' Names

LOVE Amia, Amy, Aroha, Cara, Caradoc, Caron, Ceri, Cerial, Cerys, Erasmus, Freya, Karenza, Kerenza, Phila, Venus (*see also* AFFECTION)

LOVED Angharad, Carys, Inaret, Theophilus (*see also* BELOVED)

LOVED ONE Amoretta, Darla, Darlin, Darryl

LOVELY Calista (*see also* BEAUTIFUL, BEAUTY)

LOVER Philina, Philip, Philippa, Tivian, Tivona

LOVING Aminta, Araminta, Calida, Trugaredd

LOYAL Leala

LUCK, LUCKY Chauncey, Ffodus, Ottway (*see also* FORTUNATE)

LURE Lurene

MAGIC Orenda

MAIDEN Alcina, Alina, Ancilla, Calella, Cora, Emina, Koren, Loleta, Maidie, Mayda, Morenwyn, Morwen, Nemissa, Rhian, Rhianwen, Tarum

MAJESTIC August, Augusta

MAN Farquhar, Manfred, Manning, Nestor, Newman, Scot, Swithin, Truman

MANIFESTATION Tiffany

MANKIND Aleka, Philena

MANLY Anders, Charles

MARSH Fenner, Fenton, Holmes, Kerr, Marson, Mycroft, Myer

MASTER Meldon, Sheridan

MEADOW Ackerley, Ainslie, Ardley, Arundale, Barclay, Bradley, Brinsley, Bromley, Buckley, Chesley, Dudley, Hadley, Handley, Hawley, Hayford, Hedli, Huntley, Langley, Lesley, Leslie, Lindley, Lynley, Mardella, Middleton, Shelley, Stanfield, Stanley, Wayne, Wesley, Westleigh (*see also* FIELD)

Concept Index

MEDITATION Dyana, Zen
MEETING PLACE Mala
MELODY Melodia, Melody, Thema
MELT Fonda
MEN Alexander, Alexandra
MERCY Dayala
MERMAID Morvoren
MERRY Gay, Revel, Ulani
MESSENGER Camilla, Hermes
MIDDLE, MIDWAY Midge, Milborough
MIGHTY Conal, Conan, Donal, Farold, Matilda, Rayner
MIGRANT Akan
MILD Milda, Mildred, Milena (*see also* GENTLE)
MILKY Galatea
MILL Melbourne, Meldon, Melford, Melton, Melville, Millburn, Milton
MIND Adley, Minerva, Sykie
MINSTREL Baird
MIRACLE Nasia
MIST, MISTY Haze, Kasumi, Misty
MODESTY Modesty
MONKEY Tamarin
MONTHS April, January, July, June, Novenda, September, Sivana
MOON Candra, Cynthia, Hina, Indira, Leihina, Levana, Marama, Moon, Selina
MOORLAND, MOOR Elmore, Montrose, Moreland, Morford, Morland, Morley, Merton, Muir, Seymour (*see also* HEATH)
MORNING Asa, Lamorna, Morning, Zephira, Morrow, Vaspara
MOTH Tussock, Zigena
MOTHER Abra, Ambika, Ina, Madra

The Pan Guide to Babies' Names

MOTHER, UNIVERSAL Amba
MOTHERLY Jarita
MOUNTAIN Aaron, Beaumont, Belmont, Cresta, Harel, Kelda, Lamont, Monford, Montague, Montina, Morven, Shasta, Sierra, Uta (*see also* HILL)
MOUSTACHE Algernon
MOUTH Campbell
MOVE, MOVEMENT Jet, Kineta, Lane, Zaza
MULBERRY COLOUR Morel
MUSIC, MUSICAL Alima, Liria, Lyrica, Lyris, Musette, Piper (*see also* SONG)
MUSICAL INSTRUMENT Lyra, Sarinda, Tabor, Veena
MY, MINE Mia
MYRRH Myra, Myron
MYSTERY Mystique
MYTHOLOGY Accalia, Aritha, Denia, Denis, Denisa, Diana, Dione, Elara, Freya, Griffith, Hercules, Hermes, Hestia, Hina, Idona, Inga, Irma, Irmgard, Isador, Isadora, Juno, Leda, Marius, Mark, Martin, Mera, Minerva, Naia, Nemissa, Nerine, Norna, Phenice, Ra, Seetha, Selima, Sita, Tamon, Tanith, Thor, Thora, Thurstan, Thyra, Torquil, Venus, Vesta, Wensley, Zaria, Zenobia, Zenon

NAME Heron, Jerome, Samuel, Samuela
NATURE, NATURAL Natrelle, Tivian, Tivona
NEW Naunton, Neola, Neville, Newel, Newman, Newton, Nova, Selden, Xavier
NEWS, GOOD Evangeline, Nuova
NIGHTINGALE Questa
NINTH Anona, Nona

Concept Index

NOBILITY Adelaide, Alice, Alison, Edlin
NOBLE Abelard, Acelin, Adalard, Adela, Adena, Adolph, Alaric, Albert, Albern, Aldora, Aldrich, Algar, Allard, Alonzo, Archibald, Audrey, Aylmer, Baron, Elgar, Elmer, Elmira, Elvina, Elwood, Emina, Etelka, Ethel, Hiram, Idelia, Millicent, Mona, Patricia, Patrick
NORTH Norbert, Nordica, Norman, Norris, Norton, Norwood
NORWEGIAN Fingal
NOSE Cameron, Simon
NYMPH, SEA Nerine
NYMPH, WOOD Aritha

OAK Garrick
OAK TREE Ackerley, Acton, Adair, Aiken, Chesney, Darrel, Darwin, Deri, Derry, Derwent, Oakley, Ogden
OATH Elizabeth, Sheba
OCEAN Yoko (*see also* SEA)
OFFICER Sargent, Sergeant
OIL Levani, Myron
OINTMENT Narda
OLD Alda, Aldrich, Aldwin, Alton, Alvan, Alvina, Elton, Geraint, Shannon
OLIVE, OLIVE-COLOURED Olive, Olivia, Orna, Zeta
ONE Una, Uni
ONE-POINTED Saketa
OPPRESSED Jobey, Jobina
ORACLE Pendle, Phineas
ORANGE Alani, Arani, Tangerine
ORNAMENT Adah, Adlai, Spangle
OWL Zumaya

The Pan Guide to Babies' Names

OWN Latham
OX, OXEN Lennox, Rutherford

PAGE Paige
PALACE Istana
PALE Blake, Wanetta
PALM TREE Dekel
PARK-KEEPER Warner
PASTURE Cavendish, Hayden, Marsden, Neoma, Springfield, Standish
PATH Ara, Olwen, Ordway, Rohin, Yama
PATIENT Medora
PATTERN Norma
PEACE Absalom, Eiran, Ferdinand, Frieda, Galina, Geoffrey, Godfrey, Harman, Humphrey, Irene, Jaron, Kasmira, Malu, Manfred, Paice, Paz, Peace, Salema, Salome, Shalom, Shanti, Shimonel, Shula, Siegfried, Sigrid, Solomon, Tai, Wilfrid, Zulema
PEACEFUL Frederick, Serena, Winifred
PEACE-LOVING Farica
PEACEMAKER Ferdinand
PEOPLE Fulke, Haviland, Luther, Nicholas, Theobald, Walter
PERFECT Jotham
PERFECTION Dorina, Idylla
PERFUME Chanel
PHOENIX Phenice
PIERCE Perceval
PIG Sugden
PIGEON Zorita
PILGRIM Dewar, Palmer
PIOUS Pia
PIPE PLAYER Piper

Concept Index

PITY Eleanor
PLACE Brent, Cleodel, Elmstone, Elstead, Elston, Fairley, Farley, Graham, Harrington, Heaton, Hedli, Hyman, Kennet, Kerry, Layton, Marson, Ruthven, Seaton, Sefton, Shelton, Snowden, Woodstock
PLAIN Mayo, Sharon
PLANET EARTH Ao, Ceridwen, Erda, Gaia, Gaian, Gaiane, Nedra, Terah
PLANT Azara, Bluette, Bracken, Bryony, Burrell, Campion, Caraway, Carline, Clover, Dellen, Fern, Fernley, Heather, Hedera, Hedley, Helga, Ivy, Leaf, Myrtle, Mauve, Neta, Oleanda, Oleantha, Sabra, Samphire, Shiloh, Tobira (*see also* FLOWERING PLANT, HERB, TREE)
PLAY, PLAYFUL Kori, Lila
PLEASANT Elma, Evelyn, Farand, Thirza
PLEASURE Pleasance
PLEDGE Arleigh, Arlen, Gisela
POET Devin, Teague
POETRY Ceridwen, Kavita
POINTER Obelia
POOL Lomas
POWER Emery, Geta, Orenda, Roald, Zenobia
PRAISE, PRAISED Clio, Hila, Hillela, Hilora, Jai, Jude, Judith
PRAY, PRAYED FOR Samala
PRESERVE Warren, Warrene
PRETTY Amelinda, Bonita, Del, Delyth, Linda
PRIEST Prescott, Preston
PRINCE Mylor
PRINCESS Almira, Koa, Sarah, Shimona, Zsa Zsa
PROGRESS Ayumi
PROMISE, PROMISED Amaris

The Pan Guide to Babies' Names

PROPHETESS Cassandra, Sibyl
PROSPERITY Edgar, Edith
PROSPEROUS Edlan, Zadah
PROTECTED Osmond
PROTECTING Sarana
PROTECTION Clairmond, Esmond, Faramond, Gerda, Inga, Irmgard, Raymond, Rosamond, Valmond
PROTECTOR Alexander, Alexandra, Brina, Eastman, Faramond, Freemont, Osma, Tesmond, William, Wyman, Wymond (*see also* DEFENDER)
PRUDENT Prudence, Sophronia
PURE, PURITY Agnes, Catherine, Kasia, Katherine, Kisha, Kolina, Neysa, Phoebe, Trinette, Virginia, Wynn, Zacchaeus
PURPLE Iona, Mauve

QUARRELSOME Sarai
QUARRY Dunstan
QUEEN Gevira, Juno, Morowa, Queenie, Quenby, Rani, Regine, Reina, Reinita
QUEENLY Daria, Darice
QUEST Odessa, Questor
QUIET Shizu

RADIANT Marmora, Taliesin, Zohar
RAIN Jorah, Varsha
RAINBOW Enfys, Keshet, Rainbow, Raynbow, Spectra
RAM, RAMS Ramsden, Ramsey
RAMSHORN Jubal
RAVEN Bertram, Bran, Brannan, Branwen, Brendon, Corbin, Ingram, Raven
RAVINE Corey

Concept Index

REASON Mayu
REBORN Rene
RECONCILIATION Winifred
RECORD-BREAKER Vikram
RED Radcliffe, Ralston, Redford, Rory, Roy, Ruby, Rudyard
REDDISH BROWN Russet
RED EARTH Adam, Adamina, Ruthven
RED-HAIRED Reed, Rogan, Rudge, Rufus, Russell, Rusty
REDEEM Ransom
REEDS, REEDY Radford, Redway, Sedgwick, Sefton
REFUGE Sharana
REJOICE Cai, Caius, Marni, Marnina
REMEMBER Zachariah
RENOWNED Aylmer
REPOSE, REST Layana, Noah
RESOLUTE Ernest, William
RESOLUTION Abelard, Adalard
RESURRECTION Anastasia, Anstey
REWARD Mercy
RICH Alodie, Edina, Edmar, Edmond, Edric, Hadrian
 (*see also* WEALTHY)
RICHES Jethro, Odelia, Odette, Odile, Zosima
RICHLY COVERED Richmond
RIDER Rider
RIDGE Aldridge, Chevy, Kenwyn, Ordway
RIGHT, RIGHTLY Rashida
RIGHTEOUS Zadok, Zedekiah
RIGHT-HANDED Dexter
RING Ringo
RISING GROUND Holland
RIVER Afon, Alden, Avon, Blain, Calder, Clodagh, Conway, Darcy, Darwin, Daven, Derwent, Elan,

The Pan Guide to Babies' Names

India, Isla, Kennet, Munro, Rivana, River, Sabrina, Severn, Sirion, Talbot, Teasdale, Tone, Trent, Tyne, Yeo
RIVERBANK Oram, Windsor
RIVER CROSSING *see* FORD
ROBUST Hardy
ROCK, ROCKS Chaney, Gavra, Hallam, Perrine, Peter, Petra, Rochella, Rock, Rocklin, Rockney, Sela
ROMAN NAMES Celia, Charmaine, Claud, Claudette, Claudia, Horatia, Horatio, Lelia, Lucia, Lucian, Lucius, Marius, Portia, Terence, Virginia
ROOK Rockwell
ROUGH Rawdon, Rowley
ROYAL Kendrick, Kennedy, Kenrick
RUDDER Helma
RULE, RULING Amory, Isolda, Walter
RULER Alaric, Aldrich, Auberon, Aubrey, Coromel, Cyril, Derek, Dirk, Donald, Donalda, Edric, Elric, Elrica, Emeric, Emery, Eric, Erica, Frederick, Gerald, Geraldine, Harriet, Henry, Kendal, Richard, Richenda, Richmal, Roderick, Rula, Theodoric, Waldo, Zoba, Zoltan
RUSH Bronnen
RYE Royden, Rydon, Ryford, Ryland

SACRED *see* HOLY
SACRIFICE Pascal, Pascale
SADNESS Merari, Trista
SAILS Vela
SALUTATION Alnod
SALVATION Elisha, Ezra, Isaiah
SAME KIND Ilka

Concept Index

SANCTUARY Temple
SAND, SANDY Sandford
SAUCY Sassy
SAVIOUR Moses, Salvin
SAXON Saskia, Saxon
SCARLET CLOTH Scarlett
SCEPTRE Macy
SCHOLAR Cleary
SEA Alcina, Cordelia, Delmar, Dylan, Edmar, Hyone, Kai, Lemarr, Mare, Marina, Maris, Marlin, Marne, Marola, Marsden, Marston, Marvin, Meredith, Merlin, Merlyn, Mervyn, Miriam, Moana, Morien, Morvoren, Moultrie, Muriel, Murphy, Nerita, Ocean, Oceana, Rosemary, Seabrooke, Seaton, Seward, Sewell, Seymour, Thaisa, Trevor, Ula (*see also* OCEAN)
SEABOARD Moray
SEAGULL Gwylan, Laraine, Larina
SEA-HORSE Roscoe
SEAL Ronan
SEAMAN Murdoch, Seamon
SEASHORE Delora
SEASON Spring, Summer
SEA SPORT Havelock
SEA WARRIOR Murdoch
SECOND Secunda
SECRET Raza
SEE Horace
SEED Garnet, Samara
SEEK, SEEKER Sika, Zito, Ziva
SELF-RESPECT Asmita
SENSE Kan
SENSITIVE Mimosa

The Pan Guide to Babies' Names

SENTINEL Vedette
SERVANT Amma, Launcelot, Malcolm, Malise, Obadiah, Osman
SERVES Ewart
SET, TO Seth
SETTLEMENT Bransby, Crichton, Danby, Keretta, Lincoln, Moray, Preston, Shelby, Summerton, Vanton
SETTLER Dane
SEVEN, SEVENTH Saith, Septa, Septimus
SEVERE, SEVERITY Severine, Shibui
SHADOW Ozelia, Zillah, Zilia
SHAPELY Almedha
SHELTER, SHELTERED Leland, Shelby, Sheldon, Sherlock
SHIELD Randolph, Ranscombe, Sigmund
SHIELD BEARER Squire
SHINE Gray, Koronette, Levenia
SHIP Hoyt, Kelton, Kelvin, Skipper
SHIRE Sheridan, Sherman, Sherrill, Sherwin, Sherwood
SHORE Iverna, Riva, Wharton
SHOULDER Fenella, Nuala
SHRINE Ahulani
SIGN Nissa, Zeno
SIGNPOST Herma
SILENT Tace
SILK Silky, Surah
SILVER Arian, Arianwen, Eirian, Sylver
SIMPLETON Moria
SINCERE Ernest
SINGER, SINGING, Corisande, Efrona (*see also* SONG)
SISTER Kaya

Concept Index

SKILL Finesse
SKIN Kiri, Maurice
SKY Azure, Kasota, Lani, Sky (*see also* HEAVEN)
SLENDER Kealan
SLOPE Shelley
SMALL Paul, Paula
SMILE Emi
SMOKEY Shubuta
SMOOTH Silky
SNAKE Linda, Ormond
SNOW Eira, Neva, Nevada, Snowden
SNOWDROP Galantha
SNUB-NOSED Simon
SOIL, EARTH Ralston
SOLDIER Herman, Kern, Troy
SON Benjamin, Bevis, Fitzroy, Gaynor, Keye, Reuben
SONG Ballard, Chantal, Geeta, Gita, Lirone, Questa, Shiri, Zamir, Zimri (*see also* MUSIC)
SONG THRUSH Mavis
SORROW Dolores, Loleta
SOUL Enid, Sykie
SOUND Cadence, Zona
SOUP Bree
SOUTH, SOUTHERNER Dacey, Sudy, Sutcliffe
SOW, PIG Sugden
SOWER Sholto, Shonet
SPARROW Galvin
SPEAR Algar, Barry, Berenger, Cain, Darrow, Edgar, Elgar, Garrick, Garvey, Gerald, Geraldine, Gerard, Gervase, Gervaise, Hodgson, Jarvis, Orde
SPEECH Amira, Euphemia
SPIRIT Esprit
SPIRITUAL Ohana
SPLENDOUR Zara

The Pan Guide to Babies' Names

SPORT Havelock
SPRING (fount) Chalfont, Chilton, Fontayne, Springfield
SPRING (season) April, Atherton, Idona, Laverne, Spring, Verda
SPRINKLING Zilpah, Zylpha
SPRITE, WATER Nixie, Undine (*see also* NYMPH)
SPUR OF HILL Howland
STABLE LAD Mander
STAG Hart, Hartley
STANDARD SETTER Solita
STAR Asta, Astra, Danica, Estelar, Estella, Esther, Galaxy, Hoshi, Mazal, Nemissa, Sidra, Siriol, Star, Star-child, Stella, Stellan, Tara
STARLIGHT Seren, Starlyte
STEADFAST Constance, Constant, Constantine, Costin, Duretta
STEWARD Grainger, Reeves, Stuart
STONE Alstone, Arthur, Churstan, Elstan, Flint, Galena, Giza, Mason, Oneida, Parnel, Rance, Redford, Stannard, Thurstan, Wystan
STONY Standford, Standish, Stanfield, Stanhope, Stanton
STORM Gale, Storm, Tempest
STORYTELLER Skelly
STRANGER Barbara, Dougal, Gallin, Wallace
STREAM Alton, Amaryllis, Beverley, Bourne, Brook, Burnford, Coburn, Derora, Dolan, Edlyn, Elbourne, Hamlin, Hewlett, Holbrook, Lambourn, Lynley, Lynton, Lynwood, Manford, Maxwell, Melbourne, Milburn, Rayford, Rhett, Riley, Rio, Rockwell, Seabrooke, Sidwell, Strother, Stream, Telford, Walford, Westbourne, Westbrook, Winslade, Yeo

Concept Index

STRENGTH Audrey, Bryna, Eswen, Gabriel, Gabriella, Humphrey, Maynard, Mena, Millicent, Oscar, Ozora, Treasa (*see also* STRONG)

STRIFE Edith, Kelly, Kilian, Wolfgang

STRONG Arnold, Barrett, Beavis, Brian, Briar, Brynn, Egan, Etana, Ethan, Kid, Mallard, Osborn, Reynard, Reynold, Richard, Richenda, Ronald, Ronna, Shira, Songan, Swithin, Trahern, Valeria, Valerian, Valmond, Valoria, Virgil

STYLE Elan

SUCCESS, SUCCESSFUL Seika, Winfield

SUFFER Patience

SUMMER Somerset, Summerton, Teresa

SUMMON Sumner

SUN Cyrus, Heliantha, Helius, Kanti, Keira, Keiran, Ra, Raa, Sampson, Sola, Solaire, Soleil, Sudance, Sunrey, Sunshine, Yoko

SUNRISE *see* DAWN

SUNSET Dysis

SUPPORT Josiah, Saada

SUPREME Fergus

SURE, SURER Shura

SWALLOW Celandine, Hirondelle

SWAN Elvedon

SWEET Adoncia, Coromel, Delcine, Dulcie, Islien, Melys, Miette, Vevina

SWEET-SINGING Efrona

SWEET-SMELLING Levani, Myron

SWEET-VOICED Islien

SWEETHEART Cariad

SWEETNESS OF FACE Anika

SWIFT Fleet, Gava, Skelter, Vitesse

SWORD Brand, Brenda, Saxon

SYMPATHY Maurilia

The Pan Guide to Babies' Names

TALENTS Cachel
TALK Lalla
TALKATIVE Callena
TALL Galiena, Temira, Timora
TAME, TAMING Damara, Damian
TANNERY Pelham
TEACHER Latimer, Moretta, Reshad
TENDER Malva
TENDERNESS Mahala
TENTH, TITHING Decia, Tate
THEME Motif, Thema
THIEF Larren
THIRD Tressa
THIRST Ita
THIRTY Trenton
THORN, THORNY Acantha, Thorley, Thorne, Thornton
THREAD Nema
THREEFOLD Trinita, Triune
THROW Jet
TIGER Tora
TIME Horace
TITLE Tully
TORCH Helen
TORRENT Wynford
TOUCH Caress
TOUGH Suta
TOWER Magdalene
TOWN Chadwick, Colby, Glenville, Granville, Greville, Kelton, Melville, Merville, Milborough, Neville, Orville, Pelham, Townsend, Wilber
TRANQUIL Galen
TRAVELLER Faramond, Farold, Paxton
TREASURE Joya, Sima, Takara

Concept Index

TREE Acacia, Acantha, Ackerley, Acton, Adair, Aethnen, Aiken, Alder, Ashby, Ashcroft, Ashford, Ashton, Aspen, Astley, Aston, Avelina, Barclay, Barker, Birch, Buckley, Cassena, Cassia, Cedar, Chesney, Damaris, Daphne, Darrel, Darwin, Dekel, Delaney, Deri, Derry, Derwent, Durian, Elana, Elden, Elingdon, Ellery, Elmstone, Grover, Haslam, Hawthorn, Hazel, Hazelwood, Hickory, Holly, Hyssop, Ivo, Jarrah, Juniper, Karri, Larch, Laura, Laurel, Laurelia, Linden, Lindley, Lindsay, Linford, Lingrove, Linwood, Logan, Magnolia, Maple, Mayo, Miki, Nairn, Ngaio, Oakley, Ogden, Olin, Olive, Oliver, Oren, Osmantha, Palmira, Poplar, Rowan, Samara, Saward, Selby, Sequoia, Shea, Sophora, Spruce, Taru, Thirza, Torreya, Trayton, Vernon, Wanetta, Welby, York, Zamia, Zeta (*see also* FLOWERING PLANT, HERB, PLANT)
TREE-STUMP Curzon
TREE-TRUNK Cormac, Newbold
TREMBLE Zia
TRIANGULAR Garfield
TRIBE Clancy
TROOPS Garrison
TRUST Faith
TRUTH Alethea, Emmet, Vera, Vere, Verena, Verity, Verna
TRUTHFUL Verada
TWILIGHT Twila
TWIN Tamlan, Thomas, Thomasin, Tommina

UNCLE Emer
UNDERSTAND Yavin

The Pan Guide to Babies' Names

UNFADING Amarantha
UNIQUE Angus
UNITY Unita, Unity
UNIVERSAL Amba, Irma
UNIVERSE Cosmo
UPLAND Yale
UPLIFT Jeremiah
UPPER Upton

VALLEY Arundell, Barden, Bryden, Compton, Dale, Dallas, Denman, Denna, Denver, Devon, Devona, Elsdun, Elvedon, Gayora, Glendale, Glenn, Glenna, Glenton, Glenville, Glynis, Greendale, Halden, Holden, Hyssop, Kelvedon, Kendal, Langdon, Lonsdale, Ogden, Perceval, Ramsden, Ranscombe, Rosedale, Rydon, Selden, Slade, Stanhope, Teasdale, Theydon, Tilden, Trafford, Vail, Vale, Wendell, Wildon
VALOROUS Farrel
VALUABLE Merritt, Precious
VEIN Vena
VENERABLE Sebastian, Sebastiana
VENTURE Farrant
VENUS, PLANET Esther
VERDANT Laverne
VICTORIOUS Collette, Eunice, Sewell
VICTORY Berenice, Jai, Nicholas, Sayer, Sebert, Seward, Siegfried, Sigbert, Sigmund, Sigrid, Victor, Victoria, Vijay, Wim, Wingate (*see also* VICTORIOUS)
VIGILANT Gregory
VIGOUR, VIGOROUS Arial, Valence, Valentia, Valentina, Valentine
VILLAGE Acton, Alstone, Ashton, Aston, Atherton,

Concept Index

Barrington, Barton, Benton, Bolton, Branton,
Burton, Carleton, Charlton, Chelston, Chilton,
Clifton, Clinton, Colston, Compton, Crofton,
Dalton, Darrington, Darton, Dayton, Denton,
Easton, Edlan, Elton, Elvaston, Felton, Glenton,
Hampton, Hilton, Kirton, Langston, Lauriston,
Lawton, Levington, Lytton, Lynton, Marston,
Melton, Merton, Middleton, Milton, Morton,
Newton, Norton, Rika, Somerby, Stanton,
Thornton, Trayton, Trelawney, Upton, Walton,
Welby, Winthrop
VINE Ives, Ivy, Lorimer, Vinna
VINEYARD Carmel, Wynard
VIRGIN Kanya
VIRTUE, VIRTUOUS Aretha, Kalyana, Sati
VISION Druella (*see also* DREAM)
VIVACIOUS Alvita (*see also* ALIVE, LIVELY)
VOICE Islien

WAKE/FESTIVAL Wakefield
WALK, WALKER Andeana, Tamatha
WANDER, WANDERER Errol, Peregrine, Ranger,
Wanda, Wendelin
WAR Alvey, Edith, Githa, Hedda, Serilda (*see also*
BATTLE, STRIFE)
WARLIKE Kelly, Kilian
WARRIOR Albern, Armand, Armina, Baron, Cadell,
Cador, Caldwell, Chad, Chadwick, Duncan,
Edmond, Einar, Garvin, Gertrude, Hildegarde,
Moultrie, Murdoch, Ottway, Roger, Sloane,
Turlough (*see also* SOLDIER, BATTLE, WAR)
WATCH, WATCHER Garrett, Theora
WATCHFUL Casey
WATCHMAN Ward

The Pan Guide to Babies' Names

WATER, WATERY Deron, Douglas, Ewart, Kelsey, Lindsey, Mardella, Marden, Mortimer, Rodney, Sadira, Sidney, Tallulah, Undine, Washington, Whitney
WATERWAY Layton, Mio, River
WAVE Genevieve, Guinevere, Jennifer, Nyree, Undine, Vanora, Zinevra
WAYSIDE Fairley, Farley
WEALTH, WEALTHY Jesse, Otto, Udele (*see also* RICH)
WEARY Leah
WEAVER Penelope, Webster
WEED Darnel
WEEKDAY Monday, Neda, Thursday, Tuesday
WELL Howell
WELL-BEING Keefe
WELL-BORN Eugene, Owen
WEST, WESTERN Wesley, Westbourne, Westbrook, Westleigh, Weston
WHARF Redvers
WHEAT Wheatley
WHEEL Monro
WHITE Alban, Alpin, Alva, Arianwen, Aubin, Bain, Bianca, Birch, Blanche, Bronessa, Bronwen, Candace, Candida, Dwight, Fenella, Fiona, Genevieve, Guinevere, Gwen, Jennifer, Kenwyn, Nuala, Olwen, Vanora, Wynford, Wynn, Wynne, Wynton, Zinevra
WHITE-HAIRED Gaynor
WHOLE, WHOLENESS Irma, Salim, Shalom
WHOLESOME Althea, Valeda
WIFE Aia, Medora, Sati
WILL Thelma, William, Willis, Wilmot
WILLING Joel

Concept Index

WILLOW Saward, Selby, Welby, Weldon, Wilber, Wilbert, Wiley, Wilford, Willard, Willoughby, Willow, Wilton

WINCH Windsor

WIND Canace, Keith, Mistral, Saruk, Scirocco

WING, WINGED Alette, Alula

WINTER Wentworth

WISDOM Athene, Bina, Cachel, Elra, Kyna, Linda, Minerva, Sarada, Sophia

WISE Alfred, Alim, Alura, Alyssa, Belinda, Bena, Druce, Eldridge, Jada, Keene, Konrad, Nestor, Raymond, Reynard, Sabella, Sagina

WOAD Odell

WOLF Adolph, Bardolph, Louvella, Lovell, Phelan, Ralph, Randolph, Rudolf, Ulrick, Wolfgang, Zeva

WOMAN Aisha, Alzena, Beulah, Cerelia, Delphine, Doris, Duma, Lalana, Maurilia, Trista, Vevina, Zena, Zenana

WOMANLY Carla, Charla, Quinby

WONDER, WONDERFUL Marvell, Mirabel, Shani

WOOD, WOODED, WOODLAND Arlington, Ashley, Berkeley, Boyce, Brindley, Bruce, Brucena, Burwood, Collingwood, Darley, Dashwood, Ellwood, Elwood, Firth, Forrest, Frith, Fritha, Glenn, Glenna, Glenton, Glenville, Greenwood, Hartley, Harwood, Haywood, Hazelwood, Heywood, Hurst, Ivo, Kingsley, Kingswood, Lee, Lichfield, Lockwood, Lynwood, Neoma, Norwood, Ridley, Selva, Shaw, Sherwood, Silas, Silva, Silvan, Silvana, Silvester, Silvia, Slade, Walden, Whalley, Winwood, Woodstock, Woodrow (*see also* COPSE, FORREST)

WOODSMAN Gideon

WOODWORKER Sawyer

The Pan Guide to Babies' Names

WOOL Lana
WORK Amory, Oprah
WORLD Cosina, Desmond, Donal, Donald, Donalda, Mondiale (*see also* PLANET EARTH)
WORTHY Iole, Yorath
WREATH Garland, Leihina

YELLOW Boyd, Xanthe
YEW TREE Ivo, Mayo, York
YOUNG Deirdre, Junior, Wanetta
YOUTH Hebe, Taruna
YOUTHFUL Ida

ZEALOUS Ardelia, Zelia

Index of Sources

This index is concerned with linguistic sources only. A breakdown of these are given in the Analysis of Sources on page 11.

ABORIGINE Kylie.
AFRICAN LANGUAGES *see* AKAN, HAUSA, NGONI, NIGERIAN, SWAHILI, YORUBA, ZULU.
AKAN Morowa.
AMERICAN INDIAN Hickory, Kasota, Kaya, Kiona, Kiowa, Leola, Malita, Nemissa, Ohana, Olathe, Orenda, Sakima, Songan, Sonora, Suta, Tallulah, Tawana, Wenona, Winona. (*See also* OJIBWAY, IROQUOIS, CHEROKEE, CHOCTAW AND SIOUX)
ARABIC Aisha, Alim, Alima, Almira, Alzena, Amber, Amina, Farrah, Gala, Izora, Jameela, Kalila, Karim, Leila, Medina, Najina, Rabia, Sadira, Saffron, Salim, Salima, Samira, Saruk, Scirocco, Sequin, Shakira, Shula, Sima, Tamatha, Taz, Ulema, Zadah, Zakiya, Zara, Zhara, Zoltan, Zora, Zuleika, Zulema.
ARAMAIC Bartholomew, Ila, Keshia, Martha, Raza, Samantha, Tabitha, Talia, Talitha, Talman, Tara, Thaddeus, Thomas, Thomasin, Tommina, Zacchaeus.
ASSYRIAN Sivana.

The Pan Guide to Babies' Names

BOHEMIAN Jaron.

BRETON Margaris, Talan.

CELTIC Alan, Alana, Anyon, Arlen, Bowen, Bryce, Calder, Calella, Cameron, Carlile, Carney, Caromy, Cassady, Cassidy, Chad, Cordelia, Craig, Devin, Donnell, Druce, Duncan, Eia, Evelyn, Farrel, Gallin, Galvin, Genevieve, Gilda, Gilmore, Glendale, Glendon, Glenford, Glenn, Glenna, Glenton, Glenville, Guinevere, Gwen, Innes, Islien, Isolda, Joss, Keegan, Kendal, Kennet, Maura, Moina, Mylor, Nairn, Nara, Neula, Shannon, Shonet, Sloane, Taldon, Tavis, Teague, Ula, Vanora, Watkin, Wira, York, Zinevra. (*See also* BRETON, CORNISH, GAELIC, IRISH, SCOTTISH, WELSH)

CHEROKEE Sequoia.

CHINESE Tai, Taisha, Tao, Yulan.

CHOCTAW: Shubuta.

CORNISH Bronnen, Cador, Caja, Cledra, Daymer, Dellen, Demelza, Ebrel, Elestren, Elowen, Enyon, Ervan, Gweniver, Jago, Jory, Jowan, Karenza, Kay, Kayna, Keby, Kenan, Kendern, Kenver, Kenwyn, Kerensa, Lowenna, Marya, Medwenna, Meliora, Melwyn, Meryn, Morenwyn, Morvoren, Pedrek, Peran, Piran, Rosen, Senara, Talwyn, Tecca, Trelawney, Tressa, Tristan, Wenna, Yesten.

CZECH Koruna.

DANISH Hobart, Kristian, Ulrick, Yorick.

DUTCH Anneka, Digby, Diggory, Gardner, Marieke, Riley, Saskia, Skipper, Spangle.

EGYPTIAN Akau, Aostra, Phenice, Ra.

FIJIAN Levani, Tevita.

FRENCH Aimee, Algernon, Avellane, Bayard, Beau,

Index of Sources

Beaumont, Bellamy, Bibi, Blanche, Bo, Bonnie, Boyce, Bruce, Brucena, Cachel, Cerise, Chandelle, Chandler, Chanel, Chaney, Charlotte, Cher, Cherie, Chesney, Cinderella, Clementine, Cleta, Clete, Cordelle, Darcy, Darel, Dax, Denis, Denisa, Domino, Elan, Eloise, Esma, Esme, Esprit, Fifi, Finesse, Fleur, Fonda, Fraser, Gaston, Glenville, Greville, Heloise, Henri, Henrietta, Hirondelle, Ivon, Jacqueline, Jacquetta, Janine, Jardine, Jeanette, Jet, Josephine, Josette, Jules, Julienne, Juliet, Justine, Larren, Leone, Lera, Leroy, Liam, Lian, Liana, Lisle, Lorraine, Louis, Louvella, Lovell, Lucie, Lurene, Lynette, Mabel, Madeleine, Manetta, Manville, Marvelle, Marc, Margo, Marguerite, Marie, Melville, Merle, Merville, Michele, Miette, Mistral, Mondiale, Monette, Monique, Monro, Morel, Mortimer, Motif, Nathalie, Neville, Noel, Noeleen, Noelle, Normand, Oisin, Olivier, Orabel, Orly, Orville, Panache, Paris, Perceval, Petunia, Rance, Raoul, Raymonde, Reina, Rene, Robard, Rochella, Romaine, Russell, Sacheverell, Samphire, Savilla, Severine, Sidney, Simone, Sinclair, Soleil, Spinel, Stephanie, Surah, Tamarin, Trenton, Valerie, Verdun, Verlie, Victorine, Vitesse, Wim, Yancy, Yolanda, Yvette.

GAELIC Adair, Aidan, Aideen, Ailsa, Aine, Ainslie, Alan, Alana, Alastair, Angus, Athol, Aulay, Bain, Baird, Barry, Blair, Boyd, Cailin, Caird, Callum, Campbell, Carlin, Catriona, Cleary, Colum, Corey, Dacey, Dalta, Dana, Dewar, Douglas, Erina, Erskine, Farquhar, Fenella, Fergus, Fingal, Finlay, Fiona, Grady, Hamish, Iain, Ilka, Innis, Irving, Keith, Kenneth, Keye, Kyla, Kyle,

The Pan Guide to Babies' Names

Kyna, Maise, Malcolm, Malise, Maxwell, Mayo, Morna, Mingo, Mocara, Montrose, Morag, Moray, Morna, Morven, Moultrie, Mungo, Murdoch, Myrna, Rogan, Rory, Ross, Roy, Ruthven, Ryan, Seonaid, Sheena, Sholto, Shona, Sina, Skelly, Sona, Strother, Struan, Tynan, Vevina.

GERMAN Aldous, Anneliese, Anton, Elka, Fritz, Gregor, Gretchen, Haines, Hedda, Heidi, Iloe, Imelda, Jaeger, Liesl, Magda, Meta, Mitzi, Ramina, Rainer, Rocana, Rupert, Ruperta, Susette, Wilhelmina, Wolfgang (*See also* OLD GERMAN)

GREEK Acacia, Acantha, Agatha, Agnes, Alcina, Aleka, Alethea, Alexander, Alexandra, Alexis, Alienor, Althea, Alyssa, Amarantha, Amarinda, Amaryllis, Ambrose, Ambrosine, Amethyst, Anastasia, Anders, Andra, Andrea, Andrew, Andriana, Angela, Anstey, Anthea, Aostra, Aretha, Ariadne, Ariane, Aritha, Asta, Athene, Aura, Azara, Barbara, Basil, Berenice, Beryl, Briar, Bryony, Calandra, Calantha, Caldora, Caldwell, Calista, Calla, Campion, Canace, Candace, Caraway, Caris, Carisma, Cassandra, Catherine, Cedar, Celandine, Celosia, Charis, Charmian, Chloe, Chloris, Christopher, Cleodel, Cleome, Cleone, Cleopatra, Cliantha, Clio, Cora, Coral, Coriander, Coriantha, Coris, Cormac, Corisande, Cosina, Cosmo, Cressida, Cronan, Crystal, Cyan, Cyma, Cynara, Cynthia, Cyril, Damara, Damian, Daphne, Delpha, Delphine, Delvin, Delmelda, Denia, Desma, Diamond, Diandra, Diantha, Dione, Doral, Dorcas, Dorea, Dorena, Dorian, Doris, Dorothy, Dysis, Ebony, Elara, Eleanor, Elena, Elias, Ellendea, Elma,

Index of Sources

Elora, Elodie, Emerald, Emma, Eola, Eolande, Erantha, Erasmus, Eugene, Eunice, Euphemia, Eustace, Evadne, Evangeline, Forbes, Gaia, Gaiane, Galantha, Galatea, Galaxy, Galen, Galina, Gallen, George, Georgia, Giles, Gordon, Greer, Gregory, Griffith, Hadrian, Harman, Harmonia, Harmony, Hebe, Hector, Helen, Heliantha, Helius, Hercules, Hermes, Hermione, Hestia, Homer, Horace, Hyacinth, Hyone, Ianthe, Idylla, Ileana, Iola, Iona, Irene, Irina, Iris, Isador, Isadora, Jacinta, Jason, Jasper, Jelena, Jerome, Jet, Jonas, Julian, Kalman, Katharine, Keira, Keiran, Kineta, Kolina, Koren, Kos, Lais, Lalla, Leanda, Leander, Leda, Leon, Leona, Leontine, Linus, Liria, Lois, Lotus, Luke, Lydia, Lyra, Lyrica, Lyris, Lysandra, Malva, Margaret, Marmora, Mary, Melanie, Melina, Melissa, Mellan, Melody, Mera, Monica, Moria, Myra, Myron, Myrrh, Naia, Narda, Neola, Neoma, Nerine, Nerita, Nestor, Neysa, Nicholas, Nyssa, Obelia, Ocean, Omega, Onyx, Ophelia, Otis, Pandora, Panthea, Parnell, Paul, Paula, Penelope, Penthea, Perrine, Peter, Petra, Phila, Philemon, Philena, Philip, Philippa, Philomena, Phoebe, Phyllis, Rhoda, Rhodes, Sebastian, Sebastiana, Selina, Sibyl, Sigma, Simon, Sior, Sophia, Sophronia, Stephen, Stephene, Sykie, Tansy, Tarragon, Teresa, Thaddeus, Thaisa, Thalia, Thana, Thea, Theda, Thema, Theodora, Theodore, Thelma, Theola, Theone, Theophilus, Theora, Theron, Thetis, Thion, Tiffany, Timothy, Titania, Topaz, Trinette, Tryphena, Ulysses, Vanessa, Vela, Velia, Venus, Xanthe, Xena, Zelie, Zeno, Zenobia, Zenon, Zito, Ziva, Zoe, Zola, Zosima.

The Pan Guide to Babies' Names

HAUSA Anika, Tamsha.

HAWAIIAN Ahulani, Alani, Alaula, Aolani, Helina, Iolana, Kaimana, Kanani, Lani, Leihina, Leilani, Lilliana, Luana, Makala, Malia, Malu, Miliama, Nalani, Noelani, Nolina, Noma, Ohana, Ulani, Wanaka.

HEBREW Aaron, Abel, Abigail, Abner, Abra, Abraham, Abram, Absalom, Acima, Adah, Adam, Adamina, Adena, Adina, Adlai, Adley, Aia, Aliya, Alma, Amaris, Amira, Amma, Anan, Anita, Ann, Annora, Aphra, Ardath, Arella, Ariella, Arleigh, Asa, Asher, Atara, Athalia, Babette, Barnabus, Bena, Benjamin, Bethany, Bethia, Beulah, Bina, Cain, Caleb, Carmel, Challah, Chaya, Cinnamon, Civia, Dana, Danice, Daniel, Danielle, David, Daya, Deborah, Dekel, Delilah, Derora, Dinah, Doran, Dorina, Duma, Eben, Edna, Efrona, Elana, Eli, Eliana, Elijah, Eliora, Elisha, Elizabeth, Emanuel, Emmet, Enoch, Ephraim, Erlinda, Esau, Etana, Ethan, Eva, Eve, Ezra, Gabriel, Gabriella, Gavra, Gayora, Geva, Gevira, Gideon, Gila, Gilana, Girvan, Giza, Gomer, Hannah, Harel, Haviva, Hawa, Hila, Hillela, Hilora, Hiram, Huldah, Ira, Isaac, Isaiah, Israel, Ivanna, Ivena, Jaala, Jacob, Jacoba, Jada, Jael, Jairia, Jahola, Janan, Japhet, Jared, Jed, Jemima, Jeremiah, Jeska, Jesse, Jessie, Jethro, Jevera, Joann, Job, Jobina, Joel, Johanna, John, Jonah, Jonathan, Jorah, Joram, Jordan, Jordana, Joseph, Josiah, Jotham, Jubal, Jude, Judith, Kefira, Kelila, Keren, Keretta, Keshet, Keziah, Kitra, Koa, Koronette, Leah, Lemuel, Leora, Levana, Levi, Lirone, Magdalene, Mahala, Mahira, Mara, Marni, Marnina, Marva, Masada, Matana,

Index of Sources

Matthew, Mazal, Mehetabel, Mehira, Merari,
Michah, Michael, Michaela, Miki, Miriam,
Morasha, Moretta, Moselle, Moses, Moss, Naava,
Nama, Namir, Naomi, Nasia, Nathan, Nathaniel,
Nema, Neta, Netania, Nirel, Nissa, Noah, Nofia,
Noya, Obadiah, Omar, Ophira, Oralie, Oren,
Ozella, Ozora, Pascal, Pascale, Peta, Phineas,
Rachel, Rani, Ranon, Raphael, Raphaela, Raya,
Rebecca, Rena, Reuben, Reuel, Rimmon, Rimona,
Rishona, Roni, Ruth, Saada, Sabra, Salema,
Salome, Samala, Samson, Samuel, Samuela,
Sapphira, Sarah, Sarai, Saul, Sela, Samira,
Seraphina, Seth, Shalom, Sharon, Sheba, Shifra,
Shimiah, Shimona, Shira, Shiri, Shoshona,
Simeon, Sivia, Solomon, Susan, Talia, Talma,
Talora, Tamar, Tamara, Temira, Thirza, Timora,
Tira, Tivian, Tivona, Tobias, Tova, Uriah, Varda,
Yavin, Yeda, Yehudi, Zacchaeus, Zachariah,
Zadok, Zaheera, Zaka, Zaza, Zebedee, Zedekiah,
Zehara, Zelinda, Zema, Zephaniah, Zephira, Zeta,
Zeva, Zia, Zilah, Zilia, Zilpah, Zimra, Zion, Ziona,
Zipporah, Zira, Zohar, Zohara, Zsa Zsa, Zuba,
Zylpha.

HINDI Rani.

HUNGARIAN Ilona, Jan, Margareta, Maritza, Mila.

IRISH Aingeal, Aisling, Aithne, Arthur, Brannan,
Brendan, Brian, Bridget, Bryna, Brynn, Casey,
Cathleen, Cavan, Ciara, Clancy, Clodagh,
Colleen, Colman, Coman, Conal, Conan, Conn,
Connor, Conroy, Daley, Declan, Deirdre, Dolan,
Donal, Donald, Donalda, Donnan, Dougal, Doyle,
Duane, Eamonn, Eilan, Eileen, Eiran, Elva,
Ethne, Eveleen, Finbar, Finn, Finnian, Fintan,
Fynn, Gaynor, Hogan, Ita, Juno, Kathleen,

The Pan Guide to Babies' Names

Kealan, Keefe, Kelly, Kern, Kerry, Kerwin,
Kevern, Kevin, Kiaran, Kiera, Kieran, Kilian,
Lorcan, Madigan, Maeve, Mahon, Mair, Maureen,
Meave, Mhairi, Moira, Mona, Munro, Muriel,
Murphy, Neil, Neila, Nevin, Niam, Nola, Nolan,
Nora, Nuala, Onora, Oonagh, Oran, Orla, Orna,
Padraig, Phelan, Quinn, Redmond, Regan, Roisin,
Ronan, Seamus, Sean, Shaun, Sheila, Sile, Sinead,
Sioban, Siran, Sorcha, Sullivan, Tara, Toran,
Treasa, Trent, Troy.

IROQUOIS Oneida

ITALIAN Belmont, Benedetta, Bettina, Bianca,
Cameo, Carmila, Caroline, Chiara, Clarice,
Diretta, Donna, Francesca, Gianetta, Griselda,
Imelda, Ines, Jovanna, Korenza, Leonora, Lia,
Lorenzo, Magenta, Mariana, Melita, Melodia,
Mia, Nardi, Nicolette, Nolana, Nuova, Olivia,
Orlando, Osella, Raffaela, Ringo, Riva, Roma,
Rosina, Sandra, Sera, Solange, Torin, Torina,
Unita, Vedette, Volanta, Zefira, Zigena, Zimarra,
Zingara.

JAPANESE Aki, Akira, Anzu, Asa, Ayumi, Azami,
Emi, Hoshi, Kai, Kami, Kan, Kasumi, Kichi,
Kimi, Kuni, Mayu, Miki, Mio, Reika, Reiko, Rika,
Ringo, Sai, Sakura, Seiko, Shibui, Shima, Taro,
Tora, Yoko, Zen.

LATIN Accalia, Adoncia, Akilina, Alban, Aleria,
Alette, Alpin, Alula, Alva, Alvita, Amabel,
Amanda, Amelinda, Amia, Amica, Aminta,
Amoretta, Amy, Ancilla, Annabel, Anona,
Anthony, April, Aquila, Arabella, Araminta,
Archer, Ardelia, Ardelle, Arden, Arval, Astra,
Aubin, August, Augusta, Aurea, Aurelia, Aurora,
Ava, Avalon, Beatrice, Belinda, Benedict,

Index of Sources

Benedicta, Blaise, Blandon, Brett, Burgess, Burl,
Cadence, Caius, Calendula, Caltha, Calvin,
Camilla, Candida, Caprice, Caress, Carina,
Carita, Carline, Caromel, Cecil, Cecile, Cecilia,
Celeste, Celia, Cerelia, Chantal, Charity,
Charmaine, Cherith, Chester, Christabel,
Christian, Christine, Clara, Clarence, Clarity,
Claud, Claudette, Claudia, Clemence, Clement,
Collette, Columba, Comfort, Concord, Constance,
Constant, Constantine, Coromel, Corona, Costin,
Courtenay, Crispin, Curtis, Dacia, Damita,
Damson, Decia, Delcine, Delia, Delicia, Delora,
Desi, Desmond, Dexter, Diana, Dianora, Diella,
Dominic, Dominique, Drake, Drusilla, Duke,
Dulcie, Durand, Durrant, Elian, Emile, Emily,
Emina, Enyon, Errol, Estella, Fabia, Fabian,
Faith, Fawn, Felicia, Felina, Felix, Fennel, Ferris,
Fidel, Fitzroy, Flair, Flora, Florence, Florimel,
Floris, Flower, Forrest, Frances, Francis,
Franklyn, Galena, Garner, Garnet, Gem, Gemma,
Geneva, Germaine, Geta, Gladys, Glanna, Gloria,
Grace, Hedera, Herma, Hilary, Honor, Horatia,
Horatio, Hortense, Horton, Ilaria, Imogen, Ina,
Iora, Isola, Ivor, Jane, January, Jarman, Jay, Jem,
Joy, Joyce, Julia, July, June, Junior, Juniper,
Juno, Justin, Justina, Lake, Lamont, Lana,
Laraine, Larch, Larina, Larissa, Laura, Laurel,
Laurence, Laurine, Lavender, Laverne, Lavinia,
Lelia, Lemarr, Lenis, Lenice, Leo, Leta, Letitia,
Liberty, Lilian, Lionel, Lorimer, Lucas, Lucia,
Lucian, Lucina, Lucis, Lucius, Magnus, Maia,
Maja, Marcia, Mare, Maria, Marina, Maris,
Marcius, Mark, Marlin, Marne, Marola, Martin,
Martina, Marvell, Maurice, Maurilia, Mauve,

The Pan Guide to Babies' Names

Max, Maxima, Maxime, Maxine, Mayer, Mela,
Mentha, Mercy, Merritt, Mimosa, Minerva,
Mirabel, Miranda, Modesty, Monica, Montague,
Montina, Myrtle, Natalie, Neva, Newell,
Newman, Newton, Noble, Noella, Nona, Nordica,
Norma, Nova, Octavia, Octavius, Olive, Oliver,
Oprah, Orabel, Oralia, Orban, Orella, Oriana,
Oriel, Orien, Orienne, Orion, Orlena, Orlin,
Orlina, Orson, Palmira, Pansy, Pascoe, Patience,
Patricia, Patrick, Peace, Pelham, Penta, Pentas,
Perdita, Peregrine, Pergola, Perpetua, Petula,
Pia, Poppy, Portia, Precious, Prima, Primrose,
Primula, Priscilla, Prosper, Prudence, Prunella,
Quentin, Questor, Ransom, Regine, Regis, Remy,
Rex, Reyner, Rock, Rois, Rosa, Rosalie, Rose,
Rosemary, Roxanna, Ruby, Rufus, Rula, Russet,
Sabella, Sabina, Sabrina, Sagina, Salvia, Salvin,
Samara, Secunda, Septa, September, Septimus,
Serena, Severn, Sidra, Silas, Silva, Silvan,
Silvana, Silvester, Silvia, Sola, Solace, Solita,
Solitaire, Spectra, Stella, Stellan, Sumner,
Superba, Tace, Tamarisk, Telford, Tempest,
Temple, Terah, Terence, Trinita, Trista, Triune,
Tully, Turner, Una, Undine, Uni, Unity, Urban,
Ursa, Ursula, Vail, Valence, Valentia, Valentina,
Valentine, Valeria, Valerian, Valonia, Valora,
Vena, Veneta, Vera, Verada, Verdant, Vere,
Verena, Verity, Verlin, Verna, Veronica, Vesta,
Victor, Victoria, Vidal, Vilette, Vincent, Viola,
Virgil, Virginia, Vita, Vivian, Vivien, Yelena,
Zea, Zelia, Zelinda, Zona.

MALAY Istana.

MAORI Aki, Anahera, Ao, Ara, Arani, Ariki, Arita,
Aroha, Emere, Hauora, Hilora, Kiri, Kita, Koha,

Index of Sources

Koo, Kori, Kura, Maaia, Marama, Maru, Moana, Muna, Nyree, Ora, Raa, Raiona, Rei, Roha, Tahuna, Taimana, Tara, Tarati, Tika, Tori.

MIDDLE ENGLISH Alder, Bailey, Ballard, Bluebell, Brand, Bree, Burrell, Coburn, Coleman, Colvin, Cooper, Cramer, Dara, Darby, Darla, Darnel, Dawn, Gay, Gig, Grant, Harcourt, Hardy, Harland, Haven, Hayward, Hazena, Heath, Hillman, Hoyt, Ives, Ivy, Jolie, Lamorna, Leala, Levenia, Logan, Lucky, Maidie, Marigold, Milda, Morning, Morrow, Park, Pearl, Prentice, Ranger, Sassy, Sawyer, Somerby, Spike, Teal, Twilight, Tyler, Ulla, Velvet, Violet, Warren, Warrene.

MONGOLIAN Yul.

NGONI Moyo.

NIGERIAN Alika.

NORMAN FRENCH Payn, Siri, Tracy, Wright.

NORWEGIAN Disa.

OJIBWAY Onaway.

OLD ENGLISH Abbott, Ackerley, Acton, Ada, Addison, Aiken, Ainsworth, Albern, Alden, Aldora, Aldrich, Aldridge, Aldwin, Alford, Alfred, Algar, Alnod, Alodie, Alston, Alton, Alura, Alvaston, Alvey, Anson, Ardell, Ardley, Arundale, Arundell, Ashby, Ashcroft, Ashford, Ashley, Ashton, Astley, Aston, Atherton, Audley, Audrey, Averil, Aylmer, Baden, Bamber, Bancroft, Barclay, Barden, Bardolf, Barker, Barlow, Barnes, Baron, Barrington, Barton, Beavis, Belden, Bentley, Benton, Beresford, Berkeley, Berwick, Beverley, Binnie, Birch, Blain, Blake, Blanford, Blessing, Bliss, Blossom, Bluebell, Bolton, Booth, Bosworth, Bourne, Bowden, Braden, Bradford, Bradley, Brady, Bramble, Bramley, Bramwell,

The Pan Guide to Babies' Names

Branden, Branton, Brent, Brigham, Brindley, Brinsley, Brock, Bromley, Bron, Brook, Bryden, Buck, Buckley, Burchard, Burnford, Burton, Burwood, Byram, Byrne, Byron, Calvert, Carel, Carey, Carla, Carleton, Carlile, Carson, Cavendish, Chadwick, Chalfont, Channing, Charla, Charles, Charleton, Chelsea, Chelston, Chesley, Chilton, Christmas, Churston, Clarendon, Clayton, Cleveland, Clifford, Clifton, Clinton, Clive, Clover, Cody, Colby, Collingwood, Colston, Colville, Compton, Cranford, Cranleigh, Cranston, Crawford, Crofton, Culver, Dain, Daisy, Dale, Dallas, Dalton, Dane, Darlene, Darley, Darlin, Darrel, Darren, Darrington, Darrow, Darryl, Darton, Darwin, Dashiel, Dayton, Dee, Dell, Denman, Denna, Denton, Denver, Derman, Dermot, Deron, Derry, Derwent, Devon, Devona, Dinsdale, Dixie, Dolan, Dudley, Dunstan, Dwight, Eartha, Earthan, Eastman, Easton, Edgar, Edina, Edith, Edlan, Edlyn, Edmar, Edmond, Edric, Edward, Edwin, Edwina, Egan, Elan, Elbur, Elbourne, Elden, Eldon, Eldridge, Elfin, Elford, Elgar, Elingdon, Ellwood, Elmer, Elmira, Elmore, Elmstone, Elsdun, Elstan, Elstead, Elston, Elton, Elvaston, Elvedon, Elvina, Elwood, Emer, Emmet, Erlina, Esmond, Ethel, Everton, Faine, Fairfield, Fairley, Farland, Farley, Farold, Farrar, Felton, Fenner, Fenton, Fernley, Fielding, Firth, Fisher, Flann, Flint, Fontayne, Freedman, Frith, Fritha, Fuller, Fulton, Garrick, Garvey, Garwood, Geoffrey, Giselle, Glade, Gladwin, Glendale, Glenford, Glenton, Goddard, Godwin, Golda, Goldwin, Goodwin, Graham, Grantley, Gray, Grayling, Greendale, Greenwood, Greville,

Index of Sources

Grover, Haddon, Hadley, Halden, Halford,
Hamilton, Hamlin, Hampton, Handley, Harford,
Harker, Harley, Harold, Harrington, Hart,
Hartley, Harwood, Haslam, Haviland, Hawley,
Hawthorn, Hay, Hayden, Hayford, Haymon,
Haywood, Hazel, Hazelwood, Heaton, Hedli,
Hedley, Helga, Helma, Henly, Hereward, Heron,
Hewitt, Hewlett, Heywood, Hiam, Hildreth,
Hilmer, Hilton, Holbrook, Holden, Holland, Holly,
Holman, Hope, Howard, Howell, Howland, Hunt,
Hunter, Huntley, Hurst, Hyman, Hyssop, Ilva,
Ingham, Iverna, Jarvis, Keene, Kelton, Kelvedon,
Kelvin, Kendrick, Kenley, Kenna, Kennedy,
Kenrick, Kenward, Kimberley, Kingsley,
Kingston, Kingswood, Kirby, Kireen, Kirton,
Kramer, Lambourn, Landry, Lane, Langdon,
Langford, Langley, Langston, Latham, Latimer,
Lauriston, Lawson, Lawton, Layton, Leaf, Lee,
Leland, Lennox, Lester, Levina, Levington,
Lewin, Lilly, Lincoln, Lindell, Lindley, Lindon,
Lindsay, Linford, Lingrove, Linwood, Lister,
Litton, Lockwood, Lomas, Lonsdale, Lowell,
Lyman, Lyndon, Lynford, Lynley, Lynton,
Lynwood, Macy, Maisie, Mala, Manford, Manning,
Mansfield, Maple, March, Mardella, Marden,
Markham, Marley, Marsden, Marshall, Marson,
Marston, Marvin, Maxwell, Mayda, Maynard,
Mead, Meadow, Mederick, Medora, Melbourne,
Meldon, Melford, Melton, Melville, Melvin,
Melvina, Merrie, Merry, Merton, Middleton,
Milborough, Milburn, Mildred, Millard, Milton,
Misty, Monday, Monford, Moreland, Morford,
Morland, Morley, Morton, Mycroft, Myler, Nara,
Naunton, Nayland, Nedra, Newbold, Nixon,

The Pan Guide to Babies' Names

Norman, Norris, Norton, Norwood, Oakley, Odell,
Ogden, Olin, Olinda, Oram, Orde, Ordway, Orlan,
Osborn, Oscar, Osma, Osman, Osmond, Oswald,
Oswin, Paige, Palmer, Parker, Parr, Pembroke,
Piper, Porter, Prescott, Preston, Quanda, Queenie,
Quenby, Radcliffe, Radford, Rainbow, Ralston,
Ramsden, Ramsey, Randolph, Ranscombe, Raven,
Rawden, Rayburn, Rayford, Redford, Redvers,
Redway, Reed, Reeves, Rhett, Richmal, Richmond,
Rider, Ridley, Rio, Robert, Roberta, Rockney,
Rockwell, Rodney, Roger, Rowley, Royden,
Rudyard, Rutherford, Rydon, Ryford, Rylan,
Sandford, Sargent, Saward, Scanlon, Scot,
Seabrooke, Seamon, Searle, Seaton, Sebert,
Sedgwick, Selby, Selden, Selwyn, Sergeant,
Seward, Seymour, Shaw, Shelby, Sheldon,
Shelley, Shelton, Shepherd, Sheridan, Sherlock,
Sherman, Sherrill, Sherwin, Sherwood, Shirley,
Sidney, Sidwell, Skeeter, Slade, Slim, Snowden,
Somerset, Spenser, Spring, Springfield, Stafford,
Standford, Standish, Stanfield, Stanford,
Stanhope, Stanley, Stannard, Stanton, Starkie,
Stedman, Sterling, Stratford, Stratton, Stuart,
Sudy, Sugden, Summer, Summerton, Sutcliffe,
Swithin, Talbot, Talcott, Taldon, Tate, Taylor,
Teasdale, Theydon, Thorley, Thorne, Thornton,
Thursday, Thurstan, Tilden, Tilman, Todd,
Tolman, Torben, Toria, Townsend, Trafford,
Travers, Trayton, Trillow, Truman, Tuesday,
Turlough, Tussock, Tyndall, Udele, Upton, Vale,
Van, Vance, Vanton, Vardon, Vinna, Wade,
Wadham, Wadsworth, Wainwright, Wakefield,
Walcott, Waldo, Walford, Walker, Walton,
Wanetta, Ward, Washington, Wayland, Webster,

Index of Sources

Welby, Weldon, Wendelin, Wenona, Wensley, Wentworth, Wesley, Westbourne, Westbrook, Westleigh, Weston, Whalley, Wharton, Wheatley, Whitney, Whittaker, Wilber, Wilbert, Wildon, Wiley, Wilford, Wilfrid, Willa, Willard, Willoughby, Willow, Wilona, Wilton, Windsor, Winfield, Winfred, Wingate, Winmer, Winslade, Winslow, Winston, Winthrop, Winwood, Woodrow, Woodstock, Wright, Wyman, Wymond, Wyndham, Wynton, Wynard, Wystan, Yale, Yardley, Yarrow, Yeo, Zelick.

OLD FRENCH Accord, Avelina, Bevis, Bonar, Boone, Borden, Burnett, Carden, Chauncey, Corbin, Cresta, Dasha, Dashiel, Dashwood, Dean, Delaney, Dempsey, Desiree, Elaine, Ewart, Farrant, Fay, Ferrant, Fletcher, Garland, Garrett, Garrison, Gaylord, Gifford, Grainger, Granville, Guy, Isla, Jewel, Judge, Lesley, Leslie, Linet, Mace, Maitland, Mallory, Mander, Mansel, Manton, Mason, Mavis, Mignon, Moon, Musette, Paice, Pleasance, Poplar, Raleigh, Rayner, Revel, Rivana, River, Royston, Rudge, Sable, Sorel, Squire, Tolan, Turquoise, Verda, Walden, Wallace, Warner.

OLD GERMAN Abelard, Acelin, Adalard, Adela, Adelaide, Adolph, Ahren, Alaric, Albert, Alda, Alice, Alison, Allard, Alonzo, Aloysia, Alvan, Alvar, Alvina, Alvira, Amelia, Amery, Amory, Ancel, Ansell, Ara, Arabella, Archibald, Arletta, Arlin, Arlington, Armand, Armina, Arney, Arnold, Aspen, Auberon, Aubrey, Baldwin, Barrett, Baxter, Berenger, Bernadette, Bernard, Berry, Bertha, Bertram, Bruna, Burke, Callena, Clairmond, Clay, Clayborn, Clotilda, Colvin,

The Pan Guide to Babies' Names

Conrad, Curzon, Delinda, Derek, Dirk, Druella,
Easter, Edlin, Ella, Ellery, Elra, Elric, Elrica,
Emeric, Emery, Erda, Eric, Erica, Erland, Ernest,
Everard, Fairburn, Faramond, Farand, Farica,
Felda, Ferdinand, Fern, Frederick, Freemont,
Frieda, Fulke, Galiena, Garfield, Garvin, Gerald,
Geraldine, Gerard, Gertrude, Gervaise, Gervase,
Gilbert, Godfrey, Hanford, Harriet, Harva,
Harvey, Henry, Herbert, Herman, Hertha,
Hildegarde, Hodgson, Hubert, Humbert,
Humphrey, Ida, Idelia, Ingram, Irma, Irmgard,
Ismay, Isolda, Ivo, Jocelyn, Kelby, Kelsey, King,
Konrad, Lambert, Lenna, Leonard, Leopold,
Linda, Lindo, Linden, Louis, Louisa, Luther,
Malca, Mallard, Manfred, Matilda, Mena, Milena,
Miles, Millicent, Mystique, Nixie, Norbert,
Odelia, Odette, Odile, Oliver, Orwin, Osbert, Otto,
Ottway, Paxton, Radella, Raymond, Reynard,
Richard, Richenda, Roderick, Roland, Rolanda,
Rosamond, Roscoe, Royce, Rudolf, Rue, Saxon,
Sayer, Sefton, Serilda, Serle, Sewell, Siegfried,
Sigbert, Sigmund, Tesmond, Thayer, Theobald,
Theodoric, Valda, Valdis, Valeda, Valmond,
Vernon, Walter, William, Winola, Wybert, Zoba.

OLD NORSE Alvis, Amma, Astrid, Bracken,
Bransby, Brenda, Brink, Broderick, Dalby,
Danby, Denby, Denholm, Einar, Fleet, Freya,
Garth, Gerda, Githa, Haley, Hallam, Halley,
Hally, Harper, Havelock, Hawk, Hesketh, Holm,
Holmes, Honey, Idona, Inga, Kerr, Kerra, Kirk,
Midge, Nessa, Olaf, Olave, Oleta, Olga, Ormond,
Ormsby, Ralph, Ralphina, Reynold, Ronald,
Ronna, Rosedale, Runa, Shell, Silky, Silver, Sky,

Index of Sources

Star, Starlight, Storm, Thor, Thora, Thyra, Torquil, Wanda.

PERSIAN Azura, Cyrus, Daria, Darian, Darice, Darius, Esther, Farah, Jasmin, Lilac, Roxanna, Soraya, Tabor, Tulip, Vashti, Zena, Zenda.

POLISH Irena, Kasia, Krystyna, Michal, Morela.

QUECHUA Inca.

RUMANIAN Afina.

RUSSIAN Anoushka, Anton, Antra, Anya, Boris, Ivan, Kalinka, Katinka, Katisha, Katrushka, Katya, Kisha, Koshka, Mariska, Mishka, Nadine, Natasha, Nina, Ninka, Odessa, Olena, Olga, Petrina, Radinka, Sacha, Sonia, Stefan, Stefanie, Tanya, Tatiana, Vanya, Viviana.

SANSKRIT Adara, Amara, Amba, Ambika, Amita, Ananda, Aruna, Asmita, Candra, Chandra, Darshan, Dayala, Deva, Dyana, Gavra, Geeta, Gita, India, Indira, Jai, Jana, Jarita, Kalya, Kalyana, Kandra, Kandrin, Kanti, Kanya, Kara, Kari, Karuna, Kavita, Komala, Kushuma, Lalaka, Lalana, Lalita, Layana, Lena, Lila, Maiya, Manon, Maya, Meena, Meera, Meloney, Mohan, Nalina, Nanda, Nandy, Nara, Opal, Padma, Reshad, Rohin, Saketa, Sara, Sarada, Sarana, Sarinda, Sati, Seetha, Shanti, Sharana, Sita, Tara, Taru, Tarum, Taruna, Varsha, Vasara, Veda, Veena, Vijay, Vikram, Viveka, Yama, Zenana.

SCANDINAVIAN Aina, Atalie, Axel, Dagan, Daven, Ingrid, Katarina, Kelda, Kirsten, Kristine, Nitha, Norna, Quimby, Roald, Rolf, Rowan, Yves, Yvonne.

SCOTTISH Bonnie, Chel, Davina, Drummond,

The Pan Guide to Babies' Names

Elspeth, Fife, Geordie, Ian, Isla, Jamie, Jean, Kirsty, Lorna, Muir, Ninian, Payton, Ranald, Skye, Tamlan, Toyah. (*See also* GAELIC)

SIOUX Petra, Toya.

SLAVONIC Brina, Danica, Etelka, Ilya, Ivan, Jara, Karol, Karola, Kasmira, Katarina, Katina, Katrinka, Nadia, Neda, Radman, Sandor, Sandora, Sonia, Veta, Wanda, Zenka, Zevan, Zivana.

SPANISH Alonzo, Adeana, Benita, Bettina, Bonita, Calida, Calinda, Carmen, Clarita, Davita, Delmar, Delores, Dolores, Dorita, Duretta, Eldora, Elvira, Esmeralda, Estelar, Jade, Jonquil, Joya, Juan, Juanita, Linda, Loleta, Lorenzo, Madra, Marisella, Mercedes, Mia, Montez, Morena, Nevada, Paloma, Parilee, Paulina, Paz, Pepita, Ramon, Ramona, Raquel, Reinita, Ricardo, Sanchia, Santana, Sarita, Selva, Sierra, Teresita, Tereza, Tia, Trella, Uta, Vida, Ventura, Xavier, Zaida, Zala, Zarina, Zorita, Zuma, Zumaya.

SWAHILI Shani, Simba.

SWEDISH Elna, Karna, Kristina, Marna, Ottilie.

TAHITIAN Hina.

TIBETAN Dechen.

TURKISH Kedi, Rashida.

WELSH Aderyn, Aelita, Aeres, Aerin, Aerion, Aeron, Aethnen, Afon, Aled, Almedha, Almon, Andris, Angharad, Angwen, Annwyl, Anwen, Arial, Arian, Arianwen, Arthur, Arwen, Asgell, Avon, Bevan, Blodwen, Bran, Branwen, Bronessa, Bronwen, Bryn, Cade, Cadell, Cai, Caradoc, Cariad, Caron, Carys, Cedric, Ceri, Cerial, Ceridwen, Cerys, Chevy, Clyde, Conway,

Index of Sources

Craddock, Crichton, Del, Delyth, Deri, Deryn, Dillys, Dylan, Effro, Eira, Eirian, Elain, Elan, Elfed, Elfen, Elfyn, Elphin, Elphine, Eluned, Emrys, Enfys, Enid, Eswen, Evan, Ffodus, Gavin, Gawain, Geneth, Geraint, Gildas, Glain, Glenda, Glenys, Glyn, Glynis, Gweneth, Gwylan, Gwyn, Gwyneth, Gwynfa, Gwynfor, Huw, Hywel, Iago, Ianto, Idris, Iestin, Ieuan, Ifor, Inaret, Iole, Iorwen, Jennifer, Jevan, Kane, Kiew, Leolina, Lichfield, Llewellyn, Lloyd, Lyneth, Lynwen, Madoc, Maldwyn, Malvern, Medwin, Megan, Merion, Melys, Meredith, Merlin, Merlyn, Merrick, Merryn, Morgan, Morgana, Morien, Morwen, Mostyn, Myfanwy, Nerys, Nesta, Olwen, Owen, Parry, Perl, Price, Rhian, Rhianwen, Rhonwen, Rhys, Saethydd, Saith, Seren, Shan, Sian, Sion, Taffi, Talfryn, Taliesin, Trahern, Trebor, Trent, Trevor, Trugaredd, Tudor, Tyne, Valma, Vaughan, Warwick, Wayne, Wenda, Wendell, Winifred, Wynford, Wynne, Wynton, Yorath.

YIDDISH Gita, Leeba, Raisa, Shaina, Zade, Zaida.
YORUBA Adeola.
ZULU Temba.

Special Category Index

This index lists names that are derived from different sources and complements the Concept Index on page 249.

ANAGRAMS Reva, Roneel.
BACKSPELLINGS Azile, Ronaele, Senga, Trebor,
BOOKS Alyena, Aslan, Ayla, Azea, Brion, Cal, Dursten, Elendil, Elenya, Garion, Huckleberry, Inza, Irissa, Jancis, Jyan, Kade, Kala, Kalinda, Kanga, Karanda, Kelana, Kelson, Kerrick, Kes, Kesira, Lorien, Lorna, Lythanda, Melcena, Minna, Mondy, Moriana, Morleena, Nydia, Orlene, Pamela, Phyllida, Ratha, Rhanna, Rilla, Rohan, Rohanda, Romola, Ronica, Roo, Scarlett, Shannara, Shikasta, Tallis, Taraza, Thelma, Topsy, Trilby, Vanessa, Vanna, Zana, Zazie.
COMMERCIAL PRODUCTS Chanel, Mox, Nardi.
DANCES Calinda, Sundance, Tanga.
FILMS Kes, Kira, Leia, Willow.
LAWS Nira.
MYTHOLOGY *See* MYTHOLOGY SECTION in Concept Index.
NURSERY RHYMES Bunty.
PLAYS Amanda, Berinthia, Melantha, Miranda, Norval, Orintha, Regan, Timon, Wendy, Yorick.

Special Category Index

POETRY Geraldine, Myra, Odessa, Orinda, Percival, Rosalind (*See also* PLAYS).
RADIO Zathara.
TELEVISION Caress, Sable.

Combinations Index

This index lists the combinations given in the dictionary. These names are formed by blending the elements of two or more existing names. Where the entire names are used to form a new name (eg Donnamarie or Donna-marie) the name is not given here, nor will it be found in the dictionary. This is because the result is simply a linking together of two names rather than a merging or blending: in these cases the reader is referred to the individual entries concerned.

Many of these new blends only started appearing in the 1980s, and consequently a large proportion of them are not listed in any previous dictionary. They form a fruitful area of inquiry for the parent seeking a new but attractive name.

The names given here are listed under the first element in the name.

Ada Adalee.
Adele Adeliza.
Ali Alora.
Alice Alianne, Alibeth.
Alix Aliza.
Amanda Amabeth, Amadelle, Amalina, Amalinda, Amalissa, Amanita, Amantine, Amaranda, Amathea.

Combinations Index

Amara Amarel, Amarena, Amarintha.
Amy Amera.
Angelica Anjenette.
Ann Anabeth, Andora, Anella, Anira, Anisa, Annabeth, Annada, Annalee, Annalisa, Annalyn, Annathea, Annathella, Annazette, Anella, Annina, Annona.
Anthea Anthelia.
Arleen Arlynn.
Barbara Barantha, Barina.
Bella Belantha.
Belle Beletta, Belina.
Betty Betora.
Bree Breelyn.
Brenda Brendelia, Brendella, Brendina, Brendora.
Brianna Briantha.
Bronwen Bronanda.
Brynn Bryola.
Caitlin Caitanya.
Camilla Camara, Camina, Caminda, Camira, Camita, Camora.
Cancer Canli.
Candace Candora.
Cara Carana, Caranda, Carantha, Carema, Caretta, Carissa.
Carol Caroleen, Carolinda.
Cassandra Cassantha, Cassara.
Celia Celara, Celantha.
Chana Chamara, Chamel, Chamella.
Chantal Chantelle.
Charles Charel, Charlinda.
Chere Cheredith, Chereen, Cherella, Cherette.
Cheryl Cherilyn, Cherrilyn, Cherylyn.
Chloris Chlorel.

315

The Pan Guide to Babies' Names

Christine Chrisanda, Chrisantha, Crisann, Cristella, Cristelle.
Claire Clairona.
Clara Claranda, Clarantha.
Clare Claribel, Clarina, Cloyce.
Clea Cleandra, Cleantha.
Clio Cliandra, Cliantha.
Cora Corabeth, Coranda, Corantha, Corinthe.
Cyndy Cyndora.
Daisy Damae, Damala.
Dalila Dalinda.
Danielle Danya.
Dara Daranda, Darantha, Darilyn, Darina, Darinka, Darissa.
Darren Dario, Darvin, Dary.
David Davian.
Davina Davora.
Dawn Dawnella, Dawnelle.
Deborah Debrelle.
Del Delana, Delandra, Delane, Delanne, Delanie, Delara, Delaura, Delena, Delina, Delita, Delois, Delola, Delorna, Delosa, Delshay, Delynda.
Denise Denine.
Deri Derenda.
Diamond Diamanda.
Diana Diadora.
Dionne Diorella.
Dolores Dolvene.
Dona Donella.
Dorothy Doanna.
Dora Dolinda, Dolisa, Dolita, Donya, Doranda, Dorann, Dorantha, Dorella, Dorinda, Dorna, Dorona.
Elizabeth Bethanna, Bethina, Liselotte.

Combinations Index

Elaine Eleila.
Elana Elandra, Elantha.
Elen Elenda.
Ella Elamara, Elola.
Ellen Ellana.
Elnora Elsena.
Eloise Elouisa.
Ethel Ethena.
Eva Evara.
Eve Evelia, Evinda.
Everard Everol.
Fanny Fanya.
Felina Felantha.
Fidel Fidelma.
Fiona Fiorina.
Flora Floella, Floriane, Florinda.
Fonda Fondra.
Frances Francelle.
Frederick Frenelle.
Gem Gemelle.
George Georgeana.
Glenys Glendora, Glinda.
Haley Haleen.
Hattie Hattierene.
Hazel Hazelbelle, Hazira.
Helen Helaine, Helandra, Helantha, Helinda, Helissa, Helita, Helora.
Hilda Hildelith.
Ida Idana, Idena.
Ilona Ilora.
Irene Irelda.
Jacinta Jacada, Jacanda, Jacantha, Jacenda.
Jade Jadeen.
James Jasa.

The Pan Guide to Babies' Names

Jane Jahlia, Jalene, Jances, Janda, Jandora, Jandy, Janelle, Janne, Janora, Jansue, Jantha, Janthea, Janthina, Jaomi, Jarietta.
Janet Jenelle.
Jay Jayelle.
Jean Jeanella, Jeanne, Jeony.
Jeanette Jenalyn.
Jem Jemary, Jemonica.
Jemima Jemira, Jemita.
Jennifer Jenilee.
Jeri Jerlene.
Jerry Jesmond.
Jessie Jessamy, Jeswyn.
Junior Jereva.
Jo Joella, Jola, Jolantha, Jolanta, Jolinda, Joris.
Joan Jobeth.
Joni Joneda, Jonella, Jonina.
Joseph Jolaine, Jolea.
Josie Josella.
Joy Joylene, Joylyn.
Joyce Jorel, Joycelyn.
Jude Judian.
Julia Julianne.
Julie Julanda, Julantha, Julinda, Julita.
June Junella.
Kahlia Kahlita.
Kaley Kalanda, Kalantha, Kaldora.
Kandy Kandora.
Kara Karantha, Karella.
Karen Kacy, Karena, Karetta, Karona.
Katherine Katarinda.
Kathleen Kathlyn.
Kathy Kaela, Kahlia, Kathevira, Katonna.
Keira Keiranne.

Combinations Index

Kelly Kelanda, Kelantha.
Keren Kerella, Kerena.
Kevin Kex.
Kirsten Kristen.
Kitty Ketena, Ketty, Kitena.
Kori Korinda, Korintha.
Kriss Krisha.
Kyla Kylara.
Kylie Kylanda, Kylantha, Kylene, Kylina, Kylinda, Kylora, Kylynda.
Kyra Kyrene.
Lana Landora, Lantha.
Lara Alariel, Laralyn, Larella, Laretta.
Larissa Laryetta.
Laura Laurana, Lauranda, Laurantha, Laurella, Laurelen, Lourana.
Leah Leabel, Leandra, Leanne, Leanora, Leantha, Leanza, Leatrice.
Lee Leeann.
Lily Lilanda, Lilantha, Lilimae, Lilina, Lilisa, Lilita, Lilybeth
Lilly Lillette, Lillita.
Lin Linara, Linita, Linora.
Lisa Lisanne.
Liza Lizanne.
Lola Lolana, Lolanda, Lolantha, Lolara.
Lomas Lomax
Lona Londa, Lonice.
Loretta Loretha.
Louise Louann, Louantha, Louella, Louetta.
Lovina Lovinda.
Lucy Lucetta.
Lyn Lyndal, Lyndora, Lynira, Lynita.
Lyssa Lythinda.

The Pan Guide to Babies' Names

Mabel Macinda, Macintha, Madella.
Madeleine Madelyn.
Mala Malandra, Malantha.
Malvina Malvinda.
Mandy Mandora.
Manon Manenda.
Mara Maranda, Markaya.
Marala Maralee.
Mare Marella.
Margaret Marles.
Margo Margolaine.
Marja Marjabelle, Marjalena, Marjana.
Martel Maretta.
Mary Marilene, Mairona, Mairwen, Mareetha, Mariam, Maribelle, Maribeth, Maridel, Mariel, Marijon, Marijune, Marilane, Marilou, Marilyn, Marinda, Marintha, Marita, Mariwin, Marosa, Maryam, Marybeth, Marylou, Marylyn, Maryse.
Maureen Maurita.
Mela Melana, Melanda, Melandra, Melann, Melara, Melata, Melaura, Melea, Meleila, Meleta, Melika, Melira, Melisa, Melola, Melona, Melora, Melorna, Melosa, Melyn.
Melina Melinda, Melinka, Melintha.
Melissa Meliza.
Mena Menora.
Mercia Mercille.
Merrie Merriah, Merridee, Merrion, Merrita.
Meryl Merelina, Meretta, Meribeth, Merilyn, Merissa, Merita.
Michaela Micole.
Millie Milora.
Mira Mirago, Miram, Miramer, Mirilyn, Mirjana, Mirola, Miromel, Mirora, Mirosa.

320

Combinations Index

Misa Misalyn.
Molly Molanda, Molantha, Molina, Molinda, Molissa, Molita, Molitha.
Morag Moranda, Morantha, Morita, Moritha, Moryl.
Moureen Mourilyan.
Moyra Mhorabelle.
Myra Myan, Mylynn, Myriam.
Nancy Nanella, Nanita.
Nana Narita
Nara Narelle, Narissa.
Natalie Natania, Natharina.
Ned Nedrick.
Nicola Nichelle, Nichela.
Nola Noll.
Nora Noranda, Norantha, Norella, Norissa, Norita.
Norma Norola.
Nova Novanda, Novantha.
Nyla Nylanda, Nylantha, Nylara, Nylora.
Oran Oranda, Orantha.
Pamela Pamelyn, Pamira, Pamita, Pamola, Pamora.
Pearl Pearline.
Phila Philana, Philantha.
Rae Raelaine, Raelene, Raetha.
Raya Rayanne.
Raymond Raynold.
Remi Remira.
Rene Renise, Renita.
Rhonda Rondelaine.
Rita Risa.
Roald Roanna.
Robert Robana.
Rois Rolaine.
Roland Rolantha, Rolara, Rolene, Romaire.

The Pan Guide to Babies' Names

Roma Romanda, Romantha, Romara, Romelda, Romily.

Ron Roncel, Ronelle.

Rona Ronalee.

Rose Rosabel, Rosalin, Rosalinda, Rosan, Rosanda, Rosantha, Rosaria, Rosean, Rosehanna, Roselle, Roseltha, Roselyn, Rosinda, Rosintha, Rosira, Rosita, Rosan, Rozella, Rozlyn.

Rowena Rowanda, Rowantha.

Roxanna Roxolana.

Ruth Ruthan, Ruthena.

Sally Sallianne.

Salome Salona.

Salvatore Salene.

Samantha Samana, Samanda, Samilla, Samina, Samora.

Sandra Sanderel, Sandina, Sandreena, Sandriana.

Sarah Sarala, Saran, Sarantha, Sarayn, Sarella, Sarenne, Sarinka, Sarola.

Selina Selanda, Selantha, Selara, Selinda, Selinka, Selita.

Selma Selora.

Serina Serinda, Serintha.

Shan Shanalee, Shanda, Shandy, Shanna.

Shanti Shantina, Shantrice.

Shara Sharelda, Sharella, Sharly, Sharyn.

Sharon Sharmalee, Sharolyn, Sharona, Sharonda.

Shea Sheanda, Sheantha.

Sheila Sheila, Shiona.

Sher Sherella.

Shera Sherala.

Sherie Sherilyn.

Sherry Sherralyn.

Sheryl Sheryn.

Combinations Index

Shona Shonda.
Sola Solana, Solandra, Solane, Solanne, Solantha, Solara, Solata, Solea, Soleila, Solena, Solinda, Soliza, Solola, Solorna, Solyn.
Sonia Sonda, Sondra, Sonesta, Sontara.
Sorcha Sorkina.
Star Stellanda, Stellantha, Stellara, Stellina, Stellinda, Stellise.
Sue Suella, Suellen, Sulu.
Suky Sukina.
Sula Sulaika.
Suna Sundarah, Suneetha, Sunita.
Susan Susanda, Susantha, Susita, Suzanna, Suzella.
Talia Talanda, Talantha, Talara, Talina, Talinda, Talira, Talisa, Talita, Talona.
Tamar Tamarantha.
Tamsin Tamana, Tamanda, Tamandra, Tamantha, Tamelda, Tamella, Tamia, Tamila, Tamina.
Tana Tanamara.
Tango Tanga.
Tara Taralyn, Tarika, Taryn.
Taz Tazara.
Tena Tenisha.
Tera Teranda, Terantha.
Teresa Teressa.
Terri Terena, Terice, Terina, Teranda, Terantha.
Thea Theda.
Tia Tiarella.
Tina Tinesse.
Toni Tonda.
Tora Toranda, Torantha.
Trevor Trevyn.
Tully Tuleda.
Tyrus Tyann.

The Pan Guide to Babies' Names

Vania Vanina.
Varda Varella.
Vela Velanda, Velantha, Velinda, Velintha.
Vera Verella.
Vita Vitara.
Vona Vonora.
Yolanda Yolandra, Yolantha, Yolara, Yolina,
    Yolitha, Yolonda.
Yvette Yvelda, Yvella.
Zade Zadina.
Zaida Zelma.
Zala Zakina, Zalina, Zalora.
Zane Zaneta, Zanna.
Zara Zarala, Zaranda, Zaranna, Zarantha, Zarella,
    Zarissa, Zarisha, Zarita, Zarola, Zarona.
Zelia Zelinka.
Zephira Zerelda.
Zoe Zoanna.
Zora Zorella, Zorinda, Zorna.

Bibliography

Books consulted during the preparation of this dictionary include:

Bice, Christopher *Names for the Cornish – Three Hundred Cornish Christian Names* Dyllansow Truran (1984).
Boyer, Carole *Names for Girls and Boys* Grafton Books (1974).
Brown, Michele *The New Book of First Names* Corgi Books (1985).
Cottle, Basil *The Penguin Dictionary of Surnames* Penguin Books (1967).
Cresswell, Julia *Bloomsbury Dictionary of First Names* Bloomsbury Publishing (1990).
Dunkling, Leslie *Scottish Christian Names* Johnston and Bacon (1979).
Dunkling, Leslie and Gosling, William *Everyman's Dictionary of First Names* J. M. Dent (1983).
Ekwall, Eilert *The Concise Oxford Dictionary of English Place-names* Oxford University Press (Fourth edition, 1960).
Glennon, James *4001 Babies' Names and Their Meanings* Robert Hale (1985).
Hanks, Patrick, and Hodges, Flavia *A Dictionary of First Names* Oxford University Press (1990).

The Pan Guide to Babies' Names

Hanks, Patrick, and Hodges, Flavia *A Dictionary of Surnames* Oxford University Press (1988).

Jarvis, S. M. *Discovering Christian Names* Shire Publications (1973).

John, Steven *The Right Name for Baby* W. Foulsham (1988).

Kolatch, Alfred J. *The Jonathan David Dictionary of First Names* Perigree Books (1980).

Nicholson, Louise *The Baby Name Book* Thorsons (1985).

Reaney, P. H. *A Dictionary of British Surnames* Routledge & Kegan Paul (1961).

Spence, Hilary *The Modern Books of Babies' Names*, W. Foulsham (1988).

Stephens, Ruth *Welsh Names for Children* Y. Lolfa (1970).

Withycombe, E. G. *The Oxford Dictionary of English Christian Names* Oxford University Press (Third edition, 1977).

Woulfe, Patrick *Irish Names for Children* Gill & Macmillan (1974).

Note: For further reading see more comprehensive bibliographies given in the works cited by Dunkling and Gosling, Ekwall, Hanks and Hodges, and Kolatch.